T0079918

James M. Cain

JAMES M. CAIN

By DAVID MADDEN

Carnegie Mellon University Press
Pittsburgh 1987

Carnegie Mellon University Press books are distributed
by Harper and Row, Publishers

Library of Congress Catalog Card Number 86-72297
ISBN 0-88748-045-4
Copyright © 1970 by David Madden
All rights reserved
Printed and bound in the United States of America

Preface

Among writers, critics, and other serious readers in America and abroad, James M. Cain has an unusual reputation for a so-called popular writer, who, according to several critics, has never written anything entirely out of the trash category. This reputation is based on *The Postman Always Rings Twice, Serenade,* and *The Butterfly* (which Cain feels comes closest in "theme and treatment" to art); I rank *Mildred Pierce* and *Double Indemnity* also with Cain's best. Little has been written about Cain, but the fact that he should have been discussed as he has been suggests that his novels are more important in American and in world literature than most readers have supposed.

I began writing about Cain in 1959 because as a student, teacher, and writer of fiction I saw that his novels have in a special way a significant place in literature. But his life and work have excited a somewhat gratuitous interest in me since adolescence; one cannot entirely separate a writer like Cain from the decor of one's nostalgia, separate the aura of the movies made from his novels, which one saw as a child (and now sees regularly on television) from the books one read later. If Cain as popular culture has been with us since 1934, it is with Cain as "literature" that we have to reckon now, though we risk the admonition that Cain should remain in the limbo of "camp" enthusiasms.

As I have noted, millions consider Cain an excellent popular writer; a few critics and readers consider him a trashy popular writer; a few consider him an important, though popular, writer —and he is all these. As one who agrees with all three points of view, I have written from Cain's point of view as well, quoting him quite often. Although there is no intentional ambiguity about my own opinions and attitudes, I have attempted several levels of approach. I quote a great variety of critics and reviewers (even *Time* and *Newsweek*), and do so rather frequently, because one of my major purposes is to put the shifting Cain image in focus; reader response is particularly relevant to an understanding of novels such as Cain's, and critics often behave more like ordinary readers than critics, seeming in their commentaries to be, appropriately, preoccupied with the phenomenon of reader response to Cain. When I use the pronoun "we," I refer to the collective Cain readership, though it consists of many different sorts of readers.

The ways in which popular culture and popular fiction interact upon and reflect each other has not been studied diligently enough in American literary criticism, nor has the impact of popular writing upon "serious" novels in America and abroad. But, in ways that differ from "serious" fiction, a study of popular literature is a study of the psychology of the mass mind at the time in which it appears; mere entertainment can become a source of enlightenment, as the recent "pop" art and "camp" movements in all media only begin to suggest. But it is in the realm of art that popular fiction becomes most instructive, for we experience intensely basic esthetic forces at work in their clearest manifestations and with greater lucidity comprehend the more mysterious processes in "serious" literature. We also see in sharper relief the functioning of fiction as a source of nonthematic or "pure" experience. James M. Cain's novels, along with other tough fiction of the 1930's, offer one approach to these areas of study. That Cain is interesting in his own right becomes apparent to anyone who reads his best novels, and one task of this book is to show that he deserves a place of distinction—though certainly a minor place—in American literature.

While Cain's nonfiction and his short stories are not discussed as thoroughly as they perhaps deserve, this book offers commentary on every major aspect of his work. Chapter 1 describes his place among the "hard-boiled" writers. Chapter 2 examines his life in relation to his time and to his writing. The rest of the book, interpretative in purpose, is not chronological; for that approach to Cain's work is not the most revealing. Indeed, one of the most interesting aspects of Cain's novels is the way in which he manipulates plot, theme, character, and other elements through craft. Since the love-rack and wish-come-true concepts are central to all his work, it is appropriate that in Chapter 3 we look briefly at each of his novels in light of these concepts, gaining, at the same time, an immediate familiarity with the story of each novel. Chapter 4 is an analysis of Cain's characters; we see ways in which they reflect aspects of the American character and dream. Chapter 5 examines the dubious literary and cinematic influences on Cain and the relationship between the author and his ideal reader; it offers a detailed scrutiny of the technical means Cain employs to elicit a controlled response; we see the appropriateness of point of view, style, pace, and other technical elements to his conceptions. Chapter 6 is a study of the problem of theme in Cain's work and the way his novels exemplify the concept of the "pure" novel. Chapter 7 is an examination of some reasons for studying Cain and "tough" fiction; we see their relevance to American and European literature in the 1930's and 1940's; the book closes with a general estimate of Cain's importance in literature.

DAVID MADDEN

Louisiana State University
Baton Rouge, Louisiana

Acknowledgments

I am grateful to Kenyon College for financial assistance made available to me through the kindness of Bruce Haywood; to Ohio University for covering the cost of manuscript typing; and to Edgar Whan and Arvin Wells for allowing me time off from teaching to finish this manuscript. Norman Holmes Pearson was very kind to see the value of my writing about Cain in his seminar in American Studies. I am also grateful for the advice and encouragement of Charles Shapiro, Walter Van Tilburg Clark, and George Lanning. About Sylvia Bowman I will content myself simply with saying that she is a scholar of admirable energy and enormous generosity. I hope this book is worthy of James M. Cain's unusual cooperation and kindness. Lorraine Howard prepared the manuscript, with encouraging asides. My wife Robbie has endured through many versions. My friend Margaret Myers provided a detailed and intelligent commentary on the entire manuscript. For allowing me to reprint passages which appeared in different forms in their publications, I wish to thank: Alexander Cappon, editor of *The University Review;* Ray Browne, editor of *Journal of Popular Culture;* Frank Magill, Salem Press; Warren French and Everett/Edwards Press; Nicholas Joost, editor of *Papers on Language and Literature;* and Anthony Macklin, editor of *Film Heritage.* For permission to quote from the works of James M. Cain, I wish to thank the Screen Writers Guild and Cain himself. All quotations and excerpted material used herein fall under the "fair use" concept as it applies to critical and scholarly books. Separate acknowledgments of permission to quote are therefore omitted.

Contents

Chronology

1892– July 1, James Mallahan Cain born in Annapolis, Maryland;
1903 first of five children of James William Cain, teacher, and
Rose Mallahan Cain, singer. Boyhood spent in Annapolis
where father was professor at St. John's College.

1903 Moved to Chestertown, Maryland, when father became
president of Washington College.

1910– Graduated from Washington College, 1910. Held a series
1913 of jobs; studied singing in Washington, D.C.

1914– Decided to become a writer; meanwhile, taught mathe-
1917 matics and English at Washington College.

1917 Received master's degree, Washington College.

1918 Reporter for the Baltimore *American;* then, reporter for
the Baltimore *Sun.*

1918– Enlisted as a private in the army, served in France; edited
1919 *The Lorraine Cross,* a weekly, for 79th Division.

1919 Reporter for the Baltimore *Sun,* until 1923.

1920 Married Mary Rebekah Clough (divorced, 1923).

1922 First magazine articles published in *The Atlantic Monthly*
and *The Nation.* Worked in coal mines; first efforts at
writing novels. Met H. L. Mencken in Baltimore.

1923– Professor of journalism at St. John's.
1924

1924 First major illness—tuberculosis. Moved to New York City;
began writing editorials for Walter Lippmann on the New
York *World,* and published other newspaper and magazine
pieces, until 1931. Met Vincent Lawrence, playwright, and
Philip Goodman, play producer, influences upon his writing.

1925 First play published, "Servants of the People," in *The
American Mercury. Crashing the Gates,* first produced
play, failed outside New York.

1927 Married Elina Sjösted Tyszecka of Finland (divorced,
1942).

1928   First short story, "Pastorale," published in *The American Mercury.*

1930   *Our Government,* collection of satirical dramatic dialogues, most of which appeared in *The American Mercury,* published.

1931   Managing editor for *The New Yorker* for ten months. Moved to Hollywood; remained seventeen years, writing scripts for Paramount, Columbia, Metro-Goldwyn-Mayer, Warner Brothers, Universal. Continued to write articles and syndicated columns.

1934   *The Postman Always Rings Twice.*

1936   Adapted *The Postman* to the stage; it ran seventy-two performances. *Double Indemnity* began as serial in *Liberty.*

1937   *Serenade.*

1938   Cain's father died. *Career in C Major* began as serial under title "Two Can Sing" in *The American Magazine.* Traveled in Europe.

1940   *The Embezzler* began as serial under title "Money and and the Woman" in *Liberty.*

1941   *Mildred Pierce.* Cain had second major illness—ulcer and gallstone.

1942   *Love's Lovely Counterfeit.*

1943   *Double Indemnity* appeared as movie. *Three of a Kind.*

1944   Married Aileen Pringle, movie star (divorced, 1945).

1945   *Mildred Pierce* appeared as movie.

1946   *Past All Dishonor. The Postman* appeared as movie.

1946–   Cain attempted to organize American writers into Ameri-
1947   can Authors Authority. Married Florence Macbeth, opera singer, September, 1947. *The Butterfly.* Moved to Hyattsville, Maryland, where he has remained. *Sinful Woman.*

1948   *The Moth.*

1950   *Jealous Woman.*

1951   *The Root of His Evil;* first version written in 1938.

1952   Third major illness—cholesterol condition.

1953   *Galatea.*

1958   Cain's mother, ninety-five, and two sisters died.

1963   *Mignon.*

1965   *The Magician's Wife.*

1966   Cain's wife, Florence, died in May.

1967–   Cain at work on two novels.
1969

CHAPTER 1

The Toughest Boys in the Back Room

DURING the late 1920's and the 1930's, three related genres developed in the novel: the hard-boiled private detective, the proletarian, and the tough guy.[1] Each of the five finest writers in these genres produced at least one minor classic of American literature ("tough-guy novel" as an embracive, descriptive term may be applied to all five): Dashiell Hammett's *The Maltese Falcon* (1929) and Raymond Chandler's *The Big Sleep* (1939) in the private-detective field; B. Traven's *The Death Ship* (1926) among proletarian novels; and Horace McCoy's *They Shoot Horses, Don't They?* (1935) among the "pure" tough-guy works. The twenty-minute egg of hard-boiled writers is James M. Cain; and the quintessence of the tough-guy novels is *The Postman Always Rings Twice* (1934).[2]

One of the first critics of eminence to discuss Cain seriously was Edmund Wilson. In 1940, he introduced the readers of *The New Republic* to "The Boys in the Back Room": James M. Cain and John O'Hara (later, he added John Steinbeck, Horace Mc-Coy, William Saroyan, Hans Otto Storm, Nathanael West, and a few others). Wilson called them "poets of the tabloid murder," a phrase which has echoed down the decades. Since all of these writers had lived in and written about California, "They thus constitute a sort of group to which we might add Hammett and Chandler and they suggest certain generalizations"; but the remarkably detailed similarities in the life and work of these writers are beyond the scope of this book.

The significance of the tough-guy novel as exemplified in the works of Cain and these other and similar writers extends beyond pure entertainment and basic esthetic values. The tough novel reflected the hard surfaces, inadvertently expressed the mood, and provided an impersonal vision of American civilization during the depression. It stimulated the action element in motion pictures; it

[17]

affected the tone and attitude of more "serious" writers; and it inspired certain European novelists during the 1940's.

Generally, scholars of American literature give Cain and the tough writers merely a passing glance; like travelers who must pass through the slum outskirts to reach the heart of a great city, these scholars are a little fascinated, a little repelled, and certainly relieved to have passed through. But they see immediately the tough novel's literary line of descent: the European Naturalism of Zola; the Americanized Naturalism of Frank Norris and Dreiser, commingled with the European Realism of Flaubert and Balzac; and the American selective Realism of Stephen Crane. Frederick Hoffman, who summarizes the impact of Naturalism on *The Modern Novel in America,* cites the tough novel as its latest manifestation: "The influence of Dreiser, Farrell, and Hemingway is pervasive. Beyond that, the slickness of John O'Hara's conceptions has been added to the contribution made by James Cain to the surface picture of American violence." [3]

Herbert J. Muller, in *Modern Fiction: A Study of Values* (1937), argues that of more influence upon the tough novel than Hemingway were the proletarian writers. As an extension of Naturalism, which "subordinated style to matter," and as "an expression of the post-war mood, with its distrust of rhetoric," proletarian fiction gave the tendency "toward the hard-boiled manner not only a new impetus but a new direction." [4] In "Disengagement: The Art of the Beat Generation," Kenneth Rexroth said: "Much of the best popular fiction deals with the world of the utterly disaffiliated. . . . The first, and still the greatest novelist of total disengagement" is B. Traven, a "Wobbly" of German ancestry.[5] Traven's fiction lacks both the strident commitment of much of the proletarians and the seeming indifference of the tough guys to ethical implications of human suffering. But, in some of his attitudes, in his style, and in other characteristics of his fiction, he is strikingly similar to the toughest boys in the back room.

The tough writers lacked a doctrine which would impose upon their narratives any predetermined pattern. Although Zola argued that the novelist should base his work on careful documentation— as though he were a scientist conducting an experiment, free of moral conventions and preconceived theories—such practice, and such an assertion, determined that his own dispassionate examination of phenomena would lead to conclusions as definite as natural laws—the conclusion, for instance, that heredity and environment determine the actions of men. An inverse expression of this mania to explain man's ecological context is the psychological Realism of Henry James and James Joyce. But the detachment of hard-boiled objective realism allows surface details to make their own statements; the avant-garde extension of this method is the objectivism of Robbe-Grillet.

Using the technique of selective realism, tough fiction achieves an objectivity that scorns romantic subjectivism and idealization; it reflects a lower-class, harsh, sordid environment; and it depicts character as a product of social conditions, spoiling if not rotten. Theirs is the pure vision of man the animal, which sees, but cannot (or in their case will not) evaluate. While too many of the proletarian writers wrote about the masses *to* the intellectuals, Cain and other hard-boiled writers wrote not only *about* but mainly *to* the masses, giving violent impetus to their forbidden dreams, dramatizing their darkest temptations and their basic physical drives.

A distinction must be made, however, between the traditional novel of detection and the hard-boiled mystery novel. Developed by Poe to full fruition in only four tales, the detective story was our first literary export. Attracted and repulsed by the American taste for violence, the English adopted—even before Poe could be imitated in America—and domesticated the form. W. H. Auden has testified that one became addicted to novels of detection as to tobacco or alcohol. Discriminating writers and critics read detective novels: André Gide, Robert Graves, André Malraux, T. S. Eliot, Paul Elmer More, Jacques Barzun, Somerset Maugham, Bernard De Voto, Joseph Wood Krutch; and some have even written "esoteric" defenses of the form. In a time when fiction was dominated by philosophical, psychological, and symbolic concerns, the detective story offered simple storytelling, mechanical intellectual stimulus, and a pure, though crude, esthetic pleasure.[6] Or, as Chandler put it, "There's nothing left to discuss."

The genteel English novel of detection prevailed until the 1930's. Then, with the publication of Hammett's *Red Harvest* (1929), hard-boiled detective fiction stepped out of the pulp pages of *Black Mask* and into hard-cover respectability, thus contributing to the decline and fall of the traditional "whodunit." Slightly adapted, what critics said about Hammett is descriptive of Cain and of the tough-guy novel in general as well. In *Murder for Pleasure* (1941), Howard Haycraft delineated Hammett's contribution: "Hammett's lean, dynamic, unsentimental narratives created a definitely *American style,* quite separate and distinct from the accepted English pattern." His are "penetrating if often shocking novels of manners" and of character. "Yet they are as sharply stylized and deliberately artificial as Restoration Comedy, and have been called an inverted form of romanticism. . . . Commercial in inception . . . they miss being Literature, if at all, by the narrowest margins." [7] In "The Simple Art of Murder" (1944), Chandler offered a practitioner's point of view: Hammett took murder out of the English drawing room and "dropped it into the alley." "Hammett wrote at first (and almost to the end) for people with a sharp, aggressive attitude to life. They were not afraid of the seamy side of things; they lived there. Violence did not dismay them; it was right down their street. Hammett gave murder back to the kind of people that commit it for reasons, not just to provide a corpse." [8] W. H. Auden sees Chandler himself as "interested in writing, not detective stories, but serious studies of a criminal milieu, the Great Wrong Place, and his powerful but extremely depressing books should be read and judged, not as escape literature, but as works of art." [9]

Hammett and Chandler directly aroused the fears and nightmare images of American civilization in the 1930's. Though their purpose was not to depict deliberately the social evils of the time, Hammett's and Chandler's good-bad-guy private detectives were guides who conducted Americans on a tour of the underworld, into its alleys and down its "mean streets." Hypocrisy in religion, deceit and self-interest in business, and corruption in politics seeped into these alleys and created "messes" that Sam Spade and Philip Marlowe had to clean up. Seeing life with the impartiality of the camera eye, they softened their hard-boiled attitude with neither sentiment nor moral judgment. "The private eye is not the dandy turned sleuth," says Leslie Fiedler; "he is the cowboy adapted to life on the city streets, the embodiment of innocence moving untouched through universal guilt . . . the honest proletarian, illuminating by contrast the decadent society of the rich." [10]

As for the special appeal of the private-eye novels of Hammett and Chandler, as opposed to the cool puzzle appeal of the novels of detection, Chandler's explanation also accounts in part for the appeal of Cain's "pure" tough novels. It was not violence, fine writing, originality of plot or character: "Possibly it was the smell of fear which these stories managed to generate. Their characters lived in a world gone wrong, a world in which, long before the atom bomb, civilization had created the machinery for its own destruction, and was learning to use it with all the moronic delight of a gangster trying out his first machine gun. The law was something to be manipulated for profit and power. The streets were dark with something more than night. The mystery story grew hard and cynical about motive and character, but it was not cynical about the effects it tried to produce nor about its technique of producing them." Chandler felt that a few unusual critics with "very open" minds recognized this devotion to craft (*Simple Art of Murder,* vii). "The story of our time to me is not war, nor atomic energy but the marriage of an idealist to a gangster and how their home life and children turned out." [11] To write about the world we actually live in, it took "writers with tough minds and a cool spirit of detachment." Speaking of the tough-guy hero, Chandler said, "down these mean streets a man must go who is not himself mean, who is neither tarnished nor afraid" (*Simple Art of Murder,* 193).

The typical tough-guy novel presents a vision of life that is cynical, if not pessimistic; the attitude is ironic, dispassionate, neutral; the tone is hard-boiled, having no cultural pretensions, expressing no tender emotions. The first-person point of view is used almost exclusively; the syntax, diction, and grammar are those of the characters; the imagery is stark, rarely lyrical. The characters are vivid, elemental, somewhat two-dimensional. The setting, environment, and atmosphere are those of the large cities, with a special recurrence of southern California as the locale. The authors use the scene method of writing, with a predominance of blunt, brisk dialogue. Action is swiftly paced. The technical control, given the simplicity and skeletal elements, is absolute. The impact of these novels derives from their brevity; average length is a hundred and ninety pages.

In Hemingway, Hammett, and Chandler, the raw masculine power to kill became a mystique; but few of Cain's characters use a gun, though Cain is always associated with "the false power of the gun." Cain has never written a detective story—not even in the Hammett-Chandler vein. *Double Indemnity* and *The Embezzler* have been cited as borderline novels; the little-known, low-quality *Sinful Woman* and *Jealous Woman* are even closer to the type. But Cain's stories are concerned with murder and love, from the criminal's point of view, exclusively. Cain is more interested in making action suggest an explanation of the crime *as it is being perpetrated* than in constructing a solution out of the swamps of mystification. In several novels, he even departs from the "pure" tough-guy type.

Just as one must distinguish between the formal detective story invented by Poe and the private-eye thrillers initiated by Hammett, one must also distinguish between the latter and the "pure" tough-guy novel, though they developed concurrently and cross-fertilized each other. Neither Cain nor McCoy exemplifies in his characteristic works either of these types. A product of all the forces referred to in this chapter, the pure tough novel nevertheless is a distinctly separate type which presents a hard-boiled picture of life for its own sake, without the justification of either an ideology or a conventional form, whether strictly adhered to or consciously violated.

CHAPTER *2*

Twenty-Minute Egg of the Hard-Boiled School

JAMES M. CAIN'S life illustrates many aspects of the tough-guy stance, and it also explains certain less obvious elements in his hard-boiled fiction. His several careers—as teacher, newspaperman, screenwriter, novelist—interesting in themselves, directly reflect the times that provided the raw material for and welcomed his novels. Though he was most dramatically a man of the 1920's and 1930's, he was still active in the 1940's and has drifted along through the 1950's and 1960's. He has followed his various careers over many landscapes, including Annapolis, Chestertown, and Baltimore, Maryland; France; New York; Hollywood; and Maryland again.

Cain's is mainly a success story; for, after an aimless series of jobs in the 1910's, he became a very successful and respected journalist in the 1920's and early 1930's, and, in 1934, with the publication of *The Postman Always Rings Twice,* he began his career as one of America's most successful popular novelists. His pride seems, however, to have been more intensely invested in the earlier than in the later career. And his pride suffered most in an early failure—he attempted to become a great opera singer. A later failure as a screenwriter affected his pride less than his pocketbook. In his private life, he experienced recurrent failure with his health and with marriage; but, now in his late seventies, he is in good health and is still writing; and for twenty years, until the death of his wife in 1966, he was blessed with a happy fourth marriage. Failure in the public arena as organizer of an association for writers persuaded him to retire in the late 1940's to a small town in Maryland. It is particularly appropriate when studying a popular writer to take a lingering look at his life. And Cain's especially reveals certain insights, assumptions, and atti-

[23]

tudes about the society in which he has lived so fully and for which he has written works of enormous and enduring popular appeal.

I   A Moth and a Race

Cain's grandparents were Irish immigrants, and his parents were reared in New Haven, Connecticut; his father, James William Cain, met Rose Mallahan when he was a student at Yale University. James Mallahan Cain was born July 1, 1892, in Annapolis, Maryland, where his father was vice president and professor of English at St. John's College.

James M. Cain's earliest memory is an enchanting vision of a large green luna moth on an overcast summer day. He called his mother to come look; but, when he returned to it, a thick-legged boy was beating it to pieces with a club—"a moment of horror, that has remained with me to this day." [1] That night, Cain's mother, perhaps to cheer him, recalled his frequent boast that he could beat his father running. She announced a race from the house on the college grounds down to the foot of the campus. With a flourish, the race began; but, instead of running, Cain's father walked, with long strides, looking back with a giggly grin, not even bothering to throw away his cigarette. From the bench in front of the house came waves of laughter, for Cain's mother and Aunt Mary were overcome with the spectacle of a three-year-old boy trying to outrun a tower of muscle. Infant Cain collapsed in tears upon a world that for him had suddenly caved in. This double-horned day left deep and lasting wounds. The race had a great effect upon his writing. His six-foot father, Cain believes, might have foregone the funny feat of beating a small child, and thus allowed him the illusion of victory that night. Cain always remembers this incident in his relations with children, small animals, and his readers. For instance, his left hand is constantly cut and scratched from the attention he gives his cat, Mittens; for he never forgets that being enticed with a string or a finger isn't much fun for the cat unless he *wins*. In his fiction, Cain puts his reader in place of the cat; for the reader hopes to win, too, and *must* win. Whether he is enticed by the prospect of sex, riches, violence, or whatever, the reader, Cain feels, must be indulged, must get a good full bite of what has been promised. This payoff, rather than any penchant for "violence" as such, dictates much that is in his novels; where other writers might have used indirection, Cain plunges the action along, without flinching, to give the reader what he came for.

The luna moth figures frequently and significantly in Cain's work. In *The Moth*, Jack Dillon describes "that beautiful green thing, all filled with light, fluttering off through the trees, alive and free. It was a feeling I imagine other people have when they think about God in church. It makes no sense, does it, to say that a few times in my life, when something was happening inside of me, I could tell what it meant by that pale, blue-green, all-filled-with-light color the feeling had?" Such rare moments of beauty and peace momentarily dispel the aura of evil in Cain's novels.

Symbolic sensations of guilt are constant motifs, as when Dillon feels guilt as the pink, hot-faced sensation associated with the pear he didn't give his teacher; and another episode in Cain's childhood inspired that distilled image of guilt. Bushrod Howard, a languid, aristocratic, handsome boy, three years older than Cain, was dragged one day into assembly at the Annapolis School by the principal and commanded to "apologize." The third-grader not only refused, but "in a hysterical, weeping blaze of ferocity let fly with his heels against the shins of the principal, who was holding him up bodily, in front of the whole school; and when the principal was utterly defeated, clobbered 100%, Bush went charging off through the door at the side, and disappeared." Cain never discovered what Bush's offense was. "I thrilled to his triumph over his stupid, cruel schoolmaster, and when I went home, I looked up that word 'apologize' in the dictionary. Finding out what it meant frightened me even more than the scene itself. For I had a terrible, horrible suspicion that I *would have* apologized—though I didn't even know for what!" Cain's sense of guilt, over what he *might* have done, he confesses, has stayed with him all his life. But the incident made a double impression: "It was my first encounter with gallantry. When things get tough, I always remember Bushrod, and the courage it took to smash up that principal, and, I hope, act in loyalty to that courage." [2]

Cain's childhood in Annapolis and Chestertown was rather uneventful. Cain was a precocious scholar, but in the third grade, where he was teacher's pet, occurred something that was to have a negative effect on his life. Since his father was president of the school board ("he was always president of everything"), Cain persuaded him to arrange his skipping from the third to the fifth grade so he would be with his friend and idol, Bushrod. His father's success in doing so is one of the few things Cain holds against his father—irrationally, he admits—since it was he who urged his father to arrange the double promotion. Suddenly, he was with pupils a great deal older; and, when he went on to the sixth grade, they were also a great deal wiser. He still remembers his sense of fright at the teen-age girl, "a cheap, brassy little trollop," who displayed her breasts: "I was a midget among giants, and this fact, more than anything else, I think, meant that my schooling, especially my college years, meant nothing whatever to me."

Cain was eleven when his father became president of Washington College at Chestertown, Maryland, a small institution, the eleventh oldest in the country. When Mr. Cain decided to lay a brick walk down the campus, Ike Newton, a thickset man in his fifties, worked, sitting on the ground among the bricks and sand, his legs spread open, while young Cain listened to him talk: "It was pure enchantment. I was simply enthralled—not so much by his stories or his ideas as such, as by the language he couched them in. It was pure bucolic vulgate, but so rich, so expressive, so full of color that I couldn't hear enough of him. I can't say Ike taught me how to write dialogue, but I owe this man a great debt for stirring in me a respect for his lingo and all that went with it, for exciting in me a feeling for simple speech, for the way people actually talk, for the country idiom as distinguished from the citified." His mother's speech and writing, combined with Ike Newton's influence, affected Cain's style. Her diction, terse, well-pronounced, and distinguished, was rather different from Cain senior's windy, elaborately grammatical and Yankeeish mode of utterance. And on paper she was a model of prose composition—vivid, brief, and clear, with few adjectives. "If I have any talent to write, I got it from her."

At fifteen, Cain became a student at Washington College. Perhaps unconsciously he was taking revenge upon his father when he avoided athletics and other extracurricular activities and also declined to edit the college magazine. His father looked with "wholehearted disapproval" upon Cain's complete indifference to campus affairs. His younger brother, Edward, on the other hand, proficient in sports and on the violin, was good at all those things which the father could admire and understand. In 1910, at the age of eighteen, Cain graduated "without distinction." [3]

In the pattern of his father's life and behavior at critical moments, James M. Cain's own life and the audacious acts of some of his fictional heroes are prefigured. At Yale, Mr. Cain won a cup and an oar for rowing and also played football. When he became a college president, his greatest talent quickly came into evidence; for he was not primarily a scholar, educator, or athlete, but a politician. For ten years, he made a success of sleepy, pastoral Washington College. When the new administration building burned in 1916, Mr. Cain's opponents made his life so miserable that he threw up his hands in disgust, resigned, and became vice president of the United States Fidelity and Guaranty Company of Baltimore. He gave Cain some inside information on the intrigue that goes on at the top of such a company. In 1933, he published *Financial History of the United States.*

Facing crises in his own life, James M. Cain has had the will to go on, owing much of his spirit, he feels, to his father's example. "To see, in late middle age, everything he stood for plucked from his hand, and then to turn around, and without any self-pity, to make a new life for himself, find a new sphere of usefulness, and do it so successfully that when he died in 1938 he was the lead story of both the afternoon and morning papers, and a tremendous throng gathered at his graveside, a measure of community respect—this strikes me as something."

Cain was very close to his mother, a pretty woman whose soprano voice was trained in all the intricacies of coloratura singing. Despite her potential for a singing career, as evidenced in her performances around New Haven, she preferred marriage. She was thirty when Cain was born; her other children—three girls and one boy—were born at two-year intervals. While the other three shared the Cain characteristics of good looks, easy manners, and marked gregarious impulses, Genevieve and James were withdrawn and literary, ill at ease with people. Genevieve and Cain's spinster sister Virginia died within a few months of the death of the mother (she was ninety-five) in 1958.

II *False Starts*

The three or four years preceding his decision to become a writer are so painful in Cain's recollection that he rarely talks about them. He moved "quickly from one job to another," he says, "and lost most of them" through "incompetence." [4] But he often reflects that for much of his writing he draws the background from those years. In the months just after graduation, Cain was bewildered, coming for the first time in his life to the realization that people worked. "Never once, in our house," he says, "was there so much as a hint that life was hard, that work was the lot of all. We lived in grand style, with the grubby aspects of life concealed from us children." Cain is rather proud of the fact that some traces of this lordly view of things still cling to him in his adult life through "rough times."

As a young man, he had no idea at all that one was supposed to "do something" with his life; and, after facing the visible choices offered, he did not want to do anything. The manager of Consolidated Gas and Electric Company of Baltimore, an acquaintance of Cain senior, gave the young man his first job, as a clerk filling up consumers' ledgers. Cain quit that job to work for two years on the state roads as inspector of construction. If he became bored and increasingly dubious about his qualifications to build roads, there is no doubt about the qualifications of his heroes in *Past All Dishonor, The Moth,* and *Mignon* to move the earth in various construction projects—nor about Cain's own capacity, based on this early experience and later research, to be persuasive about it.

In Baltimore and Washington, Cain had heard a great deal of serious music. Suddenly, in Vienna, Maryland, where he had taken a job as principal of the high school, he decided that he would become an opera singer. He had met a vacationing music teacher from Washington, John R. Monroe, who had taken an interest in him; Monroe, he decided, should be his teacher. Without enthusiasm, Monroe accepted the task; and Cain now feels indebted to him for the background for his four novels that deal directly with music.

Cain's mother was a major inspiration in his desire to become a singer. Although it contributed to her social popularity, Cain's mother did very little professional singing in Annapolis and Chestertown. In his childhood, he had heard her sing many times; but her voice had made no impression on him, though her capacity to read music and to conduct choirs and orchestras fascinated him. But at fourteen, when he heard her sing the "Inflammatus" from Rossini's *Stabat Mater*, "a fiendishly difficult thing for solo soprano," he suddenly realized how good both she and the music were. Such a performance, such a spectacle, was to appear repeatedly, in one form or another, in Cain's novels. "It wasn't so much," Cain says of her singing, "that she could do it, that interested me—but that she *knew* she could do it, and never even got excited about it, or nervous, or worried. All this, to me then, and to me now, was black magic. Subconsciously, my novels about singers are really votive offerings to her."

But, when the mother was confronted with her son's ambition to become a singer, she was aghast and forcefully informed him that he had little talent. However, understandably obstinate, since this was the first big decision he had ever made in his life, Cain quit his teaching job and went to study in Washington. This plunge, he realizes now, was as preposterous as his mother had said; but it at least caused him to break with ledgers, transits, blackboards, and all sorts of things that bored him to distraction and made him feel that his life was slipping away in a meaningless series of jobs whose only object was to make a living. Though he couldn't ignore the fact that no one in Washington took his singing seriously, he continued to work at two jobs he had taken to support his singing lessons, one selling accident insurance, or trying to; this experience enabled him to depict the insurance angle in *Double Indemnity* with an impressive sureness. But, finally, he decided he had little talent and quit music after one year.

Then one day, while sitting on a bench in Lafayette Park in Washington and catching his breath after an excursion to sell Victrolas for a department store, he suddenly resolved to become a writer: "It was a full-fledged bulky resolve, with seemingly good reasons back of it." Having quit his job, he went home to inform his father, who, to his astonishment, offered no opposition, but considerable encouragement, verging on enthusiasm, mixed with relief. His first efforts were short stories, which magazines speedily returned. Chiefly efforts to project local color or background, they lacked narrative thrust.

But Cain's literary output was interrupted by something that was to have an enduring effect on his writing. When an instructor at Washington College became ill, Cain's father asked his son to teach the man's classes. Cain accepted the offer. To face the boys, Cain had to learn the subjects—English and mathematics—thoroughly. He performed so well that, when the instructor took a job elsewhere, Cain was kept on. His father asked him to manage the entire preparatory department, a task which required that he live in the dormitory with the boys and also be in charge of discipline.

Cain's handling of discipline and grades foreshadows his heroes' behavior in parallel situations. For many years, the dormitory had been "slopped up with water thrown for a gag, and other problems created by young boys, which the colored clean-up men had to sweat over." His first night in the dormitory, Cain assembled his charges for a lecture:

I intend to live in a place that my mother, my sisters, or any woman can drop in on any time, and find fit for them to visit. I assume that that's the kind of place you, too, would maintain if it weren't for a few clowns trying to be funny. Well, that's the kind of place we're going to have—I'm telling you, not asking you. This isn't an invitation for you to vote on *whether*. We're going to *have* that kind of place, and the only question is, *how*. If you want to co-operate, I'm willing, even glad to let you, and we can adjust the rules to that co-operation, so you have certain liberties you don't now enjoy. If you don't want to co-operate, we're going to have that kind of place anyhow, but you'll find the screws tightened in a way you may not enjoy. So, I'm leaving the room now for a few minutes, and you can talk it over, and then we'll all talk together.

The boys agreed to cooperate, and "No water, orange peels, or other comedy props were thrown the rest of the time I served. It taught me something about the teen-age mind. Apparently, they like the iron mike—being told what they have to do lets them know where they're at, and they get the point without resentment. At the same time, being allowed to participate—the real point of co-operation—seems to stimulate their pride, and once they get that concession, they'll respond in an astonishing way."

When Cain became convinced that pupils did not seek knowledge, but *grades,* his notions along this line colored his next few years. In the mathematics classes, he set up the rule that there could be only two marks—perfect and zero; and his students seemed to accept this dictum. "There's no such thing in math, as being pretty nearly right," he told them. "It's all right or it's all wrong." Though his stories got sidetracked for a while, Cain looks back with some satisfaction on these three years he spent on this job, and feels he learned "a bit about education and what makes it tick—as well as what doesn't." Moreover, he was compelled to learn the principles of English composition so thoroughly they never left him.

Charles Louis Townsend, professor of French at the college, who later became a "big academic mogul," encouraged Cain's writing aspirations, and insisted that Cain get his master's degree while at Washington. Reluctantly, Cain did the required work, some of it under Townsend, minoring in drama, and received his degree in 1917.

III   *Newspaper Career: Baltimore, France, Baltimore Again*

Teaching was just another interim job for Cain. In 1917, he decided to make a break. In Baltimore, he applied at Swift & Company and quickly got a job as weighmaster in the cold storage room. He rather enjoyed the work, and he so pleased the management that he and Swift are friends to this day. Decades later, for researches on *Galatea* and *The Magician's Wife,* officials gave him the "red carpet."

One day, like one of his own fictional heroes, Cain went impulsively to the city room of the Baltimore *American* and persuaded William Kines, the city editor, to give him the job of covering one of the police districts. He turned in his first story, an account of a drowning, which was accepted with compliments by the city editor. Later Cain was made financial writer, covering war-bond drives, large financial "combos," and war conferences. Then, the Baltimore *Sun,* a much better paper, he felt, made him an offer. At twenty-five, he began work in January, 1918; and he went back on the police beat. But during that year Cain's new and long-lasting career in journalism was interrupted by service in the army.

Although he was far from persuaded of the necessity for America's participation in World War I, Cain told himself that, before he could be certain of his feelings and convictions, he would have to go into the army. The draft board and various recruiting outfits turned down his applications because of a weak lung; but, when his case was reviewed, Cain persuaded the doctor to pass him. At Camp Meade, when he heard of an outfit going overseas that needed men, he went to Captain Edward O. Maderia (later a close friend) and misrepresented himself as being able to do all sorts of things he could do a little, but not well. (This behavior is standard for most of his fictional heroes.) That afternoon Cain was transferred to 1st Headquarters Infantry Troop, Seventy-ninth Division, as a private in the rear rank. There he met Gilbert Malcolm, a tall, rawboned, red-haired graduate of Dickinson Law School (later, in the 1950's, president of the college), who had misrepresented his qualifications as Cain had, and for the same reason: so long as they were in the war, despite their misgivings about its justifications, they wanted to be in all the way. Among other campaigns, they participated in the big drive out of Verdun.

Meanwhile, Cain's younger brother Edward had joined the Marines and was commissioned as a lieutenant. On February 15, 1919, Edward was taking a farewell spin in his plane just before a luncheon in his honor, to celebrate his discharge from the corps, when his plane crashed. His death was a dreadful blow to the family, especially to Cain, who learned of it while in France. After the armistice, Cain spent a dreary winter in Souilly, until he was placed on special duty as editor of *The Lorraine Cross*, the division's limping, two-column, four-page newspaper, which wasn't doing well. Malcolm was appointed Cain's sports editor and took charge of the printing and manufacturing of the paper. "Except for identifiable contributions by occasional outsiders," Cain says, "I wrote the whole paper." [5]

One day Donald F. Cronin appeared. His pitch was to be circulation manager; and, like a true Cain hero, he had all the angles figured. By the second week, this dynamic trio was producing a six-page, five-column "sockdollinger," made up in big-city style, with snappy headlines and much division news. Some of Cain's maneuvers to get paper, stamps, and other necessities were larcenous and highly ingenious; but "the papers went down and the papers came out." It was one of the most successful weeklies of the American Expeditionary Force. With Malcolm, Cain also wrote a troop history, published in 1919.

Discharged from the army, Cain returned to Baltimore. Promoted to copy editor, with a raise, Cain went back to work for the *Sun*. But correcting grammar and writing headlines to fit seemed painfully unrelated to his aspiration to become a novelist. However, aware that he was learning still more about language, especially its possibilities for terseness, he stuck with it.

In 1920, he entered into the first of four marriages. His marriage to Mary Rebekah Clough, "though sincere enough in intention, and carried on with real effort on both sides, was doomed from the start, and didn't get far enough off the ground to count," he says. A classmate of Cain's at Washington College, Mary Clough was beautiful and had a taste for "high-brow things"; but she was also in significant ways a genuine member of the Eastern Shore Maryland squirearchy, and her incompatibility with Cain's attitude toward life, letters, love, and alcohol immediately became apparent.

When Cain became state editor of the *Sun*, he gained wide knowledge of Maryland, Pennsylvania, Delaware, and Virginia. To get into the streets again, he became financial writer. Taking courses in labor and economics at Johns Hopkins, reading Marx's *Das Kapital*, John Common's *History of the Labor Movement*, and other background material, he became interested in political and industrial strife. He managed to have the *Sun* assign him to the treason trial at Charles Town of William Blizzard, a United Mine Workers official indicted in connection with a 1921 armed march in West Virginia. Out of this experience came his first magazine piece, "The Battleground of Coal" (*The Atlantic Monthly*, October, 1922).

The trial, other trips to West Virginia, and considerable meditation convinced Cain that he was accumulating enough background for the long-postponed novel. He "studied, trudged, and crammed" firsthand information on labor conditions and worked in the mines in the fall of 1922, at Ward, West Virginia; then he took three months off to write. He came out of that winter, having discarded three novels, with the bitter conviction that he could not write.

A feeling he was going nowhere on the *Sun* led Cain to accept an offer from incoming President Enoch Barton Garey to be professor of journalism at St. John's College in Annapolis. Though Cain's previous enthusiasm for teaching English had waned, he made a great effort during this one-year interim. But, when Garey precipitated a student strike by expelling four boys without a hearing of the evidence, Cain resigned, though he agreed to serve out the year. He rallied the faculty to a realization of their duty under the charter to oppose such high-handed tactics as Garey's, but in other ways he tried to restore calm. However, this incident led him to his first serious misgivings about himself—as to whether he was not "a stormy petrel of controversy, with the capacity to stir up much more trouble than his convictions were really worth."

The first conscious influence, outside his own family, on Cain's style and attitudes was H. L. Mencken. Mencken's tone and debunking compulsion, if not his gift for invective, were contagious to Cain. Having read all the Mencken he could find and knowing he had encountered a spirit so exciting to him that his writing would never be the same, Cain began to send pieces to *The Smart Set*. They were rejected, but a correspondence between Cain and Mencken began. In 1923, Mencken told Cain about a new magazine he was starting and invited him to submit to the first number. When Cain suggested an essay portrait of the labor leaders he had encountered in recent years, Mencken was delighted. One of the great disappointments of Cain's life is that the essay did not appear in the premiere issue of *The American Mercury* because the union printers refused to set it! "The first issue, I knew, was literary history; the second was just a magazine."

Cain saw Mencken often. He was helpful to him in many ways, and Cain feels a "tremendous obligation to him." Mencken's antiprovincial, cosmopolitan air impressed and influenced Cain: "He freed me from the thrall of local literarians" and "urged me to bail out of Baltimore." But, though they liked each other, Cain and Mencken never became intimate friends: "We saw each other often . . . but I could never forget I was in the presence of genius. Every word he uttered proclaimed it, and I was always adjusting to it. It is a fatal blow to intimacy." Most of Cain's nonfiction appeared in Mencken's *The American Mercury*. Debunker in the manner of Mencken though Cain often is, he usually shows a fair-mindedness toward his target—a willingness, at times even an eagerness, to acknowledge the *earned* positive possibilities in the most negative situation.

Between 1922 and 1948, Cain wrote essays and articles for *The American Mercury, The Nation, The Saturday Evening Post, The Atlantic Monthly, Esquire, Vanity Fair, The Screen Writer,* and *Saturday Review of Literature.* The tough characteristics of these essays offer perspective on Cain's fiction, and they are so suffused with his own personality that he reminds one at times of Sinclair Lewis, Philip Wylie, and even Ayn Rand. As a long-time student and critic of the American character, Cain is most ferocious in the series of eight essays and in the dramatic dialogues which appeared in *The American Mercury.* The dialogues were collected in the volume *Our Government* (1930) and published by Knopf in its series "The American Scene."

In a pretentious preface, Cain declares that his "little book represents an effort to make a beginning" in the direction of a scientific examination "of our American government. . . . There is no book, so far as I know, which sets out . . . to depict, without bias or comment, the machine which passes our laws, educates our children, and polices our streets. . . . It was to fill this hiatus that I set to work. . . . For if the field proves attractive to scholarship, and others take up the work where I have left off, the United States will be unique among nations." This extreme claim for so modest a book is one of the most transparent instances of Cain's tendency, shared with his own characters, to endow every project with absolute significance.

In this book, Cain starts at the top with the chief executive and goes down the governmental pyramid to the lowest local bedrock. To "achieve complete verisimilitude," his "method of approach" was "to select some typical problem of a particular branch of government, usually on the basis of newspaper clippings, and then reconstruct the manner in which it would be dealt with by the typical agents of that branch." Although reviewers praised *Our Government* as a "cruel, satirical" sequence of "caricatures, ironic distortions that bring home the inefficiency, the hopelessness, the downright asininity of phases of popular government," and called it "an objective work of almost sadistic skill," the dialogues are not objective at all.

Almost without exception the dialogues exaggerate for satiric

effect, so that public officials and members of the public who figure in them come out in the main as irresponsible, self-deluded,
moronic yokels. Given what he shows us, the miracle of democracy is that it works at all; but Cain's final point is that it *does*
work. The dialect and the colloquialisms are authentic and demonstrate Cain's ability to listen carefully. Above all, the dialogues
are richly comic; and the irony, rampant in all of them and quite
suitable in most of them, is amusingly achieved. If these dialogues
fail to justify Cain's claims, to demonstrate his intentions, and to
instruct, they certainly entertain.

IV *New York: the* World, *the* Stage, *and* The New Yorker

The St. John's controversy, the aggravation of Cain's lung problem, and the breakup of his marriage to Mary (they were divorced in 1923) left Cain, in 1924, "at the end of the plank."
Cain's health has influenced his life and affected his literary
output for years: "From childhood, I was a deceptive figure, physically. Large for my age, I looked strong. Actually, there was
never such a weakling, kinetically, as I. I've always had soft,
squashy muscles, with no real strength to them, and along with
this, low blood pressure and low temperature." Alcohol, a factor
in the breakup of his marriage, undermined his health over the
years.

The discovery that he had tuberculosis marked a turning point
in his life: "Until then, I had had this driving compulsion to avoid
being a 'failure in life,' to be a credit to my father. But with the
T.B. I was relieved of that—after all, who can hold a lunger to a
high ambition? I began doing what I wanted to do, having so
little time to live, it seemed, and that was how I made the big
writing try again, after initial failures, and after envisioning instead some unspecified but wished-for high-pressure career." A
bad mustard-gas attack had aggravated his "incipient" tuberculosis, and he had to enter the state sanatorium. Twice in his life,
new techniques saved Cain from mortal illnesses; the new thera-
peutical treatment of tuberculosis was the first.

During the summer "seminar" of "chasing the cure" at the sanatorium, Cain was for the first time in years free of commitments;
but he was compelled to think over his life and to look realistically
at his future. So, upon his release from the sanatorium, Cain went

to New York, where he shared an apartment with editorial writer Malcolm Ross and began to look for a job, starting with Ross's paper, the rather conservative but respected New York *World*. Mencken had given Cain a letter of introduction to Arthur Krock, who escorted him to an office where Walter Lippmann, chief editorial writer, somewhat curtly interviewed him. Cain, feeling that he had been given the "brush-off," was depressed; and he delivered a few sweeping observations about the editorial page; it could do, he said, with some articles by qualified writers which would amplify or "orchestrate" the themes of the editorials. Lippmann asked to see some specimen Cain pieces, and, a few days later, he wired Cain and offered to give him a trial.

Cain was instructed to write several editorials. "Actually," says Cain, "I'm not sure that up to that time I had ever read an editorial. To a working stiff in the news departments, they are think pieces, not respected at all, done by trained seals with green eyeshades, most of them very elderly." Neither the editorials he glimpsed nor the news about the Teapot Dome scandal, the tariff, Calvin Coolidge, or John W. Davis and the coming election campaign sparked any ideas. A sourceless bit of advice kept running through his mind: "You must be in favor of motherhood, and against the man-eating shark." So, he recalls, "with some imp of the perverse sitting on my shoulder, I got off my bit of gallows humor—a passionate piece proclaiming that the man-eating shark *is* motherhood; that she brings her young forth alive, provides for their food, minds her own business, keeps quiet, and molests not unless molested." He dashed off two other columns of the same kind, sneaked down the stairs, tossed them into Lippmann's basket, slunk out into the street, and told Ross that he had blown it. But the editorials appeared in the evening paper, and Cain reported for work the next day.

Unable to think of anything that was what he imagined to be appropriate, Cain "turned in more japes, and again, his japes were published." Indeed they soon began to excite the trivial controversies that continue for weeks in the letter columns. But he was still uneasy; aware in his heart that he was a fake, he was getting by less with work well done than with a series of "black-humor" pieces that were to him impudent admissions of failure. "If you think you're flopping," said Krock, "you're wrong. You're doing fine, and Lippmann is very pleased." With success thrust upon him, Cain was launched upon a seven-year career—in some ways, says Cain, "the pleasantest working years of my life—for Lippmann was the pleasantest man to work under that anyone could possibly want." With the dialogue sketches he contributed regularly to the Sunday paper, the editorials for the evening *World,* and the magazine writings for Mencken's *Mercury* and for other periodicals, Cain was making about fourteen thousand dollars a year.

His "foolish controversies" continued to score. One of the first to have great repercussions was entitled "This Evil Must Cease," a diatribe against the "Pie Trust" for spiking its products with cornstarch "so they will stack," instead of putting honest filling in, with free-running juice and fine flavor. Another was a simple inquiry as to how hogs are called; this one caused a national furor, one chronicled at length in *Literary Digest* and "given a play" on the National Broadcasting network. "This was the beginning of hog-calling as a national institution."

It is amazing that Cain could function so well in a role apparently so inimical to his nature, personality, and interests.[6] More in character was his attack on other *World* editorial writers who had preached some sort of censorship of Broadway plays. But these inflated, prolonged, ridiculous controversies taught Cain a great deal about the popular imagination, mass emotions, and what stirs them—particularly his items on food, a major subject of popular interest, which he was to exploit in his novels.

Cain feels privileged to have been a long-time friend of Arthur Krock, but the man on the *World* who had the greatest influence on Cain was Walter Lippmann. Cain's first encounter with Lippmann was the book *Public Opinion,* which struck him as the intellectualization of a subject not really intellectual. Lippmann in person, however, had a different effect upon him. As the years passed, says Cain,

I found myself under every kind of obligation to him. He seemed to understand intrinsically that writing editorial opinions can't be commanded, and he didn't want men around him who could be coerced into thinking a certain way.

He didn't laugh at me, or sneer at me, or look down on me for rewriting my editorials, some of which went through the chopper a dozen times, something the newspaper business scorns. Probably I would have done it anyhow, but that this fine intellect respected my doing it made him, at such a time in my development, a tremendous inspiration to me. . . . His style is one of the finest to be read anywhere. That he would respect my style, and the pains I took to achieve it, was a big thing in my life.

Cain is in the tradition of the American journalist turned writer. Like Twain and Hemingway, he reported from the scene; like Ambrose Bierce and Mencken, he wrote essays on public affairs and manners. But there is no direct carry-over of his journalistic background into his fiction; none of his heroes are newspapermen. However, he did acquire much background information in numerous areas during those years: the 1920's are amply chronicled and analyzed in Cain's nonfiction, in a few short stories, in sections of *The Moth,* and his own life is exemplary of the spirit of the decade; but, since he did not begin publishing novels until 1934, there is little of the 1920's in them. Perhaps his concern with the present, or at least a sense of the present moment in his narratives, is influenced by the immediacy of his newspaper work.

Beginning with William Rose Benét's review of *The Postman,* reviewers frequently comment on tabloid inspirations of Cain's fictive world. Benét notes that newspaper training teaches compact writing, and "Mr. Cain has learned it." Having compared Cain's toughness to that of Frank Norris, Benét observes that "this novel derives from the sensationalism of America fostered by the daily press." [7] Commenting on Cain's approach to the American scene in *Three of a Kind,* a *Newsweek* reviewer noted "the rancid air of authenticity which Cain obtains by screwing down his competent microscope on a drop of that social seepage which discharges daily into U.S. tabloids and criminal courts." In contributors' notes for articles and stories that appeared after he left the newspaper business, he is consistently identified as a well-known journalist; and in *Who's Who* he still lists his occupation as "a newspaperman."

Cain wrote his most important novels during the period of his second marriage which began in 1927 and lasted fifteen years—through much of the newspaper and the Hollywood careers. He met Elina Tyszecka "by accident in New York one night, not long after moving there; and fell for her wildly, on the basis of a pretty face and strange Finnish gravity that was new to me. She had a beautiful mind—sardonic, ironic, sometimes almost savage in its comprehensions of basic things. That helped a lot with the kind of writing I did." In 1931, Cain took his wife and her children by a previous marriage to Hollywood. "But she was gone to Finland too often, too long. We learned we could live apart. . . . We broke up in 1942 on a Sunday morning, quietly, and sadly."

Before going to Hollywood, Cain made two important, though brief, excursions into other media: the theater and magazine management. During Cain's years in New York, many of the best plays reflected a "tough" attitude: Eugene O'Neill's *The Hairy Ape*, Charles MacArthur's and Ben Hecht's *The Front Page*, Laurence Stallings' and Maxwell Anderson's *What Price Glory?*, George Sklar's *Stevedore*, Robert Sherwood's *The Petrified Forest*, Clifford Odets' "Waiting for Lefty," Maxwell Anderson's *Winterset*, Sidney Kingsley's *Dead End*, the Federal Theater's *One-Third of a Nation*. From the viewpoint of various sorts of tough, outsider characters, these plays took a cold look at society. But, although the motive for writing them may have been outrage and the intent to reform, the *mere show* had the kind of primitive impact Cain was to achieve.

At his house in Baltimore, Mencken arranged for Cain to meet Philip Goodman, a theatrical producer, and "by far the closest friend" Cain was ever to have. In Paris, Goodman had read some of Cain's dramatic dialogues in the *Mercury* and thought Cain could do a play for him. Cain discussed with Goodman the possibilities in an idea based on a widely prevalent feeling in the West Virginia minefields that the Second Coming was near. In 1925, *Crashing the Gates*, which resulted from this discussion, was tried out on the road in New England. Though badly received, it taught Cain a few things about writing, mainly that "you should never jeopardize a big design by insistence on small imperfections"—it had not occurred to Cain, nor even to Goodman, that profanity in a play about a minefield Jesus would be objectionable to an audience. Until then, Cain had used profanity in his writing to the extent that men use it in speech. Except "as a matter of cadence," it wasn't at all important; and Cain abruptly abandoned it almost entirely in this play.

When Goodman called in Vincent Lawrence as play doctor, Cain first met "this tall, gaunt" man who was to have a great influence upon his writing. For a year or more, Cain and Lawrence wrestled with the play; then Lawrence came up with a dictum Cain never forgot. "Goddamn it," he exclaimed one night, throwing up the window of Cain's apartment on East Nineteenth Street, "Let's let some of this smoke out of here! Listen, Cain, I'm not paying five-fifty to see a play about a guy that tried to be Jesus and couldn't be. I'm capable of that myself. This guy has to *be* Jesus or someone must *think* he is." Cain rewrote the play to suit Lawrence, but Goodman never again produced it. Cain let it die, with some relief; and he never mentions it in any biographical sketch of himself.[8] More importantly, perhaps, Goodman not only taught Cain a sense of what works in theater, but also, as a "phenomenal" advertising man, about newspapers and the reading habits of the public. Goodman's comments, which, Cain insists, were based on insight into the heart of things, "rather than on cheap mercantilism," were to shape Cain's awareness of his reader as a fiction writer. At a time when Cain needed the belief of someone he respected, Goodman often expressed reverence for Cain's literary talent.

In 1931, with the *World* dead, Cain knew he would have difficulty finding a job which would equal the pay he had received from various writings for the *World* papers. But a friend who worked for *The New Yorker* recommended him to Harold Ross as the "26th Jesus," or as managing editor, when Ogden Nash wanted to quit. Cain had misgivings about his ability to adjust to the idea that a magazine sells entertainment instead of news or information. What Ross wanted out of Cain was suggested by Ross's constant repetition of the line: "Cain, we got to get this place organized." A cursory glimpse of the setup convinced Cain that that was exactly what *The New Yorker* needed, but he quickly learned that Ross was perversely opposed to the realization in sensible terms of his own desire. Cain's solution was simple: fire the utterly incompetent secretaries Ross had hired at subquality wages—who were making it impossible for the editorial staff, E. B. White, James Thurber, Wolcott Gibbs, Robert Coates, and others to function—and replace them with top talent at competitive wages. Cain, who had charge of the budget, knew this could be done. But from Ross he got "frost, verging on ice." "Cain, we got to find new talent," Ross would say. Cain's reply that first they must make efficient use of the talent they had had no effect.

But Cain—who was acting like a true Cain hero by stepping into a mess and setting things back on the track—went ahead making the changes he thought imperative. And everywhere he turned, he encountered instances of Ross's famous crankiness. Of his ten-month "seminar" under Ross, Cain says: "It was, for some reason, the most compromising to self-respect of any period in my life. Ross was a fascinating man, and his relations with 'talent' were brilliant. He had an original mind, with enough naiveté about it to go questing for fundamentals, sometimes the fundamentals everyone takes for granted. But he wasn't for me." Since *The New Yorker* was no place for a man of action, Cain began looking around for an exit.

V *Hollywood: Failure as a Scriptwriter*

Cain urged his agent to secure a Hollywood offer. Within a few weeks, Cain's reputation, based on his columns and on the dramatic dialogues and essays in *The American Mercury*, secured him a six-month contract at four hundred dollars a week, twice his *New Yorker* salary. As a result, he wrote movie scripts before he wrote *The Postman* and before a movie was made from any of his writings. Like his newspaper experience, his Hollywood experience as such produced little background for novels, although Cain, who went to Hollywood in 1931, stayed about seventeen years. He was not a successful scriptwriter, but he claims to have learned a little about writing from the experience and from other movie people. While literary critics charge that the movies were a negative influence on Cain's novels, film critics think well of three movies made from those novels: *Double Indemnity, Mildred Pierce,* and *The Postman Always Rings Twice.*

The tough-guy novel and its movie counterpart have cross-fertilized each other. Not only have classic gangster movies been made from tough novels, but most of the best tough writers have worked for Hollywood; Hammett and Chandler were two of Hollywood's most successful screenwriters, and their own novels —Hammett's *The Maltese Falcon* and Chandler's *The Big Sleep* and *Farewell, My Lovely*—were made into celebrated movies. Essential to tough movies and novels is speed of impact. The short tough novel, like a movie, may be experienced in one sitting; like the movies, tough novels are particularly expressive products of our fast-moving culture. As Edmund Wilson has pointed out, many serious novelists who do not write for the movies have been influenced by their pace, themes, characters, tone, and attitudes.[9] The disillusioned hangover of the roaring 1920's in the 1930's produced a cynicism that welcomed a cycle of gangster films; *Little Caesar* (1931) was the first great success.[10]

These novels and movies reflected dramatic aspects of the national spirit of the times. At home and abroad, the tough guy became *the* American image. With his fast car and tommy gun, the gangster and others resembled the cowboy with his fast horse and sixshooter. But the cowboy was a folk hero of the distant, romantic past; the gangster's romantic image had a hard metallic sheen. If the cowboy offered escape from the depression, the gangster mastered, if only for the hour, conditions that the average American felt helpless to control. The emphasis upon violence in movies inheres in the nature of the medium itself, for "effects of rapid and cataclysmic action are especially adaptable to the cinema medium." Perhaps this quality explains why tough novels seem cinematic in structure and technique.[11]

When John Howard Sharp in *Serenade* says, "Understand, for my money, no picture is any good, really any good," he summarizes Cain's lifelong attitude. Cain's judgment of the movies was formed when he attended the "Nickelodeon" with a boyhood friend in Chestertown in 1906 and was repelled by comic John Bunny and by *The Great Train Robbery:* "It never occurred to either of us that this was history of a sort, that it was good, or that it was anything but a proper subject of scorn from two young intellectuals, who of course knew what was good." Yet, Cain insists, the contempt that he shared with his friend was honest contempt: "And it has never left me. It explains, I think, more than anything else, why I flopped in Hollywood. I wanted the picture money, I worked like a dog to get it, I parked my pride, my aesthetic convictions, my mind outside on the street, and did everything to be a success at this highly paid trade." (Cain speaks only once of taking this mercenary approach to his novels.) "I studied the 'Technique' of moving pictures, I did everything to become adept at them. The one thing I could not park was my nose. My dislike of pictures went down to my guts, and that's why I couldn't possibly write them." Cain has little patience with failure. To fail in the early stages of preparation to become a singer was

one thing—singing is a high art; but to fail at the movies, a low
form of entertainment to him, was degrading.

Cain arrived in Los Angeles in May, 1931, in a driving rain
storm. His first glimpse of the city included a man in a boat, rowing around under some palm trees. Next day, he was taken to
the studio. Shocked to discover that the story editor had read
none of his writings, Cain could not understand how he expected
to get good work out of his writers if he never read their published stories. But everything in Hollywood, to Cain, was done on
a lunatic basis. Thus, Cain was given a remake of De Mille's *Ten
Commandments* as his first assignment. The original was one of
the biggest hits of all time: "That it stank, that it was a glaring,
monstrous piece of slimy, phony hokum, seemed to make no
difference." But with Sam Mintz, a writer Cain came to like, he
went to work on this "masterpiece of hokum"—and before Christ-
mas Cain had flopped.

Cain sat around for three months, waiting to get assigned. In
April, he was suddenly assigned to work on a picture called *Hot
Saturday,* from a novel by Harvey Fergusson. He heard little of
his efforts on this one, but presently he was closed out, and then
faced the reality of his impulsive switch to pictures: he had
moved lock, stock, and barrel to California; he was a failure; he
had no dependable income and no idea what was next.[12]

Cain counted as friends and influences some of the best and
highest-paid scriptwriters in the business. Vincent Lawrence had
provided a bridge for Cain from the stage to the screen. They had
moved to Hollywood at about the same time, Lawrence "to zoom
to incredible wealth, I to hit the deck like a watermelon that has
rolled off the stevedore's truck. . . . Lawrence, bringing a gospel
that made sense to a picture business reeling from the tangle of
problems brought on by the talkies," learned "the difficult art of
giving $20 tips without being sent to psychopathic. I, faced with a
financial problem if I wanted to stay west, was thinking technique
in grim earnest." [13] Cain wrote in his preface to *Three of a Kind*
(1943): Lawrence's "influence in Hollywood goes considerably
beyond the scripts he has written. . . . He has laid down principles that are pretty generally incorporated into pictures by now,
and for that reason, as well as personal idiosyncrasies that are to
say the least odd, has become something of a legend. . . . So
when this wight got me by the lapel, and talked technique at me,

I was a little hostile." Cain lovingly quotes three pages of Lawrence's tough-guy-as-story-craftsman talk about the classic Romeo-and-Juliet formula. Theory in action, delivered theatrically, with the force of authority of a very lively human being—this kind of literary talk Cain respected.

Scrutiny of a man's hero is one of the best ways to reveal the man himself. *The Postman* is dedicated to Lawrence "in part because of encouragement, in part because of technical help, but in part also because he lent me the money to eat on while I was writing it, and he felt I rated steak, not beans." Though Lawrence suffered for sixteen years from alcoholism, he managed to write a good many movies; *Test Pilot* was his best. He was the first in Hollywood "to articulate the philosophy of the love story into an intellectual whole." George Jean Nathan called him "the first high comedy writer of the American stage," and Cain says that "the core of his thinking is also the core of my novels; if ever a man had an intellectual parent . . . I must acknowledge such a relationship with Lawrence." Cain never wrote the ending of a story without wondering what Lawrence was going to think of it. "That such a speculation with the death of Lawrence can no longer enter my mind is, believe me, something I shall be a long time getting used to." [14]

When Cain failed to fashion a script based on the Insull scandal in Chicago, Cain was "closed out"; his last day on the Columbia lot (he had been there six weeks), he was directed to report to Robert Riskin. Though Harry Cohn, president of Columbia, had not liked Cain's work, he had been impressed by Cain himself; and Riskin was therefore instructed to find out what was blocking him. Riskin, the highest paid screenwriter and one of the most admired by other scriptwriters, worked for Columbia and turned out, usually with Frank Capra, such successes as *It Happened One Night*. A handsome, black-eyed man a little younger than Cain, Riskin got Cain to talking. After a few hours, Riskin said: "I don't think I ever met anyone with quite the slant that you have on story-writing. You seem to regard any story as a sort of algebraic equation, to be transformed and worked out until it yields *the* inevitable story that lurks in the idea somewhere. But it's not like that at all. It has to be your story, even if you're working for a picture company. There's no ultimate, inevitable, perfect 'move' that's going to give you an outline, determine your situation. It's not mathematics. It's a living thing. It's *you*." Cain, who laughed, felt some sense of gratitude and no resentment to Riskin for expressing a characteristic of his mind that he had half realized himself. "I still have a compulsion," he says, "to grind a theme through the wringer, to extract from it somehow the ultimate, ironic point that it has in it, and I am not at all disposed to think that is bad. On the contrary, I suspect it is one of my strong points."

After *The Postman* caused a sensation, Metro-Goldwyn-Mayer hired Cain to write a script. Feeling that the assignment was getting nowhere, Cain, to release himself from his obligation, returned the down payment. But studios had no way, Cain learned, to book the return of money paid to an author. (So much for the self-righteous, often repeated charge that Cain sold out to the movies.) After Metro-Goldwyn-Mayer bought both film and dramatic rights to *The Postman*, Cain heard that one of their writers was going to adapt it to the stage; but although Cain personally liked the writer assigned to the task, he was filled with horror at the idea of someone else's doing a play based on something he had written. Though he did not want to do it, he let it be known that he would write the play version himself. He conceived it somewhat in the impressionistic style of "Waiting for Lefty." A decade before the movie appeared, the play was given a full-scale Broadway production, with a massive set, designed by Jo Mielziner (in the year of his famous designs for *Winterset* and *Dead End*). The play required ten scene changes; there were two outdoor scenes with real cars. The action, Cain says, was rather slow. It opened on February 25, 1936, and ran seventy-two performances, with Richard Barthelmess (returning to the stage from Hollywood) as Frank. The play was not a success, but Burns Mantle listed it in his *Best Plays of 1935–36:* "This is the type of play that whatever its technical perfections is pretty sure to miss popularity, for the simple reason . . . that it is hard to write an appealing story about repellent humans." [15] About the play, he was, perhaps, right, but the novel had been a tremendous popular success. *The Postman* was revived in the 1950's, starring the notorious Hollywood lovers Tom Neal and Barbara Payton, and had performances in Chicago, Pittsburgh, and other cities. Another of Cain's plays, *7–11*, which was produced in 1937, failed; it was to have "lured Lupe Velez back to the stage."

VI *The Hand of the Potter, Secondhand*

"What a pity," Edmund Wilson said, prompted by the cine-matic qualities in Cain's fiction, "that it is impossible for such a writer to create and produce his own pictures!" If Cain's own screenplays had no effect on the movies, several films made from his novels had an enormous impact. Movies made from Cain's novels influenced the work of other screenwriters; through these movies, other novelists, in turn, have been influenced by Cain. The ten or eleven movies made from Cain's novels have provoked much discussion in film criticism, from Parker Tyler's rarefied psy-chological insights into *Double Indemnity* and *Mildred Pierce* to James Agee's succinct evaluations.

Cain had been in Hollywood two years when "The Baby in the Icebox" (1933), his second story, was made into a movie, *She Made Her Bed* (1933). In 1938, *Career in C Major*, written in January, 1937, in twenty-eight days ("until then a record for me"), was sold by the middle of February to Twentieth Century Fox for eight thousand dollars (this money enabled Cain to go to Mexico to get background for *Serenade*) and appeared as *Wife, Husband, Friend* (1938), with Loretta Young and Warner Bax-ter. Several of Cain's novels had their inception in story-confer-ence situations. *The Root of His Evil* was conceived in a luncheon conversation with Kenneth Littauer of *Collier's*, who wanted a modern Cinderella story. Almost ten years later, in 1938, Cain's father was dying; during the long, grim wait in Baltimore, Cain dictated the story—the only one he ever dictated to a secretary. *Collier's* turned it down; but, before Cain got back to Hollywood, James Geller had sold the story (titled *The Modern Cinderella* in manuscript) to Universal for seventeen thousand, five hundred dollars. The movie, called *When Tomorrow Comes*, with Irene Dunne and Charles Boyer, appeared in the same year; but it was not published as a novel until 1951, when Avon presented it under the title *The Root of His Evil*. In 1940, *The Embezzler* was re-leased as *Money and the Woman*. While these movies offered good, solid, glittery commercial entertainment, they attracted very little critical attention; and they are almost never mentioned today in film chronicles or criticism.

But some of Cain's novels were "legendary successes" when

adapted for the screen. In his study of movie and television censorship, *The Face on the Cutting Room Floor*, Murray Schumach chronicles the long struggle of movie producers with the Breen office over *Double Indemnity*, "a trail-blazer in movie history . . . the first movie in which both the male and female protagonists were thorough villains." *Double Indemnity*, says Schumach, was one of the most important movies to ease interpretations of the censorship code, to force "the watchdogs . . . to become more aware of the considerable changes in American morals, mores and educational standards since the early thirties when the code was written" (63–70). When Paramount released *Double Indemnity* in 1943, which was written for the screen by Billy Wilder and Raymond Chandler, it starred Fred MacMurray, Barbara Stanwyck, and Edward G. Robinson. It is generally considered "a landmark in the art of the cinema, in solid entertainment and everything else good that can be said of a motion picture." [16] Chandler, whose attitude toward Hollywood was similar to Cain's, received an Academy Award nomination for the best-written screenplay for *Double Indemnity*. It was not *The Maltese Falcon* that started a trend in high-budget private-eye pictures, but *Double Indemnity* and Chandler's own *Murder, My Sweet* (adapted from his novel *Farewell, My Lovely*). In a letter to his producer, Joseph Sistrom, Chandler said that there was "no question but that *Double Indemnity* started it, although it was not exactly a mystery." [17]

Some reviewers of Cain's novels saw quite clearly their positive congruence with movies. It "took a while for the little men who make movies," says Jay Adams, "to recognize the wonderful possibilities of *Mildred Pierce*." In 1945, Warner Brothers released *Mildred Pierce*, with screenplay by Ranald MacDougall; produced by Jerry Wald, it was directed by Michael Curtiz. James Agee called "the tawdry, bitter *Mildred Pierce*" one of the finest of the year, and Joan Crawford's performance her best. [18]

Many critics, Edmund Wilson and Max Lerner, particularly, early predicted that *The Postman Always Rings Twice* could not be filmed. But an expertly mechanized, slick movie of hard surfaces, almost a literal transcription of the novel (except for the sex scenes), appeared in 1946; produced by Metro-Goldwyn-Mayer and written by Harry Ruskin and Nevin Busch, it starred John Garfield and Lana Turner. Thus, for Cain, *The Postman* rang thrice: as novel, play, and movie. Although not much has been written about this movie, I find it as memorable as *Double Indemnity* and *Mildred Pierce*. Roger Manvell in *New Cinema in Europe* saw greater significance in the Italian version. After continual interference, Luchino Visconti's *Obsession* (1942) was passed by Mussolini himself. "It was like a bomb exploding in the cinema," Visconti said. "People saw a film which they had not thought possible" (18). Manvell would agree with Arthur Knight's claim in *The Liveliest Art* that Visconti's version was "a true masterpiece that contained all the seeds of the postwar neorealist movement." Manvell's description of its concerns makes it sound like a proletarian novel of the 1930's. Visconti flagrantly violated copyright laws, and to this day Metro-Goldwyn-Mayer has refused to allow prints of his movie to enter the United States. There was also a French version, *Le Dernier Tournant* (1939).

Among other movies made from Cain novels was a remake of *Career in C Major* as *Everybody Does It* (1949), with screenplay by Nunnally Johnson. An incredibly mutilated movie of *Serenade* appeared in 1955, with Mario Lanza and Joan Fontaine. Cain insists that he does not write novels with the movies in mind, or with any expectation of pleasing producers. "The exception was *Love's Lovely Counterfeit*, which I thought, and still think, is a slick plot for a movie, and I executed it well enough." [19] Said Albert Van Nostrand smugly: "But even the movies would not buy this one." [20] However, it did appear in 1956 as *Slightly Scarlet*, with Rhonda Fleming and John Payne. Also in 1956, Universal remade *When Tomorrow Comes* (*Root of His Evil*) as *Interlude*. Daniel Fuchs worked on the screenplay. In 1965, a producer took an option on *Past All Dishonor*, but later dropped it; in 1968 another was taken.

In 1933, after losing his last Hollywood contract, Cain moved from Hollywood to Burbank in the San Fernando Valley and tried to assess his situation. For three years, Cain had earned a weekly wage writing a column for the New York *American* and other Hearst papers. Meanwhile, he had begun thinking once more of his ambition to write fiction. Since his early failures, he had treated his role in regard to "the world of words" as somewhat of a racket. But now, desperately needing some "re-promotion," he returned to the novel form. To Robert Riskin he owes a sudden decision: to tell *his* story, regardless of how preposterous others might think it. Two or three days after their conversation in February, 1933, Cain sat down at the typewriter to begin *The Postman Always Rings Twice.*

VII   *Cain's Career as a Novelist*

Cain published his first short story, "Pastorale," in 1928 when he was thirty-six. He was forty-two when his first novel, *The Postman,* was published in 1934. Knopf rejected it; Lippmann asked to see it, praised it, and asked permission to submit it to Macmillan, who also rejected it; and then Lippmann finally persuaded his friend Knopf to publish it.[21] When the novel appeared, it caused a sensation. Geoffrey Grigson has said that Cain wrote "one remarkable book that deserved its immediate fame." [22]

Cain wrote *Double Indemnity* (1936) to get money to finance the continued run of his play version of *The Postman.* He derived the story from an anecdote that Arthur Krock told at lunch one day at the *World,* and the title was suggested by James Geller, Cain's agent. A shorter version appeared in *Liberty* in 1936. *Career in C Major* originally appeared in 1938 as a serial in *The American Magazine* under the title "Two Can Sing." Then, in 1940, a shorter version of *The Embezzler* appeared as a serial in *Liberty* as "Money and the Woman." In his preface to *Three of a Kind* (1944), Cain said, "These novels, though written fairly recently, really belong to the depression, rather than the war, and make interesting footnotes to an era."

Serenade (1938) began in a conversation with Dr. Charles Townsend, Cain's friend and teacher at Washington College, just after Cain's ill-starred venture into music. Townsend's fascination with the idea lingered with Cain for twenty years. It was to be the tale of a singer who would commit a crime, probably murder; escape; and then not be able to sing for fear of giving himself away. As the years went by, it seemed more workable that someone else, probably a girl, should commit the crime; after visits to Agua Caliente, during his Hollywood sojourn, Cain decided to make her a Mexican: "Then the homosexual angle got into it. Then it seemed to me that only two people might possibly understand the implications of it—a psychiatrist, who simply seemed dull; or, a prostitute, who knows all about men, especially their offbeat characteristics. So the Mexican girl became a Mexican whore." But for years, he held off writing it, feeling it clinically too pat. However, all Cain needed was "the go-ahead from a man in the know," and he got this one night in Hollywood at Samson Raphaelson's house. When Cain related the story to Dr. Samuel Hirshfeld, a prominent Los Angeles physician, the doctor asked Cain why he did not write it; and Cain replied that he "didn't want to do a book a doctor might laugh at." The effect of homosexuality on a man's singing voice might not be clinically sound. Hirshfeld said *he* was not laughing; he found the idea one of the most interesting he had ever heard. After Cain wrote *Serenade*, he heard that it was prescribed reading in psychiatry courses all over the country. "You," said Dr. James M. Neilson, a Los Angeles psychiatrist, "found one that Krafft-Ebing missed, that's all. That's why the book has kicked up such excitement."

In *Mildred Pierce* (1941), Cain presents a detailed picture of the depression's middle class and one of its most convincing female archetypes: Mildred. In *The Moth* (1948), he deliberately presents a detailed picture of the life of the hobo, the migrant worker. These two novels, in many sections, come closer to the proletarian writing of the 1930's than to the tough-guy school. *The Moth*, Cain's twelfth book in fourteen years, appeared when he was fifty-six years old; but the story had its inception during the years 1932 to 1934. The road from Warner Brothers' studio to the main street of Burbank led past a railroad station at the edge of town; and there, night after night, Cain was held up by freights. As he waited, he often saw, silhouetted against the Verdugo Hills, the heads of hundreds of tramps who were riding the tops of boxcars. And gradually he felt he might write a book about them: "To get up the dope, I went to great lengths, going to the missions on Los Angeles street, and finally connecting with a mentor, a tutor, a guide to Hobohemia who was willing, for a consideration, to take me in hand and teach me." "The most erudite man" Cain ever met, the tramp got his knowledge of literature from the public library in which he took refuge from the cold. *The Moth* was an effort to let the Great Depression happen to one man. This simple intention might have produced one of Cain's finest novels; but, strangely, certain apparently autobiographical elements entered into his conception and delayed the novel's thrust into the depression material.

Meanwhile, Cain's second major illness necessitated surgery in

1941. With the excision of the lower part of his stomach went most of the acid-forming tissue, and now he "could drink with no after-effects at all, not even a hangover. The temptation was too much. I gained weight, until I was up to two hundred and forty-four, so that by the end of the forties, I was a hog-fat, pink carica-ture of a man, and knew I had come to a point in my life. I drank because I liked it, because I wanted it, because I had to." Then one night in the fall of 1949, he told Florence (his fourth wife), who took no interest in liquor, that he thought he would skip the evening cocktail, for it had come to him that if a drunk is always only one drink from disaster, he is equally only one drink from salvation. He has not taken a drink since that night.

In Cain's novels of the early 1940's, there is almost no sense of the war. Two novels dealt with things remote in time or geogra-phy: *Past All Dishonor* is set during the Civil War; in *The Butterfly*, set along the creeks of the West Virginia mountains, he finally realized his minefield material. In his preface to *Three of Hearts*, he says: "These novels will come as a surprise to readers of my previous works, for there is a never-never-land quality in all of them; a flight, not so much from reality as from actuality, not to be found in any of my previous work." Although the time is pres-ent in *The Butterfly*, "Each story, in its own way, recoils from the present as it existed at the time it was written." 23

While Cain was writing his tough, present-day novels, Edna Ferber, Walter D. Edmonds, Ernest Boyd, Margaret Mitchell, Hervey Allen, and Kenneth Roberts were establishing the histori-cal genre that became very popular in the 1940's along with the works of Frank Yerby, Thomas B. Costain, Van Wyck Mason, and others. If novelists seduce audiences, audiences also seduce novel-ists: in *Past All Dishonor* Cain responded to that interest in histor-ical fiction, while infusing his novel with elements of the tough-guy fiction for which he was famous. The book evokes the Civil War era in the same economical way his modern novels evoke contemporary times. *Past All Dishonor* was, as reviewers noted, very unlike *Forever Amber* and other historical novels of those years.

Cain, who is interested in the past for its own sake, states his intention in his historical novels in his comment on the jacket of *Past All Dishonor:* "I have tried to present the life of the time as it was." Speaking of *Mignon*, his second historical novel, Cain sees the dictates of the period novel as rigidly set: "The given events . . . can't be changed, of course, as to wind, weather, tide, or number of soldiers killed. . . . It becomes indeed a sort of étude in algebra to fit the characters to the events, with no possible relation to proper narrative, so you come out with something that looks like fiction, and with luck may be mistaken for it." After ten years' work on *Mignon* he was moved to vow: "I shall never, as long as I live, try a period novel again. It is like a sentence in the penitentiary . . . you refuse to leave your cell until your time is up." Soon after *Mignon* was published, he said of such novels, "All that reading and labor, and a kind of mouse is born." [24]

Cain presents an odd argument for writing about things remote from the war. With a war going on, it was difficult, Cain strangely assumes, for a writer to write as he was accustomed to "of this time, this place, and this world." The search for what he calls "firmer footing" led to an increased output of historical novels (preface, *Three of Hearts*). His first break with his immediate scene was *Love's Lovely Counterfeit*. What seemed in 1941 "a gay idea, seasoned with malice," to write of some "highly amusing skulduggeries around my home city," Los Angeles, "suddenly seemed somehow a dirty trick." Therefore, he set the story in a fictitious Midwestern town so he would at least have "nothing very grievous" on his conscience. "By 1942 anything current had become a complete impossibility, and like many of my colleagues I turned the calender back many years to find a time when at least the values that men cherished were fixed and comprehensible." So he wrote *Past All Dishonor* and *The Butterfly* as being "unassociated with the perplexities then plaguing us" (preface, *Three of Hearts*). One wonders which writers he considers his "colleagues"; Cain's attitude is perhaps that of the commercial writer whose values and assumptions differ from writers like James T. Farrell, William Faulkner, Robert Penn Warren, Ira Wolfert, and Saul Bellow, who wrote novels during the war and who did not feel that to take a merely glancing look at the contemporary American scene was a way of supporting the war.

Discussing the effect of the war on the American writer, in the preface to *Three of Hearts*, Cain becomes uncharacteristically poetic in a "four score and seven years ago" way. Another indication of the strange effect the war had on Cain are the jackets of *Love's Lovely Counterfeit* and *Three of a Kind*; they carried a picture of Cain looking very solemn, strong, and statesmanlike; and they presented, in excellent proclamation rhetoric, "A Word to You from James M. Cain," urging the multitudes to buy bonds. He warns, predicts, sternly advises, and promises: "To us, who are primarily makers of things, the chance to start afresh, with all molds broken and no hampering link with the preconceptions of the past, and supply a world that must have the progeny of our skill, is indeed an exciting prospect." Another, more practical, appeal reads: "Unless this investment pays, all other investments collapse."

In the spring of 1944, Cain met at a party in Hollywood Aileen Pringle, once a successful movie star. Says Cain: "We were both passing through a dark period, so we became very close friends. But friendship, no matter how close, how gay, how pleasant, isn't the stuff of which marriage is made. . . . We woke up next morning [after the marriage] total strangers, and though we both tried, conscientiously, honestly, and highmindedly to make a marriage out of our wedding, it wouldn't come alive. After a year and a half, we gave up." After the divorce, "we were the same warm friends as we had been."

Cain displayed both a sort of social consciousness, stimulated perhaps by the war, and a characteristic toughness when, in 1946, he set out to organize all the writers in America into an American Authors' Authority, a project which occupied him for several years. Cain approached the project with all of the great energy, sense of authority, arrogance, and drama of one of his characters. (Carrie Selden in *The Root of His Evil* organizes workers with a similar sweeping expeditiousness; his fourth wife Florence had proposed and helped organize a Los Angeles Opera Guild in 1940.) Cain's position is set forth in four articles in *The Screen Writer*, official organ of the Guild, and in one in *The Saturday Review*. In "The Opening Gun" (May, 1946), concerned with a typical instance of a producer's abuse of a screenwriter, Cain set the stage with his premise that "any case involving property rights and their enforcement . . . involves all writers. . . . And some of you, who read this, I expect to see down there in court, when Miss Frings' case comes to trial, going on the witness stand with me."

Three months later, Cain presented the entire plan in "An American Authors' Authority." The members of the executive board of the Screen Writers' Guild unanimously approved Cain's proposals and recommended them as the collective program of writers in America. The article is a long, witty, strongly written description of the plight of writers in all fields. But, says Cain, the writer's most formidable enemy is himself: "A gang of plumbers can sew up a city with extortionist regulations and hang together like wolves. But anybody who has tried to get three writers to act as a unit on the simplest matter knows what the difficulties are."

In September, Harrison Smith responded to Cain's proposal in an editorial in *The Saturday Review:* "This glamorous proposal is written with all the enthusiasm and confidence of a wildcat oil company's prospectus," and it is a " 'blue sky' proposal with a vengeance." Cain is naïve in his claims, said Smith, who anticipated that all the independent writers in the country would resist such an organization, for it seemed obvious that any agency with such power could strangle free speech and free literary enterprise. Smith aligns himself with those who question the political ideology of "the backers of this fabulous scheme. . . . Whether there are Communists in Hollywood and in radio studios or not, it is our opinion that the American Authors' Authority is dangerous and unworkable." [25]

In mid-November, *The Saturday Review* carried a debate, featured on the cover, between James T. Farrell and Cain. Regarding the struggle as between rich and poor writers, Farrell charges that the materialistic, inartistic commercial Hollywood writers would control the market to keep out independents. A major reason for artistic decline in America, says Farrell, is an overemphasis on money.[26] Indeed, Cain's slogan was taken from Philip Goodman's response to an inaccurate cashier in Paris: "And remember, it's not the principle of the thing, it's the money." To Farrell, "This idea is stamped in the crude conceptions of the artist which Mr. Cain holds, the notion that the artist is a kind of idiot who thinks that he is a God, but who has only the defects and none of the virtues of a God."

In his reply to Farrell, Cain observes that his opponents conceive the issue in terms of freedom versus control. Ironically, this freedom is illusory for reasons that prompted the proposal in the first place. He sees among his opponents established, wealthy writers: Louis Bromfield, Clarence Budington Kelland, John Erskine, Philip Wylie, Katherine Brush. (Cain himself, who pub-

lished four novels within two or three years of the project, must
have been doing well at this time.) Fear of reprisals from publishers, Cain said, is the real cause of opposition from well-to-do writers. Unfairly, Cain calls Farrell's argument "twittering nonsense."
He does not believe, as Farrell does, that "art can be consciously
'created' . . . these ideas, to me, are simply weird, and downright silly. . . . I believe the conscious creating of art is a form of
literary smugness." Cain's is, of course, a form of antiliterary
smugness.

Characteristically, when Cain has written several times before
on the same subject, he is at his best in a "sign-off" article. Immersed as he was, out of personal interest, in direct action,
Cain is even better than usual in "Respectfully Submitted" (Supplement to *The Screen Writer*, March, 1947). He reports that six
hundred writers attended the meeting he called in New York.
This was "said to be the largest number of them ever assembled at
one spot in the history of literature." Nobody else, Cain pointed
out, had offered a solution to the desperate plight of the American
writer, who works on an archaic copyright law framed in 1909.
What was needed was a full-time tough mug, for "pugnacity
would help more than a calm, reasonable disposition." (Cain himself looked the part: in 1942, he was described as a dark-complex-
ioned, burly man, with green eyes, black hair worn in a pompa-
dour—turning into a "bush" of gray—heavy black beetle brows,
looking "more like a schoolmaster or an amiable priest than a sophisticated novelist"; but in 1946, Cain himself said he weighed
two hundred and twenty pounds and looked "like the chief dis-
patcher of a long-distance hauling concern.") But the first full-
scale attempt in American history to organize *all* writers collapsed
in 1948, and Cain's major involvement in public affairs ended.
With his fourth wife, Florence, he retired from Hollywood to
Hyattsville, Maryland, near Washington; he has lived there since.

Cain's marriage to Florence Macbeth in 1947 changed his life.
As Cain proudly points out, she has been listed in *Who's Who in
America* longer (fifty years) than any woman, and in various encyclopedias on music. She came from Mankato, Minnesota, a de-
scendant of the Macbeths of Shakespeare. She debuted in Germany under Richard Strauss's sponsorship; in England, under
Beecham's; in Chicago, under Campanini's. A coloratura, praised
for her accuracy and adherence to score, she sang many famous

roles. For twenty years, she was first coloratura of the Chicago opera, a somewhat "legendary success."

Cain, who first become aware of her while he was studying music in Washington in 1914, had followed her career through the years quite closely. Shortly after his breakup with Aileen, he finally met her at a tea party in Hollywood. Cain hesitated at fifty-five to make a fourth try at marriage. And Florence, four years a widow, was reluctant to risk the memory of a happy marriage in a new one. But they were married in September, 1947, with many factors in favor of its lasting, as it did, for twenty years: "Physically, and I don't just mean sexually, she delighted me, and never once got 'on my nerves.' Something more elusive than that—some chemical harmony of touch, sound, even of smell, that makes for peace and tranquility. It has meant a tremendous change in my life, in my outlook. We're not young any more," he said, in 1965, "yet we are as close now as we ever were, perhaps a little closer. She unkinked me in all sorts of strange ways." Florence died in May, 1966.

In the 1950's, not much was heard from Cain. He wrote *Jealous Woman* (1950); *The Root of His Evil* was finally published in 1951. Both were published by Avon and in England. Cain's third major illness came in his sixties, a high cholesterol condition. Again, recent techniques saved him. His doctor in Hyattsville cured him in twenty-four hours with a special diet. "From having become a nitwit, one who couldn't remember anything, or think to any purpose, I was myself again." During this time, he concocted *Galatea* (1953), the tale of a fat girl, her prize-ring trainer boy friend who put her through a special reducing diet, and her restaurant-keeper husband. It was not well received. Then for ten years, Cain was silent.

In a *Newsweek* interview, he spoke of having been ill from 1957 to 1962: "I wasn't worth a damn." [27] Frightened, he finally reduced from two hundred and fifty to one hundred and eighty-five pounds on another diet. In 1962, he had an automobile crash, which led him to give up his car, thus making his life rather reclusive. Florence herself was for many years an invalid requiring a regimen of absolute quiet. Cain's various illnesses have had direct and indirect effect on his writing. The "new life" theme is one of his favorites, and he has survived several physical "wrecks" to begin again in his own life.

Recovering from his illness in 1962, Cain returned to work on *Mignon*. Into this novel he put ten years of research on the cotton racket during the Civil War; but the elements would not cohere: "It seemed a promising thing, just up my alley, with sardonic overtones and everything I like to deal with. But though I finally got the book out, I didn't pull it off. It was the most ill-starred venture I ever embarked on."

A few years later *The Magician's Wife* (1965) appeared; it was modeled on *The Postman;* and it was received with contempt. Cain simply wanted to write a story about a masculine, average guy in the meat business. "It wasn't too good an effort." Cain could not end what he had started, and the suicide was the sort of "ending few readers accept. The ending of a tale carries, or should carry, its point, and this story didn't seem to have one. But it's a hit in Japan, where hara-kiri is an honorable way out!"

At seventy-eight Cain lives in a house on a quiet Hyattsville street. He is working on two novels. One, totally different from his previous books, concerns the psychological conflict between a little girl who is given a tiger cub to raise and her domineering mother who refuses to allow the child to raise it in her own way. The other novel in progress derives from Cain's usual stock in trade.

James T. Farrell, who stresses the fact that Cain's background is intimately associated with "the twenties of Mencken," observes that in the early 1940's his writing still suggested the sophistication of *The Mercury*. But, while Mencken encouraged a more serious exploration of American experience in fiction and created an audience for it, Cain, Farrell charges, failed to grow with the positive side of Mencken's approach. "I think it not unfair to say that writing like Cain's exploits rather than explores the material of life in America." [28] Critics like Farrell accuse Cain of presenting violence without context, sadism without motive, death without dignity, sex without love, money without comfort, and murder without malice—as though these things were not to be observed everywhere around Cain—and they also lament his failure to make his work socially significant.

It is not enough for Farrell, and others, that Cain provides images, typical characters, and situations of the times in which he writes; it is not sufficient therefore that the novels themselves are characteristic artifacts of the times—Cain must render, like Farrell, some judgment on what he depicts. Farrell concedes that Cain possesses "the taste for reality" which he acquired in the 1920's; but "to it he has added lessons learned from Hollywood. Cain now shocks with his calculated thrills the yokels he attacked in *Our Government.*" Cain once suggested, says Farrell, that the yokels got what they deserved: "These same yokels deserve the realist they now have and that realist deserves his audience." But it is an audience, Cain has often remarked, of which he strives to be worthy.

Cain, then, is preeminently a man of the 1920's and 1930's whose fiction somehow evokes a sense also of the early 1940's; but he has less to say, directly or indirectly, to the 1950's and 1960's in his novels of those decades. His early works continue to be relevant, but his new ones do little to enrich his contribution to the tough-guy vision of American land, character, and dream.

CHAPTER *3*

The Love-Rack and the Wish-Come-True

WITH the success of *The Postman,* Cain realized that he would always have only one story to tell—"a love-story." Once he had invented "the big situation," the rest was "a matter of polarities." The lovers would come together; then be divided by some twist of the situation; then be brought still closer together, and, in the end, either win each other, with the dilemma resolved, or meet absolute disaster. He found he was usually better in those novels in which the perilous situation finally closed in on the characters, as in *The Postman, Serenade,* and *The Butterfly.* He discovered that his novels were "studies of emotion," which "has a dialectic all its own, a syntax, a logic, unlike the logic of reason." The effort to unravel this pattern, to reweave it again into narrative, he feels, is really his "trick."

While talking endlessly with his friend Vincent Lawrence in California, Cain first glimpsed what he wanted to do in the novel. Lawrence talked repeatedly about what he called "the love-rack." Said Cain: "I haven't the faintest idea whether this is a rack on which the lovers are tortured, or something with pegs to hold the shining cloak of romance." In some Cain novels, the rack holds the "shining cloak of romance," but in others the lovers share a bed of torture. Although this situation became obvious to Cain later, it was rather new to him at the time that the reader or spectator must first care that the lovers are on the love-rack and sympathize with them. Lawrence helped him to clarify an idea he already vaguely had in mind: "I wanted to know why every episode in the story couldn't be invented and molded and written with a view to its effect on the love story." So he made the love-rack the whole novel, not just a scene or two, and his lovers were to be viewed in respect to nothing but the experience itself. Most of his novels are concerned, therefore, with "some high adventure on which a man and woman embark" (preface, *Three of a Kind*).

Lawrence's chance anecdote about the famous Ruth Snyder-Judd Gray case made Cain see this concept more vividly: "I heard that when Ruth Snyder packed Gray off to Syracuse (where he was supposed to be staying at a hotel all this gruesome night), she gave him a bottle of wine, which he desperately wanted on the train. But he had no corkscrew with him, and dared not ask the porter for one, for fear it would be the one thing they'd remember him by. When the police lab analyzed it, they found enough arsenic to kill a regiment of men. Did you ever hear that, Cain?" Cain had not, but it gave him an idea for a story: "Your idea of a love-rack interests me, and I would think a murder would be a terrific love-rack." *The Postman* was the result of this conception.

Murder is the best love-rack, and money is at the heart of most of the love affairs. For sex and money, the lovers lose themselves in an audacious endeavor, usually the murder of the husband, "the unwanted end of the triangle." A crime must be committed, the lovers feel, before the course of love can run smoothly. Their indulgence in sex requires the money; but the pursuit of money frustrates the pursuit of sex, and vice versa. Money is sometimes a momentary substitute for sex, a source of sublimated power; but, when sex comes into play again, it becomes the motive force, and a precipice is not far away. Whether for love or money, but usually for both, the Cain hero is always leaning over the edge of the cliff for a better look at "the wish." Always he gets the woman and the money, but when he does, he usually falls over the precipice, clutching both.

"I, so far as I can sense the pattern of my mind, write of the wish that comes true," said Cain in 1947 in the preface to *The Butterfly*, "for some reason a terrifying concept, at least to my imagination. Of course, the wish must really have terror in it." He claims Pandora, "the first woman," as his inspiration, "a conceit that pleases me, somehow, and often helps my thinking. I think my stories have some quality of the opening of a forbidden box, and that it is this, rather than violence, sex, or any of the things usually cited by way of explanation, that gives them the drive so often noted. Their appeal is first to the mind, and the reader is carried along as much by his own realization that the characters cannot have this particular wish and survive, and his curiosity to see what happens to them, as by the effect on him of incident, dialogue, or character."

The wish-come-true and the love-rack theories of story-building dictate theme, character, action, and technique in most of Cain's best novels; they operate somehow in all sixteen, but in many variations. In only a few of the novels do the lovers commit no crime; in only three, there is no desperate love situation from beginning to end; in several, the lovers' exploits are clean and praiseworthy. But half of the novels end in violent death for one or both lovers.

The classic expression of what is recognized as the composite Cain image is *The Postman Always Rings Twice*. Frank Chambers, a young drifter, is thrown off a truck near a roadside restaurant in California. He meets and immediately lusts for Cora Papadakis, whose husband, Nick, the proprietor, an obese, middle-aged Greek, offers Frank a job. Frank's wish is to have Cora; Cora's desire is to have Frank, but not without money and respectability. So she urges Frank to kill Nick; the restaurant will then be hers. Thus, the lovers go on the love-rack, and acts of violence follow. As soon as Frank and Cora believe that their wish has come true, that they have committed the perfect murder and have acquired money, property, and freedom, they turn on each other. Toward the end, they become reconciled; but Cora soon dies in a car accident, and Frank ends up in the death house. He is ironically convicted of intentionally killing Cora in order to have all the money for himself.

Cain's most recent novel, *The Magician's Wife* (1965), depends, with an almost complete lack of success, upon the same formula. Clay Lockwood, a meat-packing executive, lusts for Sally Alexis, a waitress. More than sex, she craves money; and she uses Clay to get it. Together, they murder her husband, a magician, to collect insurance. Clay is on a double love-rack; for, midway in the novel, he falls genuinely in love with Sally's mother. His wish comes true, but he kills Sally and commits suicide.

The Postman and *The Butterfly* are two of the best examples of what I will discuss later as "pure" novels. Set in the mountains of eastern Kentucky, *The Butterfly* is a story of supposed incest. Jess Tyler, a farmer, and his "daughter" Kady desire to make love. They go on the love-rack, and their wish comes true. Later, Jess kills Moke Blue, a loafing banjo-picker, who stole his wife and seduced Kady earlier. Betrayed by Kady, Jess is about to be killed by Moke's kinfolk as the novel ends.

Serenade and *Mildred Pierce* are Cain's most successful character studies. In *Serenade,* John Howard Sharp is stranded in Mexico City when, as has been noted, his singing voice fails as a psychological expression of his fear of responding to the homosexual advances of his conductor, Winston Hawes. As the novel begins, Sharp's wish is to regain his voice and become a great opera singer. When he meets Juana, a Mexican Indian whore, he wishes to possess her magnificent body. The two wishes come true; but, when Hawes's homosexuality poses a threat to both, Juana impales him with a bullfighter's sword. Juana is killed by Mexican police, and Sharp gives up singing.

Mildred Pierce's wish is to have her daughter Veda's love and respect; this wish spawns another—one for money and respectability so that she can win her daughter from competing forces, manifested mainly in Monty Beragon, a rich playboy, whom she unknowingly shares with Veda. Mildred begins as a housewife and becomes a waitress, and consequently owner of a chain of restaurants; she ends as a housewife, reunited with her weak husband Bert, and finally freed of Veda. It was when her wish for money came true that she suffered the greatest pain on the love-rack.

Carrie Selden, in *The Root of His Evil,* is an interesting variation of the Mildred character. Like Mildred, she is a waitress who devotes her energies and employs her feminine wiles to make a great deal of money to win the person she loves. Too much money is "the root of evil" for Carrie's husband, Grant Harris, who would rather study Indians than make more money. The main obstacle to matrimonial contentment is Grant's mother, a society priestess. Carrie's wish comes true, and the end is a happy one, as in *Mildred Pierce.*

The Moth, Cain's longest novel, is another character study. Jack Dillon is a man of many wishes, one of which is to avoid making love to a nymphet. With its numerous subplots, this is a picaresque novel of the Great Depression—that massive expression of the futility of the wish-come-true; for in the 1920's war-weary America's wish for prosperity and freedom *had* come true. The love-rack concept, too, takes multiple forms. After years of wandering, Dillon comes home to discover that his nymphet has grown up; his wish comes true, and his many trials end happily.

Mildred Pierce, The Root of His Evil, and *The Moth*—character studies that end happily—employ the wish-come-true and love-

rack concepts in a rather diffuse way; and the audacious endeavors of the main characters are rather solitary. But in what I call
Cain's "romance novels," *Career in C Major* and *Galatea*, the two
concepts are fully explored, with interesting variations. In *Career*,
Leonard Borland wishes to live with his wife, Doris, a Veda-like
bitch, without the disruptive effect of her wish to become a famous opera singer. He is on the love-rack alone; but a lovely
opera singer, Cecil Carver, helps him make his wish come true:
Borland, an engineer, becomes a very good singer himself and
upstages his wife. This comic romance, this *opéra bouffe*, ends
happily, as does *Galatea*.

In *Galatea*, Duke Webster, ex-boxer, does not wish to make
love to his boss's wife, Holly Valenti; but, after he succeeds in
transforming her from "a tub of lard" into a trim and lovely
woman by having her use a special fighter's diet, he falls in love
with her. Their audacious adventure is the diet itself, conducted
in secrecy because Holly's husband has deliberately fed her abnormal appetite to imprison her in blubber and thus keep a hold
on her. His attempt to murder Holly and Duke (a switch from the
usual Cain pattern) fails, and he is killed himself.

Cain's two historical novels, *Past All Dishonor* and *Mignon*, are
second-rate demonstrations of the wish-come-true and the love-
rack concepts. In *Past All Dishonor*, Roger Duval, a Confederate
soldier, falls in love with Morina Crockett, a mining-camp whore,
in Sacramento and follows her to Virginia City. Before they can
fully enjoy each other, Roger must kill his wealthy rival, Brewer,
and rob and kill other men for Morina. But, in the end, their
wishes having come true, Roger accidentally shoots Morina; and
he supposedly dies shooting it out with a posse.

In *Mignon*, Bill Cresap, recently discharged from the Union
army with a leg wound, dreams of cutting a canal to the Gulf of
Mexico; but civilians draw him back into the war. In New Or-
leans, he falls in love with Mignon, a beautiful, fiery widow. If his
wish to have her is to come true, he must reject his other dream
and devote his time as a lawyer to freeing her father from the jail
where he is held on a false charge as a traitor. Frank Burke, a wily
Irish trader, a masterful liar and murderer, stands between
Mignon and Bill. He repeatedly tempts his partner, Mignon's father, a merchant of dangerously wavering patriotism, and Mignon
herself into scheming for a rich shipment of "hoodooed" cotton.

The conflict ends with everyone dead except Bill; though he loses Mignon, another wish—to serve his country well—comes true.

Cain's five other books are crime novels which employ these recurrent concepts with varying degrees of success. In *Double Indemnity* (the best of these), Walter Huff, insurance agent, lusts for Phyllis Nirdlinger, whose main interests are murder and money. Their adventure is the murder of her husband, which is arranged to look like an accident so she can claim insurance. When the wish comes true for both, they doublecross each other. Huff meanwhile falls genuinely in love with Lola, the victim's daughter by a previous marriage. The novel ends in a suicide pact between Phyllis and Huff.

Jealous Woman, another insurance story, and Cain's only mystery novel (the reader doesn't witness the crime), ends happily for the lovers. The great adventure for Ed Horner, insurance agent, and Jane Delavan, movie actress, is their effort to solve the murder of her husband, whom she is in Reno to divorce. Ed's secondary wish is to win the award cup for the best salesman. *Sinful Woman,* also set in Reno, is about the efforts of Sheriff Parker Lucas to solve the "murder" of Sylvia Shoreham's husband, whom Sylvia is in Reno to divorce. His wish to meet his favorite movie actress, Sylvia, comes true; but he is miserable for a while, as he suspects her of hoodwinking him concerning her own involvement in the "murder" of her husband. Cain's usual conception is disjointedly employed in these two mystery romances; if there is a case to be made against Cain as a cheap writer, these two novels (which he virtually disowns) are chief exhibits.

In *The Embezzler,* Dave Bennett, bank executive, is on the love-rack with Sheila Brent; their wish is to have each other, but hers is also to clear her husband of the crime of embezzlement to save her children's name. So she persuades Bennett to help her doctor the records and replace the money. Her husband is killed in a gun battle with police, and their wish comes true. *The Embezzler* is one of Cain's most effective short novels in the hard-boiled manner.

Love's Lovely Counterfeit is one of his worst. Ben Grace, ex-professional football player, now working for a crime syndicate in a small Midwestern town, wishes to be a big-time operator instead of a chiseler. He *uses* June Lyons, a political secretary; makes love to her; and gives her money to help her get her sister

Dorothy out of trouble. When Ben meets Dorothy, his wishes for money and sex come true; but his fortunes immediately change—Dorothy shoots Ben's former hoodlum boss; later, a cop shoots Ben; on his deathbed, he marries Dorothy.

Cain appeals to the child in every adult who still believes in fairy tales—or at least in the necessity of telling them. To the question, "If you had three wishes, what would you wish for?" Cain adds: "If they came true, what would happen to you?" The wish inspires most human stories, from "I wish I were Beowulf" to "I wish I were James Bond." The story the ordinary man wants to hear is true to his own daydreams. Edmund Wilson said of the typical Cain hero: "His fate is . . . forecast from the beginning; but in the meantime he has fabulous adventures—samples, as it were, from a *Thousand and One Nights* of the screwy Pacific Coast."

Cain has therefore taken the essentially masculine cliché of the "pipe-dream" and transformed it into a universal action which, he feels, bears repeating. The pipe-dream metaphor is appropriate for Cain's heroes; they seem to move in a state of narcosis, oblivious to the world beyond their circle of black enchantment. Yet few get literally drunk; none take narcotics. High on sex, often apotheosized into home-brewed mysticism, drugged with orgasmic optimism, and gorged on food, they set out from their caves, make the kill, and consummate the ritual with another orgy of sex and food. While Cain seems most interested in the characteristic male wish, in several novels he makes us experience the Cinderella wish. Many waitresses and other working girls desire to marry a millionaire prince. But that's a dream; real millionaires have ordinary human problems. In *Root of His Evil*, Carrie gets not only the millionaire but his problems as well. Ironically, she does not consciously desire to be a Cinderella; chance thrusts her into a Cinderella situation. Her wish then becomes a desire to earn her own wealth to cancel out the "prince-like" qualifications of the man she loves. Several of Cain's men go through the Cinderella syndrome, as when Sharp and Borland become famous singers overnight; but, in both instances, they return to their original situations. Cain never presents his characters in idle daydreams; we usually meet the hero at the moment he meets the object of his wish. *Serenade*'s opening lines are typical: "I was in the Tupinamba, having a *bizcocho* and coffee, when this girl came in. . . ."

In *Public Journal: Marginal Notes on Wartime America*, Max Lerner says that Cain's general theme is one "of love and death coiled up with each other like fatal serpents. It is love-in-death and death-and-rebirth-in-love. Cain's idea as a writing technician is that if you mix a potion of love with the powerful ingredient of murder, then you get the strongest light possible shed on the love story." [1] The hero is often reluctant to attempt a consummation of the wish, knowing, like the rest of us, that one attempts to fulfill such wishes at one's peril. He tries to avoid the girl, he often has premonitions of disaster; but chance, will, or recklessness throws him into the first impulsive and precipitous act. Just after meeting Phyllis, Huff says: "I lit a fire and sat there, trying to figure out where I was at. I knew where I was at, of course. I was standing right on the deep end, looking over the edge, and I kept telling myself to get out of there, and get quick, and never come back. But that was what I kept telling myself. What I was doing was peeping over the edge, and all the time I was trying to pull away from it, there was something in me that kept edging a little closer, trying to get a better look." Because we know that we, too, are capable of making the same fatal plunge—of letting our dreams lure us over the precipice into nightmare, we experience fear for the character as he goes ahead and does what we, as sensible onlookers, know he should not do.

If pipe-dreams and illusions sustain most men, Cain goes further: most men do not need the *fulfillment* of their wishes because the realization is often as lethal as inhaling gas fumes. In most fairy tales the granting of the wishes is intermingled with horrors, and we willingly suspend our disbelief that it will not all end happily. In Cain, the horror is implicit in the wish itself. To force such forbidden or unrealistic wishes as his lovers do is often to will death in disguise. Huff's dream of sex is the bitch Phyllis, but having her means having the witch, the nightmare of death, within.

Dreams are only for dreaming, not living, as the Pandora myth once and for all showed long ago. In one version, Pandora imprudently opened a jar and all the ills and evils flew into the world, but on the bottom was hope; in another version, she opened a box of good things, all of which fled. On both versions of this myth,

Cain constructs many variations. In the same act, the wish comes
true and is transformed, usually, into terror and destruction; the
dream-come-true is a false climax; the end of the nightmare, from
which the lovers often fail to awaken, is the true climax. Cain's
hero may commit the perfect murder, but somehow "perfection
itself must blow up in his face . . . a theme that attracts us all,"
says Cain in the preface to *Three of a Kind.* "They would get
away with it, and then what? They would find . . . that the earth
is not big enough for two persons who share such a dreadful secret." Immediately after the wish comes true—they've killed the
husband and have each other and stand to collect the money—
Huff and Phyllis, Clay and Sally, Frank and Cora begin to run
away from each other, the law, or both; they turn against, and
eventually doublecross, each other. But Frank discovers, when he
runs away with a female cat-trainer, that the world is not large
enough to offer escape from his passion for Cora. Caring about
nothing but themselves, Cain's lovers are condemned by situations
produced by their own characters; for to be granted one's wishes
is to be condemned to some kind of hell. And, in his best novels,
Cain creates an all-pervading stench of doom and death.

I *Overreachers on a Precipice*

Edmund Wilson's description of the "hero of the typical Cain
novel" suggests possibilities which Cain often achieves: "Cain's
heroes are capable of extraordinary exploits, but they are always
treading the edge of a precipice; and they are doomed, like the
heroes of Hemingway, for they will eventually fall off the precipice. But whereas in Hemingway's stories, it is simply that these
brave and decent men have had a dirty deal from life, the hero of
a novel by Cain is an individual of mixed unstable character, who
carries his precipice with him like Pascal."

In *The Novel of Violence in America: 1920–1950,* W. M.
Frohock expresses the negative view: he claims that Cain's
"valueless" characters are uncomplicated. Frank's "emotional
life was stunted. His physical appetites expressed themselves
without, apparently, modifying his other attitudes in any way." [2]
Frohock admits that Frank's ambivalent attitude toward people
reveals a little more complexity than that found in most 1934
murder novels: Frank can like Nick, but he can also coldbloodedly

kill him; he can love Cora, yet betray her. But, if he were really complicated, he wouldn't be Frank Chambers—a simple man in a simple situation. Through Frank's voice, the novel does exactly, with very little waste or excess, what it sets out to do.

In a review of *Mildred*, Stanley Edgar Hyman declared that "Cain deals with ciphers, picturesque cardboard characters whom he cuts into attractive designs." But, as Cain's "flat" heroes—and I use the term "flat" in Edwin Muir's positive sense—move among other flat characters, they are rounded out by the surrounding action. Cain's interest in the criminal himself, as opposed to pursuit of criminals, is expressed not in a scrutiny of character motives but rather in a character's collision with the consequences of his motives. Going against the American insistence on being told *why* a criminal does what he does—on simplifying the complex origins of an act until the act itself is submerged beneath explanations—Cain confronts us with the man and his action as a single thrust, whatever its psychological springs. Cain shows *how* a man plunges into the action, not *why*.

Although Cain's novels express various notions and aspects of masculinity, there is no conscious overemphasis: "The muscle-flexing is often there, all right, and it is real, but it is not, as so many assume, born of a desire to be tough." Neither Cain nor his characters declare their masculinity as stridently as did Hemingway and his characters; but the mystical American tough stance is as definitely associated with Cain in fiction as with Bogart in movies. However, in all Cain's heroes, there is a streak of something that is, by American tough-guy standards, unmanly—something that verges on physical or moral cowardice. The more the "normal" American male is aware of some deficiency in himself as regards the locker-room notion of masculinity, the more recklessly he pushes himself into greater masculine exploits. Sharp's tough-guy stance is one way of dealing with his fear that his homosexual inclinations will re-emerge; but, when Juana carries violence to the extreme of murder, Sharp reacts most intensely: "She spit into the blood, stepped back, and picked up the cape. . . . I sat there, still looking at that thing that was pinned to the sofa, with its head hanging over the back, and the blood drying on the shirt. . . . I picked up a rug to throw on it. Then something twisted in my stomach, and I stumbled back to a bathroom." All Cain's men weep or vomit when the sex is out of reach or the violence goes wrong (the women almost never do): "My characters always have gotten scared. My guys always get the girl in their arms and then are too scared to do anything about it," said Cain, in an interview with Luther Nichols. In *Galatea*, Duke, ex-prize-fighter, refers quite often to his yellow streak; fear of cowardice is his main character trait.

The element of cowardliness that is in most of Cain's heroes does not finally, ever, reduce any one of them to being a coward. Within the whole character makeup, this cowardice is not really cowardice, because more than enough courage offsets it; but the character's fear of it is exaggerated in typically American fashion. Cain seems to be trying to portray fully and fascinatingly the American male by showing that he has an effeminate streak—and the American female by showing her ruthlessness and almost masculine ambition and drive. While Cain has a typical American admiration of courage, he criticizes the exaggeration of courage into boorishness by introducing this element of understandable cowardliness: "My men get scared and admit it. If this makes them 'effeminate,' I hope it also makes them real."

"Tribute to a Hero" (1933), a reminiscence of Cain's early days at Washington College, ends with a long autobiographical anecdote about a football hero who had a yellow streak but overcame it. This early encounter with such a hero probably helped to form Cain's concept of a real man—the inner conflict that gives off enough heat to propel him through various adventures. "When you get older there are no more great men," but an encounter with a hero when you're young "stays with you through life, and warms you when you think of it. . . . To me now . . . a football player is rather less than a superman. Just the same, I lay this wreath at his feet unashamed as he still seems great to me." Then, almost as though aware of an unseemly soft streak in himself, Cain feels compelled to end the essay with wise-guy humor.

One of the striking correlative features of American toughness is sentimentality. We detect it in Hammett, Chandler, and McCoy. Just as Cain consciously shows that there is a little of the parakeet in every hawk, he also deliberately allows his tough characters to expose hidden springs of sentiment. Some of Frank's and Cora's pseudo-cosmic love talk, objectively examined, is silly; but we could not accuse the author himself of sentimentality in that novel. Cain is skillful at creating conditions for a *genuine* expression of sentiment by his heroes; and, while they seldom indulge in self-pity, they are capable of demonstrating pity for others. Certain situations in his novels are inherently sentimental; sentimentality degenerates sometimes into bathos. Irishman Cain often attacks sentimentality in his nonfiction; but, in the emotive context of a fictional situation, an author's usually well-concealed qualities are frequently released in disguise, even as he sneers at the behavior of his own characters.

Perhaps the objectivity of tough-guy writers and their heroes is only the tough, romantic stance of the American reluctant to show his feelings. Cain's tough heroes see life as one fierce adventure; and, with a romantic readiness, sometimes eagerness, they plunge into every situation heedless of realities; often they have the capacity to transform sordid reality into a closed world of romantic endeavor. Frank is a proletarian, a simple-minded Whitman; but his romantic subjectivity is absolutely internalized, except for his desire to have a woman in his arms on the open road:

> "Just you and me and the road, Cora."
> "Just you and me and the road."
> "Just a couple of tramps."
> "Just a couple of gypsies, but we'll be together."
> "That's it. We'll be together."

In *The Moth*, Cain takes a closer took at Frank's open but crowded road—and, to say the very least, life on the road is hell. Still, male readers, besieged by material and personal worries, probably read the long hobo section (the best in the novel) with fascination and envy. Sackett's recital of Frank's criminal record of petty offenses evokes a sense of Frank's far-reaching wandering; he belongs to that legion of unemployed who became tramps of the road, hoboes of the rails, or migrant workers. In "Dead Man," a young tramp kills a railroad cop; in "The Girl in the Storm," a tramp gets off a train in a flooded landscape and takes refuge with a girl in a supermarket. We have an explicit sense in Cain of constant movement—within a confined locale, over a region, or over the country as a whole. Cain's tramps move out of a desire to explore the country, to find employment, or to evade the law; Jack, finally, moves about for all three reasons. In depicting the American of the 1930's and early 1940's as a bum on the move, Cain captures an aspect of American land and character within

the context of the depression and of a persistent American trait
—the urge to move. Cain's fiction belongs, in this respect, with the
literature of a romance without end—the romance of the open
road.

Perhaps some characteristics of the tough-guy attitude are bru-
talizations of romanticism. As an individual in conflict with organized society and its strictures, the tough guy moves alone
through the endless streets of the city, or from city to city, having
adventures, encountering people in all their variety, living in relation to the same kinds of people, situations, and landscapes as the
Romantics; but his responses are almost willfully insensitive. For
instance, the Romantic ego fancies that it will encounter in the
open world of possibilities *the* girl worthy of all his own attributes; it is in that manner that most Cain tough guys meet their
women, but usually they enter into a compact of sexual gratification at the expense of another man's life and property, and that
is *not* in the Romantic tradition. Either to facilitate her ensnare-
ment of him or to keep him, the realistic woman encourages the
male in his romantic attitude. Even the Cain lovers who do not
kill or commit a crime clash with hostile forces and cleave to each
other as isolates from the quotidian, non-romantic world. Though
they may have a romantic outlook, Cain's characters are also capable of hard-boiled self-appraisal. Even as he faces execution at
the end, Frank accepts the fact that he is a "punk."

Long before Cain wrote *The Postman,* he had written in his
nonfiction about dramatic developments in the relationships between male and female in America as the transition from the Vic-
torian into the Jazz Age was being made. In his fiction, he does not
analyze; he depicts the sexual relationship in action; if the male
does not succumb immediately to the female's sexual power, he
enters into some sort of combat with her, which always proves
unequal. Since there is a woman behind every male hero, it may
be well to look more closely at Cain's women.

While Mildred has much in common with Donald Henderson
Clarke's ordinary working girls (*Millie,* 1930; *Millie's Daughter,*
1939; *Kelly,* 1935), she is a synthesis of them all; but she is a more
complete and convincing characterization. If some of Cain's
women appear to be mere personifications of female sexuality, he
proves in *Mildred* his ability to scrutinize women in more detail.
One day in 1933, a producer at Columbia observed: "Of course,

there's one story that has never missed yet, and that's the story of a woman who uses men to gain her ends." But it seemed to Cain that "an average femme fatale run up to this blueprint would have been obvious to the point of nausea." Then it occurred to him that if a commonplace, folksy, colorless woman should bend men to her will that might make a different story. He pictured her as a victim of the depression, "a venal American housewife, a 'grass widow with two children to support,' that great American institution that never gets mentioned on the fourth of July, who didn't know she was using men, but imagined herself quite noble—this I thought a challenge." Writing the book took over a year and gave Cain much trouble: "But when I remembered my original premise," and had Mildred reach for some man to help her out, had her "use some trick, such as stealing Bert's car key, to advance herself one step, it worked fine and she seemed alive." The woman's ability to survive in a man's world, a world which often defeats the man, is suggested in Cain's handling of another novel which focuses on the female protagonist: *Root of His Evil*. Mildred and Carrie are much alike; the circular plot in both novels is comic; both women end up where they began. Both are waitresses for a time; both have weak husbands and are pursued by seemingly strong lovers. They are forced, because of male weakness or insufficiency, to make good in the male world, even to best the man.

Cain's women are rigorously realistic in their outlook; not one has the faintest streak of romanticism; though several dream of becoming something they are not, they go about realizing their dreams in a coldblooded, practical way. Cutthroat business techniques, tough bargaining, the ability to overcome hardships, to do without love and affection while in pursuit of goals, to fight the solitary fight, to endure—these are characteristics common to them. The strong women never commit crimes; *their* strength enables the weak man to dare that.

Cain's women appeal to the male reader because they are so unpredictable. They often provide an exhilarating element of surprise, in both small and important ways, by showing an ability to do male-like things, by knowing how to handle a problem traditionally considered the male's job. They never even *pretend* to be shrinking violets who need men. Still, it is rather astonishing when they suddenly act on resources they seem to have had in reserve all the time. This spectacle, new in the 1920's perhaps, fascinated writers like Cain and Donald Henderson Clarke. When Cain shows that there is a good deal of the masculine in most women they accept the trait; but, when a Cain hero discovers that there is a little of the feminine in all men, he is at least disturbed, at most panicky.

Although the women often seem more mature in their outlook than the men, a certain innocence animates the most evil of them. Phyllis' evil is so cleanly and purely presented that it lacks the sordidness of a more realistically presented evil; it has the purity of an abstraction, of a force that is suddenly, luminously present. Morina's excessive lust for gold and blood is as honestly aggressive as her candor about herself as a whore. We, and the narrators, see these women only when they dramatically assert their wishes; and, though the wishes are monstrous, the declaration of desire, the spectacular reaching, is so pure that their evil lacks the aura of grimness that would make them despicable. On the other hand, the men—because of their constant awareness of their own weaknesses in giving in to temptation, and because of their consequent guilt and torment of conscience—have about them an aura of the squalor of evil.

Cain is a masterful creator of bitches. Veda Pierce, from age eleven when we first meet her until she finally leaves her mother at age twenty-one, is a thoroughgoing bitch—one so loathsome that even reviewers expressed intense hatred of her. (Cain sketched her earlier in the character of Doris, also a singer, in *Career*.) Veda is beautiful, talented as a singer, obnoxiously precocious, ruthlessly ambitious, a social climber and/or an opportunist—she is an absolutely selfish, deceitful, guileful, snobbish, sarcastic egoist. Although her personality has not a single redeeming facet and although she seems monstrously exaggerated, Cain depicts ways in which certain aspects of the American character and dream produce grotesque women like her. In the depression, when everything is suddenly taken from her, when her father, who represents class and the dream of better things, leaves, and when her mother becomes a drudge to acquire basic necessities, Veda alone holds on desperately and arrogantly to all the dreams of affluence which society and her father inculcated in her through mass media and by example; and she is the flowering of the seed of corruption in the American dream of success.

Having discovered her failure as a pianist, she yells at her optimistic mother: "You damned, silly-looking cluck, are you trying to drive me *insane?* . . . Punks. Like you. God, now I know where I get it from. Isn't that funny? You start out a Wunderkind, then find out you're just a goddam punk. . . . In this racket you've got it or you haven't, and—*will you wipe that stupid look off your face* . . . ? Can't you understand anything at all? They don't pay off on work, they pay off on talent! *I'm just* . . . NO GOD-DAMN GOOD . . . !" Cain is so aware of the deadly fascination of this sort of bitch that, in redoing the basic plot of *The Postman*, he replaces the more elemental and honestly brutal woman, Cora, with a Veda-Phyllis-Doris type—Sally.

Cain once said that he writes about life among "the heels and the harpies" and uses "characters off the top of the pile, plain, average people scarcely worth describing in detail, people everyone knows"; these characters leave him room in which to develop what he calls "theme," but what turns out to be action. Except for Frank and Duke, it is more accurate to call the typical Cain hero an "educated roughneck." Jack, a handyman, quickly learns the oil business, among many others; other heroes are insurance agents, bank executives, engineers, singers, sheriffs, ex-boxers, farmers, and industrial tycoons. Cain's heroes run the gamut from bum of the road to sophisticated executive; all are typical American examples of their professions as they are pushed, lured, or tempted into breaking violently out of their straitjackets. While Cain may seem to use these occupations for sensational effect, his triumph is often to charge the most banal aspects of an occupation with dramatic force. In fact, it is often against banal alternatives that these men act out their more violent choices.

II *Cain Universals: Sex, Religion, Food, Money, Violence*

Beating at the heart of every Cain novel are basic, simple, universal elements, presented baldly in bold action: sex, love, evil, religion, food, money, violence, the lure of the forbidden, among others. Of course, there is a sense in which no story, from the worst to the best, lacks universal elements, or at least overtones of them. As a literary value term, "universal" has had more than its share of mileage. Who *cannot* be universal? Are not most predicaments universal? The shape of experience is *given*. The writer's task is

to persuade us to experience once more the constant *nowness* of
the experience.

Sex was presented so memorably in *The Postman* that it immediately became a predictable element in Cain, and many reviewers were confused by those novels which departed from the basic
sex formula. Cain dramatizes sex in every conceivable form: adul-
tery, jealousy, simple passion and lust, manifest sensuality,
psychological emasculation, debauchery, perversion, incest, and
sex stimulated by hate and fear.

Cain creates just enough of a sense of the banal about the ordinary male fantasy *as it comes true* to make it seem real. A bum
like Frank in *The Postman* would imagine strolling into a restaurant very hungry and later making love to the waitress who serves
him. Men like Sharp in *Serenade* and Roger Duval in *Past All
Dishonor* would imagine falling in love with a whore whose other
qualities transcend her whorehood. Insurance men like Walter
Huff in *Double Indemnity* and Ed Horner in *Jealous Woman*
daydream of ending up in bed with their customers' wives just
after making a sales pitch. Some men like Jess Tyler fantasize
making love to their daughters; others like Jack Dillon imagine
loving a nymphet; another like Duke might imagine transforming
a fat lady into something luscious. And Clay Lockwood brings us
back to Frank, for the business executive as well as the bum imagines seducing a lovely waitress. At least once in nearly every man's
life such a dream is experienced—and Cain is interested in the
man who has already half realized his fantasy before he recognizes that such things normally do not, and most likely should not,
happen.

Cain's heroes meet their women as the male has always
dreamed; therefore, a bizarre setting, another male wish, enhances the sex. With his characteristically Byronic audacity, Sharp
wins Juana in a lottery from a bullfighter; and they make love in a
rural Mexican church. Jess and his "daughter" make love in an
abandoned mine shaft. Rain storms help create an aura of sensuality and enhance the love mystique, as in the short story "Girl in
the Storm"; a sense of isolation is evoked which intensifies the
partaking of food and sex. Cain even conceived of certain locales
as sex scenes; indeed, *Mildred* was the satisfaction of his desire to
write a novel about the adventure of sex in southern California.
With his bizarre settings for murder Cain exerts a controlled fasci-

nation over the reader; the rear platform of a moving train, a beach cliff, a rooftop, the top of a water tower, a swamp road, a gravel pit, an isolated lake, a mine shaft, a "pansy" party. "The scenes of his novels," says Frohock in *The Novel of Violence in America*, "had much to do with the success of the Cain legerdemain. Somehow the phoniness of *Postman* was less phony because the action was set in and around a hamburger joint in a part of California which had magnified the tawdriness of such places until the neon light and the false front created what was almost a special cosmos."

Postman is characteristic of many Cain novels in its depiction of sex as enhanced vividly and palpably by the elements of violence, food, drunkenness, and relatively genuine love. Immediately, in Frank's and Cora's first meeting, there is a sense of sexual violence straining to erupt: "Then I saw her. . . . Except for the shape, she really wasn't any raving beauty, but she had a sulky look to her, and her lips stuck out in a way that made me want to mash them in for her." None of Cain's femmes fatales are "raving beauties"; knowing that many such women are not, Cain deliberately turns away from the Hollywood conception of beauty. Frank stimulates Cora subtly by comparing her body with that of a Mexican woman: "She knew what I meant, and she knew I had her number." Later, he can't eat the potatoes she brings him in her food-stained dress, and the Greek wine makes him nauseous. Love for him is somatic: "I let everything come up. . . . I wanted that woman so bad I couldn't even keep anything on my stomach." Because she feels he is greasy, her Greek husband Nick disgusts Cora; but, although Frank handles mechanic's grease as Cora handles food grease, she thinks of Frank as clean. It is in the kitchen, when both are grease-stained, that they first begin to make love. The sex and food motifs are violently juxtaposed when she screams: "Bite me! Bite me!" After they kill the Greek, Frank's sudden ripping of her blouse to make the wreck look like an accident excites her: "Rip me! Rip me!"

In such situations as this one, melodrama normally breaks down, but it is perfectly believable as Cain sets it up. "I ripped her. I shoved my hand in her blouse and jerked. She was wide open, from her throat to her belly." This is the high point of violent sexual impact in this novel, and perhaps in all of Cain. "I had to have her, if I hung for it. I had her." Drunkenness is necessary if the lust is to be complete. When they first get the notion of murdering the Greek, she says she has to get drunk with Frank. After the Greek's burial, she says, "We ain't never had that drunk yet." They have it. In Cain, the terrific pace itself, with its climaxes, is almost sexual, especially in *Postman* and *Butterfly*.

Sex in Cain is usually animalistic; it lacks the niceties of conventional romance. Frohock speaks of Frank's "response to stimuli" as "automatic and completely physical. . . . Love itself was indistinguishable from animal brutality and he killed what thwarted his animal need (although he did so as no animal could, calculatingly)." Seldom is the woman odor attributed to perfume. In *The Magician's Wife*, Clay sniffs an odor that fills the car: "Adrenalin —from me," says Sally. "Things affect me that way sometimes. Like the bang I got, Clay, when that jerk went down off the road, and I knew it was going to work, this thing we've been fixing up. You'll never know what you did to me. . . . Gives me a funny smell—like a rattlesnake, kind of. Want some nice rattlesnake love?" Animal odors associated with sex and violence are a constant motif. Sharp says of Juana: "A whiff of her smell hit me in the face." Her smell is associated with the odor of the ugly bull's ear which a *torero* had given her.

But primitive, animalistic sex can also be a kind of solution. The ritual of pagan lovemaking with Juana in the church brings the *toro* back into Sharp's singing voice and he later becomes famous. But, in New York, Winston Hawes threatens to devitalize Sharp's recently regained masculinity. Sharp tells Juana he has loved her; he had not told her before because *feeling* it meant "a hell of a sight more." But the Mexican Aztec whore offers a more direct, immediate remedy for what ails Sharp: "All of a sudden she broke from me, shoved the dress down from her shoulder, slipped the brassiere and shoved a nipple in my mouth. 'Eat. Eat much. Make big *toro*! 'I know now, my whole life comes from there.' 'Yes, eat.'" Perhaps critics have this scene in mind when they refer to sordid sex in Cain, but this scene is about as explicit as Cain ever gets—and, from this second book on, there is less sex.

This particular graphic moment is not salacious, and it has a simple symbolic function. Juana, part mother, part lover, gives Sharp a fresh start. He tells her everything, and she seems to understand a great deal: "Then I'd take her in my arms, and afterward we'd sleep, and I felt a peace I hadn't felt for years.

. . . I'd think about Church, and confession, and what it must mean to people that have something lying heavy on their soul." Juana is more than a body, but as such she is the earth-source of peace and wholeness for Sharp. She is also the physical agent of redemption; for, when Winston, the corrupt homosexual sophisticate, clearly threatens to bring out again the homosexual in Sharp, Juana, the pure female force, kills her rival in a mock bullfight (another pagan ritual) with a sword; it happens at one of his "faggot" parties, when, ironically, Winston is impersonating the bull. "I tried to tell myself I had hooked up with a savage, that it was horrible," says Sharp. "It was no use. I wanted to laugh, and cheer, and yell *Olé!* I knew I was looking at the most magnificent thing I had ever seen in my life."

Often, the sex or love is somewhat abnormal. Though Cain was one of the first to write frankly about homosexuality, he was for a long while shy of incest; even so, Jess and Kady do not in fact commit it in *The Butterfly,* and it is sublimated in *Root of His Evil.* James T. Farrell refers to Mildred's "almost unnatural love for her daughter," and Parker Tyler even sees multiple layers of forbidden meanings in the movie version. Another heightening of the sexual element is the tendency of the hero, always presented with an air of the forbidden, to shift his lechery from one woman to her daughter, a younger sister, or a mother: Monty makes love to both Mildred and Veda; Clay Lockwood turns from Sally to her handsome, gray-haired mother, Grace. But more obvious instances of perversion occur. In a fit of passion partly generated by the violence, Frank and Cora make love beside the still warm corpse of their victim and his mangled car on the deserted beach. Cora, Phyllis, Morina, and Sally are sexually stimulated by murder.

In *The Moth,* Cain seems to echo Poe's love of young girls and to have also anticipated a kind of Lolita figure. But Helen is never so aggressive as Lolita, and Jack is nothing like the world-weary European Humbert Humbert. Jack's relationship with Helen is explicitly healthy, for the protection of her purity is his primary concern; Cain simply recognizes in this athletic American the presence of what might be considered an abnormal desire. As soon as his desire for Helen hits him, he flees. In the end, Jack is rewarded for his prudence; for he is reunited with a Helen who is mature enough to prefer older men. "*The Moth,* I thought," says

Cain, "had some vitality as an étude in the love life of a twelve-year-old girl, but in many ways it was faulty. I may be taking another try at a similar theme, perhaps really carrying on that story in a different setting."

Some Cain heroes have a purity complex about women. In *Dishonor*, Roger's attitude is a perverse exaggeration of Jack's. Even after he learns that Morina is a whore—and a particularly eager, obliging, and satisfied one at that—Roger is so insistent on her purity that, after she has given up trying to repulse him, she plays the game with him; she plays it so earnestly that she begins to believe it herself. In the end, sexual purity becomes a corollary to murder. Morina is about to marry Brewer for money; Roger kills him. "She closed her eyes before she kissed me, and her face looked like she was in church. . . . And so in Brewer's blood we washed out all she had been, and said we were married, and that she was a virgin until this night, and that I was." In other novels, particularly *Mildred,* there is no hint of this purity notion.

Left to respond naturally, without male coaxing, Cain's women lack this sexual mysticism, as does Mildred, whose sexual giving is basically barter (Cain tends to show a streak of the whore in all women). Like most of Cain's women, Mildred enjoys sex without an aftermath of guilt. Probably her sense of owning material things satisfies her more deeply than sex; for, after using seductive wiles to steal the car keys from her estranged husband, Bert, she takes possession of the car: "Then she eased off a little on the gas, breathed a long, tremulous sigh. The car was pumping something into her veins, something of pride, of arrogance, of regained self-respect, that no talk, no liquor, no love, could possibly give."

Cain has been accused of salaciousness at least, obscenity perhaps, pornography at worst. But, in all of the Cain novels, few scenes of actual seduction exist; and none are nearly so explicit as the novels of the 1960's that Babbitt's descendants read without a tremor. "James M. Cain," says Edmund Fuller, "established the now large school of clothes-ripping technicians, who have shredded enough lingerie to clothe the poor of the world." [3] A witty passage, it is written at the expense of truth. Frank rips Cora's clothing twice, and the act is perfectly right in the contexts. Fuller's faulty memory is a tribute to Cain's achievement as a writer doing his job of work—making a single stroke count for several. Benét, reviewing *Serenade*, praised Cain's "deliberate and even brutal sexual honesty," and he claimed that it accounts for his "intensely readable quality."

Like Hemingway and D. H. Lawrence in most of their works, Cain is actually rather reticent about sex. He leaves the action to the imaginations of those readers who are capable of handling it: "Sex is another universal theme in my books, but not as much as is thought. I seem to imply it even where it's not directly brought in, and this is somewhat deliberate. About sex, I think, in stories, if you earn it you don't have to claim it. If the situation is hot, pregnant, and passionate, you needn't get too excited. It's a sort of inevitable corollary to some things in life, such as triumphs shared by two lovers." In the essay "Politician: Female," Cain emphasizes the importance of mystery in sex; the woman's place, he insists, is in sex intrigues or in the home; politics takes away from the female her glamor, mystery, and romantic surface allure.

Cain is even ambiguous sometimes and thus more suggestive perhaps than he intends. Roger pleads with Morina to leave the whorehouse with him. Wanting to show him just how low she is, she stands on top of a piano with an empty beer bottle. But Roger leaves before she gets started with her stunt. Later, a man tries to tell him what she did for one hundred dollars extra: "She stood on one foot, and—" But Roger won't let him finish: "I never did find out what she did." Though the episode as described is extremely suggestive, Cain rejects certain extreme interpretations: "I have to know what it was, of course, and do know, but I prefer not to say." Whatever he intended, it was certainly meant to seem as repulsive a sexual act to the reader as it is to the narrator.

Frohock (speaking of Cain in the past tense in 1957, as though he were no longer read) doubts Cain's own assessment—that it is not so much sex as the opening of Pandora's box which is the source of interest in his novels: "What Pandora's box contained turned out invariably to be sex, experienced always with great intensity and sometimes with just a hint of the abnormal or the taboo about it. Sex, so conceived, was inseparable from violence. Violence was both associated with the sexual act itself and made an inevitable accompaniment of anything tending to frustrate the act. . . . In other words, sex and violence were necessary accessories of Cain's plots." Frohock is correct, but we also see evidence that Cain intends to dramatize the reality of those elements in life and not treat them as mere "accessories." He is one of those rare writers who can use effectively the method of extremes to render a truthful semblance of human nature and experience. Sex *is* at the heart of Cain's stories, but honest scrutiny fails to support the charge of sordidness. Beginning with Frank and Cora in *The Postman,* passion evolves into deeper love as often as not in Cain's novels. Moments after Frank has doublecrossed her, Cora is capable of spontaneous kindness; she tucks in his blanket as he lies on a stretcher in the courtroom. And Cain's lovers often sacrifice for each other.

Cain dramatizes the relationship between sex and religion. Sham religious mystiques enhance the sex. The lovers strive antisocially to be together, to exclude all others from their world. Outside society and its morality, they respond within their murderous love affairs to a mystique of their own, requiring acts of purification and rebirth, and sometimes of redemption or atonement, if the sex is to continue, if the money is to be enjoyed. Ironically, their actions increasingly shrink that world, until both their mutual goodness and evil come face to face; they achieve what is goodness and purity for *them* in the very moment when their evil —which they have forgotten while creating the goodness—threatens to destroy them by turning them against each other.

Postman best illustrates this irony. For Frank and Cora, sex, money, murder, religion, and food are facets of a single passion. Though they kill to be together, they surround their actions from the beginning with a homespun mysticism. Just after Cora persuades Frank to murder Nick, Frank has a feeling that, in his terms, is crudely religious: "I kissed her. Her eyes were shining up at me like two blue stars. It was like being in church." We might charge Cain with a facile manipulation of the trappings of religion for effect and place him alongside the fraudulent evangelist. But, regardless of Cain's actual intentions, it is perfectly credible that, for two such people, murder might elevate lust to resemble love and create a misty aura that looks to them like religious transport. While Nick lies in the hospital after their first abortive attempt to kill him, the lovers are free to play in the ocean: "We lay there, face to face, and held hands under water. I looked up at the sky. It was all you could see. I thought about God." But, grasping for heaven on earth, they sleep with the devil.

After they kill Nick, Cora forgives Frank for turning against her the moment they were separated: "We were up on a mountain.

. . . We had it all, out there, that night. I didn't know I could feel anything like that. And we kissed and sealed it so it would be there forever, no matter what happened. We had more than any two people in the world. And then we fell down. First you, and then me. . . . We're down here together. . . ." "Well what the hell? We're together, ain't we?" Frank tries to break with Cora once but comes back because, as he tells her, he loves her. Later, Frank, afraid Cora will turn him over to the district attorney, and Cora, afraid Frank will kill her, turn on each other.

But, when the tension is strongest, Cora admits she loves Frank, and informs him that she is pregnant (perhaps it was the night of the murder that she conceived). She was going to run away when he caught her. She could not call the district attorney and make the baby's father a hanged murderer. Because she had her chance to get even and didn't, she knows that she loves Frank, but Frank has to have his chance, she says, to prove he loves her. Before she will even let him kiss her, she insists on a test of love and a ritual of purification in the ocean; he can let her drown, as though it were a normal accident: "Tomorrow night, if I come back, there'll be kisses. . . . Not drunken kisses. Kisses with dreams in them. Kisses that come from life not death." At the funeral of her mother, she had felt what it would mean to Frank and her to have the baby: "Because we took a life, didn't we? And now we're going to give one back." They get married, and go to the ocean; Frank proves his love by taking her back to shore when she swims out too far and becomes exhausted.

As they lie together on their backs, laved by the waves, she shows him how the swells lift her breasts; and they speak of the physical change that will occur. "It's not only knowing you're going to make another life," she says. "It's what it does to you. My breasts feel so big, and I want you to kiss them. Pretty soon my belly is going to get big, and I'll love that, and want everybody to see it. It's life. I can feel it in me. It's a new life for us both, Frank." Then, as he dives deep into the water, feeling the pressure of depth, Frank begins to feel what she has been talking about: "I looked at the green water. And with my ears ringing and that weight on my back and chest, it seemed to me that all the devilment, and meanness, and shiftlessness, and no-account stuff in my life had been pressed out and washed off, and I was all ready to start out with her again clean, and do like she said, have a new life." Ironically, just after they have purified themselves in this ritual and are revitalized, they have a wreck going home and Cora is killed—bloodily, as Nick was. This fate is a typical one for Cain lovers: at the bottom of Pandora's box waits not hope but a trap door.

On the eve of his execution, Frank puts his faith in a mystical reunion with Cora. Feeling no guilt in the eyes of men, they knew that they must redeem themselves together if they were to live together. Frank hopes he will get a stay of execution, but he has no religious faith in a celestial rescue, nor does he fully trust Father McConnell, who is trying to help him. He hopes the priest is right about the afterlife but only so he can tell Cora the truth; he is afraid she may have thought the wreck intentional:

> I'm up awful tight now. . . . I try not to think. Whenever I can make it, I'm out there with Cora, with the sky above us, and the water around us, talking about how happy we're going to be, and how it's going to last forever. I guess I'm over the big river, when I'm there with her. That's when it seems real, about another life, not with all this stuff how Father McConnell has got it figured out. When I'm with her I believe it. When I start to figure, it all goes blooey.
>
> No stay.
>
> Here they come. Father McConnell says prayers help. If you've got this far, send up one for me, and Cora, and make it that we're together, wherever it is.

This passage is grossly sentimental, perhaps, but are not these the very sentiments such a man would have? *Postman* sets a pattern that Cain's best novels continue to vary and develop. For instance, in *The Butterfly*, Cain depicts ways in which sex and religious emotions are often confused in Fundamentalist sects. For such people as Jess Tyler, sex has to be sanctified by religion, and religion has to be invigorated by undertones of sex.

Perhaps sacrilege is to religion what perversion is to sex. A strong pagan pulse beats in most of these emotional religious moments in Cain. Often the Christian and pagan clash, especially in *Serenade*. To get out of a terrific rain storm, Sharp rams his car through the locked door of a rural Mexican Catholic church; a forty-page episode follows. Juana, in her simple piety, objects to the desecration, but she is just as afraid of the lightning as of the *sacrilegio.* Feeling as though he is returning to the primitive, Sharp, naked, makes use of whatever he finds in the church to provide physical comfort. It suddenly occurs to him that he has been genuflecting when passing the altar. (As a Catholic boy in Chicago, he had sung in the choir.) Later, as Sharp plays the organ and sings in the weird light, dressed in a cassock, Juana tells him he sounds like a priest, a eunuch; and he realizes she is right. Then, he is startled to see her kneeling stark naked in the dark at the altar—before her, a food offering to the Aztec gods. He senses the primitive sexual energy in that pagan, worshiping position: "There she was at last, stripped to what God put there. She had been sliding back to the jungle ever since she took off that first shoe, coming out of Taxco, and now she was right in it." Light moves over her hip: "I blew out the candle, knelt down, and turned her over." After the near-rape, she seems to crave sex more than she fears the lightning or the *sacrilegio.*

An atmosphere of evil—often pagan in mood and enhanced by superstition and a sense of the supernatural—broods over events in many of the tales. But evil is less a thematic expression of Cain's vision of life than a narrative element with a strong melodramatic value. Its manifestations are described with an odd air of assurance that his readers *do* believe in spirits and dark forces. In *Past All Dishonor,* Morina cures Roger of bullet wounds with black-magic conjuring, using a weird rattlesnake compound; and there is talk of the devil's having lived in Virginia City and having possessed Roger. Cain often conceives of the present as "hoo-dooed" by the past. In *Galatea,* the ghost of John Wilkes Booth, a lingering on of the sins of the past, walks when evil is about to be done around Holly's house in Maryland. The impure in heart hear his spurs, and Holly and Duke are cleared of murdering her husband when Holly testifies that she heard no bell. This near-hokum is handled with technical subtlety. Superstition and the supernatural are also at the center of *Mignon;* for the great quantity of cotton for which most of the characters cheat, betray, connive, kill, suffer, and die is constantly described as being "hoo-dooed." Cain creates *some* interest in this element; still, when Mignon's ghost disturbs Bill's sleep and inspires him to write his story, hokum is not far away.

Though usually made appropriate in the novels, concepts such as physical and mystical reunion, redemption and atonement, purification and rebirth, and transformation may appear to be bogus elements in the work of a so-called popular writer, especially when we look at Cain's few nonfiction statements about religion and the clergy: "As to whether there is a God or not, I have no means of knowing and cannot say." At thirteen, Cain left the Catholic Church "from a disbelief in trans-substantiation." He is a typical agnostic priest, however, whose mission is to defend God from his worshipers: "This much I know: if we are to believe in God, the only concept of Him acceptable to imaginative men is a God of the most exalted sublimity, a God of thunder and ocean, of the hushed forest; a God of great cathedrals and beautiful chalices, a God of exquisitely wrought poetry, painting, and music; a God of David, Ambrose, Gregory, da Vinci, Palestrina, Mozart, and Bach. Such a God we may conceive without impiety, and having conceived Him so, we have conceived something as near the divine essence as is possible to the puny mind of man" ("The Pastor").

Cain charges the Protestant with destroying "the poetic conception of religion" in "a wholesale trading of beauty for ugliness," with "demanding religion with common sense in it, religion you could wolf down like meat and gravy, religion you didn't have to fast all night to understand," with selling God for a profit. "The net result . . . is to inspire those of us who have any surviving respect for God with an unspeakable loathing."

Cain examines the relation between evangelical religion, art, and sex: "I have come to the conclusion that religion is one of the two main phases of the sublimated amative impulse. The other phase is the aesthetic, and I think the two are usually mutually exclusive." A very religious person is rarely esthetic, and vice versa. Exaltation is common to the romantic, religious, and esthetic experiences. "Everybody is entitled to a trance"—and that is very nearly what Cain himself gives his readers, an esthetic trance, charged with sex, imbued with religion. The conceptions about human nature which Cain's novels dramatize are perhaps as crudely perceived as they are expressed, but his intense confidence in his perceptions generates the power and sense of certainty in his work.

As a journalist, Cain wrote a great many editorials on food; he discovered that "it is a topic of compelling interest to the whole human race!" As a gourmet, he wrote three excellent "how to" essays for *Esquire* in 1934 and 1935: "Them Ducks," "How to Carve That Bird," and "Oh, *les Crêpes Suzettes*." In the first, he tells the reader how to impress other men; in the second, the family; in the third, a lady. The art of making crepes suzettes is part of a more embracive art: "What she is doing in your apartment in the first place, what gave you this idea of *crêpes suzettes*, what your intentions are after she has gobbled the dish—these things are none of my business. They hire me to tell you how to make the cakes, not to make dirty cracks about your conduct." His closing advice comes, however, *after* the food is down: "Sit back. Look at her. Forget to turn on the lights. Estimate your chances. If you have done it right, you ought to rate an even break."

Cain comments on the dominant role of food in his novels: "My lovers share food in hunger. They eat, and sometimes, eat with almost religious fervor." Food, like God, is intricately related to sex or love, illicit or not. After a dionysian sex orgy comes a dionysian food orgy in *Serenade;* Sharp and Juana catch, kill, then ritualistically prepare (using sacramental wine) and eat a wild iguana; Sharp smears her nipples with iguana grease to see if they will stick together. In *Galatea,* Duke is digging up roots when Holly approaches him with food and falls into the pit he has dug. As we have noted, Duke persuades her to diet under his guidance; when she slims down, he falls for her. Both are very conscious of God; Duke, like many Cain men, often prays. As the novel ends with a brief scene in a little church in Nevada, the name of God is on the lovers' lips. In some novels, food and sex work magic without God. With her cooking, Mildred persuades Wally, Bert, and other men to do as she wills. Sally serves a meal to Clay (an executive in a meat-processing firm), simultaneously luring him with her body.

One of the central thematic and raw material preoccupations in American literature is money. Robie Macauley argues in "Let Me Tell You About the Rich . . ." that "most American stories about the rich have their psychic beginnings in a fairy story. It is the one in which the good spirit (= money) grants three wishes to the hero or heroine—and the story goes on to develop how they use the gift wisely or foolishly, for good or ill. But good or ill just in terms of the few characters in the story's magically exclusive world." [4] Cain's own variations on this theme embrace all classes, from hoboes to decayed aristocracy. Few writers have permeated their characters' consciousnesses and saturated their dialogue so thoroughly with the remote smell, the hot reaching anticipation, the grubby feel of money. One of the wishes the average reader most often wants to come true is his wish for money. "Well, what's wrong with money, and who's indifferent to it?" asks Cain. "It's hard to bring to life, but when made vivid in a story, as perhaps it is in *Mildred Pierce*, I think it's an element all can react to." Even Farrell reacted: "Things and money creep out of every page of this book." With the help of sex, housewife Mildred invades the male world and proves audacious in business; but sex and money ultimately fail her, and she returns to being wife and homemaker.

Though the girl may already love him, the Cain hero often must get money to keep her. In *Past All Dishonor,* Roger and Morina search for an isolated place to hide, and the devouring of food symbolizes sex and money hunger. They live in a mine and hunt their food in the forest. Roger feels he must set up Morina as well as Brewer would have, so he robs a train and kills a man; she wants to think he killed in cold blood, for her: "So we can have one more night, like that night in the mine, when we first found out what living could be like." They discover gold. As usual, the woman cannot wait to have the money. One scheme leads to another, and they are doomed. Their relationship itself dooms them: in the beginning, he is decent and she is foul; he becomes obsessed with his desire for the forbidden; she resists, for his sake, but finally succumbs; then he becomes so submerged in evil that he finally tries to resist her. She is dressed in golden jewels and diamonds when he mistakes her for a deer and kills her.

Chance operates for, but ultimately against, most of the characters. The lovers meet by chance, and immediately a train of events is set in motion that can be affected at every curve, favorably or unfavorably, by chance. Chance and coincidence form an intricate pattern in *The Postman.* By chance, Frank stops at Twin Oaks Tavern; the wind blows Nick's sign down; Nick goes into town, leaving Frank and Cora alone. Cain knows that readers are fascinated by the operations of chance; as we pursue our own wishes, we fear or hope chance will intervene. It is all the more frightening to watch the wish come true when the reader remembers what the characters have momentarily forgotten—that, finally, chance is the force that determines events.

Fortuity also functions in Cain's work. Not only do the lovers contrive an "accident," but genuine accidents happen frequently in Cain. Cora and Frank make Nick's death look like a car accident; and, ironically, Cora later dies in a real car accident. Luck encourages Cain's characters to pursue a luckless enterprise. (In "Dead Man," an early short story, "Lucky" himself becomes the victim of his own luck.) At the first attempt at murder, Frank says, "Just our dumb luck that pulled us through." Ill-luck begins when they succeed. Cain's characters are willing to gamble against all odds. What Dawn Powell says of insurance agent Huff in her review of *Double Indemnity* is true of several Cain heroes: "knowing all the mysterious machinery of his business, it is a gambling challenge to beat it."

Chance, coincidence, accident, luck, and gambling construct a maze of possibilities. Cain's narrator often lucidly points out the possibilities and alternatives implicit in every situation. These factors create an *aura* of destiny or fate. But fate demands the context of a grand theme, noble characters, high endeavors, with subordinate elements that approach the grandiose. Sex, religion, food, money, chance—these elements are not unique with Cain and, in a discussion of most writers, hardly warrant attention as isolates. But Cain is so conscious, explicitly and implicitly, of these elements as dominant factors in the love-rack experience that he involves his characters in them within clearly constructed contexts. These elements, we might charge, defeat Cain. In his poorer works, they *do*; but, in his best, they operate with such frequency that, given Cain's extensive control of other aspects, we see that he deliberately depicts the dynamic interplay of these forces as operating in a world in which his lovers experience, momentarily, the wish-come-true.

And one of the most obvious elements in Cain's simple, melodramatic, terse fables of sex, murder, and money is violence. It takes many forms: sexual, physical, verbal, violence of nature, and even, we might say, violence of literary technique, perpetrated upon the reader. He satisfies the average American's inexhaustible craving for details of crime and punishment. Cain's characters commit robbery, embezzlement, graft, bribery, assault, fraud, perjury, treason, and other crimes. Many men wish to commit a crime, if they can get away with it; his characters do, for a while, and we live their success. The mere tension of being on the love-rack erupts in violence. If the wish for sex and money is to come true, violence must be resorted to. In a conversation with Vincent Lawrence about *Postman*, Cain said in his preface to *Three of a Kind:* "Murder . . . had always been written from its least interesting angle, which was whether the police would catch the murderer. I was considering . . . a story in which murder was the love-rack, as it must be to any man and woman who conspire to commit it." The typical rhythm of violence in Cain is from crime climax to sex climax to the fall of one or both of the lovers.

Except for the fact that the lovers' criminal acts sometimes oblige Cain to describe other brutal, sadistic, or vicious encounters, Cain indulges in no unmotivated, no gratuitous or incidental thrill-violence, such as we find in Hammett, Chandler, or even Horace McCoy. Most of the characters set circumstances in motion that cause their own violent destruction. Sometimes the lovers plan their suicides (Huff and Phyllis); sometimes suicide is impulsive (Clay slays Sally, then tosses himself off a high building). But not all the acts of violence are criminal or, if criminal, totally reprehensible: Juana seems partly justified in killing Hawes; and Val brings on his own death by his sadistic abuse of his wife Holly.

Frohock charges Cain with "a knowing exploitation of violence," but that charge, like the one of obscenity, is difficult to document and prove. Cain lends little power to the long-existing tendency in various forms of mass entertainment to glamorize criminals and crime. His lovers are lovers first, criminals second, but never mobsters, except for Ben Grace, who is not glamorous. While a thorough examination of all Cain's works may expose a high incidence of violence, at least a fourth of them is almost devoid of what might be called "lurid violence," suggesting that exploitation is not, at least, his sole aim.

With the frequent violence of the 1920's and 1930's covered extensively in the news media and fictionalized in mass entertainment, the public became particularly bemused by violence in the 1930's. Popular culture expresses not only the spontaneity of violence in America but also the American's eagerness, even while condemning it as "evil," to experience it vicariously as "entertainment." As Dillinger walked toward the woman in red, thus signaling his execution in the streets of Chicago, Clark Gable, on the screen of the Biograph Theater, was walking to the electric chair in *Manhattan Melodrama.* Lerner declares that gangster movies and detective novels are appropriate daily entertainment for Americans, "a people who never spared violence in opening the continent, and subduing it to the uses of profit and exploit." These are the experiences the *children* of the 1930's *really* had, some say; and the French seemed to agree, appearing to mistake American popular culture images for the genuine article; in a sense it really was, for in a cultural perspective, violence imagined approaches that of violence committed.

Cain has been active in several of the mass media that disseminated the tough-guy attitude: drama, movies, journalism, popular novel, slick magazine. His own experience as an on-the-scene observer of the disillusionment and violence of the 1930's must have urged upon him the view of American history as a long panorama of violence. In his essays and novels, he directly examines these and other media; and his fiction deliberately answers certain needs and demands of mass culture. Contemporary events, as well as various entertainment models, are always in the background; for instance, *Postman* was not only inspired by the Ruth Snyder murder, but also resembles Sidney Howard's play *They Knew What They Wanted* (1924). Cain has explored the psychological basis of this public nostalgia for the violence of the past and this fascination with "show of violence" in the present; he has observed the cheap and vulgar curiosity in the news coverage of violence; the hunger for it is symbolized by the way spectators of both movie and actual violence ferociously eat hot dogs and popcorn as they watch.

Thus, Cain's works reflect a vision of popular culture, based on assumptions which his observations of society have encouraged. Without deliberately attempting to depict the world of his times, Cain does evoke it. Though he may criticize it and his own tastes may turn elsewhere, it is out of *this* culture that Cain writes and to this culture that his novels belong. That American readers have blessed his novels with their approval is in itself a comment on society. Even in his less violent novels, Cain depicts a world produced by violent conditions, revealing a vision that sees "American tragedy colored by American farce."

CHAPTER *4*

The American Character in Shadow

I N THE 1930's, Cain's novels and the tough-guy vision related, in a special way, to the persistent theme of the American Dream. Lacking the context of significance that "justified" the proletarian novels, they show the failure of the dream by a camera-cold recording of the nightmare. *Mildred* and *The Moth* show the breakdown of the dream in the depression of the 1930's; *Indemnity* shows the perversion of the dream of success; *Serenade* shows how one man seizes that dream. Cain's themes are often inherently serious, his character relationships are at least potentially complex, and the milieus in his novels often promise the richness of association we find in less commercial writers. A close look at his novels reveals their contribution to the tradition of American literature that is concerned with American character, land, and dream.

Farrell, predictably enough, charged that in *Mildred* Cain "squanders what could have been a very good and representative American story," even "a great one." Having described Bert and Mildred as a specimen depression couple, Farrell observed that "one of the striking and promising features in the early portions of this novel is that the two main characters are presented with reference to objects." Things, "commodities," become the basis for the "spiritual content of Mildred's life. . . . Much has been written about the standardization of human beings in modern American society. But here was the promise of a vivid, empirically grasped, and well-presented fictional account of the structure of American standardization." But Mildred's problems are falsified by "plot involvements," distorted by "cheap glamour and cynical melodrama," and developed in terms of the simplicities of "movietone realism." Cain began with a genuine social problem, and *Mildred* "could have been a poignant account of the middle class housewife." To see the deeper possibilities of Cain's characters, few critics and reviewers look as closely as Farrell does. Cain's most fully realized characters—Frank Chambers, John Howard Sharp, Mildred Pierce, Jess Tyler, Walter Huff, Jack Dillon—are representative and effective simplifications of many traits, good and bad, in the American character. Although Cain never explicitly depicts those traits as being particularly American, but strives for universality, we sense the assumptions behind the absolute authority with which he presents them. Perhaps he assumes, for one thing, that his dramatic demonstration of these traits will move the reader to identify with his characters and to believe in the urgency of the action. Whether Cain's image of the American tough guy who acts on impulse and instinct, who moves through "violent extremes of conduct," is as authentic as the author seems to believe, the image is certainly true to the one many Americans have of themselves.

I *Qualities of the Aggressive Voice*

The exploits of Cain's characters offer an interesting perspective on the element of motivation. They do what they do not only because they want sex or money, but also because they *want* to do what they do—the adventure has its own intrinsic value. Success is an abstract goal, amid more immediate and clearly defined objectives. Just as men often think that money motivates them to perform a certain job, while the doing is actually what they enjoy most, Cain's characters set about their exploits with such zeal and absolute involvement that we sense their pure excitement in the doing; and we often see that, when they get what they thought they wanted, the atmosphere around them suddenly turns dull and their lives slump, vitality and spontaneity go, and Cain himself seems to be doing what he must with situations that have been depleted of energy.

The American notion that anything is possible, given determination, perseverance, and audacity, is fully illustrated in the behavior of Cain's heroes and of several of his women. Cain proceeds with such a strong assumption that this attitude is a typical American one that he never examines it closely, as though it were so obvious that all we require is to see instances of it. Some charge that Cain exploits this American self-image. Whether his intellect, which attacks so much hokum in his essays, accepts a quasi-superman idea, it is clear in his fiction that his imagination unhesitatingly responds to the image. The Cain hero certainly proceeds on the assumption that he *is* something of a superman, and consequently he overcomes great obstacles. These men never let an opportunity slip by; they are sufficient to whatever the day demands, and they spontaneously seize the chance to act and to carry that action to its full realization. For example, we have Sharp's career in Hollywood and New York, or Jack's exploits as he seizes the day, day after day.

Cain depicts the consequences of the assertion of will. Even the man who lacks the will to resist lust asserts, under the spell of a woman, abnormal will power to execute a crime; the failure of several exploits to win Mignon's love acts as a push to success in an area which Bill has neglected while serving her—service to his country; near the end, Bill attempts to solve the whole Union army's problems by building a bridge. Most of Cain's men *stumble* onto the opportunity for success; only a few *set out* to become successful. Cain's men venture out with absolute confidence in themselves, marshaling the limited talents of those around them. (Cain's own life has often been like that.) As much as such behavior strains our credulity, it is presented with such ease and naturalness that we are usually persuaded.

Cain's heroes, then, often act as *real* heroes. Cain assumes a public readiness, created by comics and movies, to believe, or at least to go along with such actions. In America's past, there certainly were such men, and Cain apparently wants to believe in them. At peak moments, Cain's sometimes exceptional and unusual characters are impressive; and, when conscious delight accompanies our awareness of this impressiveness, we feel that Cain himself is impressive in the way he conducts himself as an author, managing the affairs of such bulldozers against obstacles. This impressiveness comes from the sense of bravura with which the Cain hero moves into a situation and begins to mobilize all forces toward success.

There is remarkable energy, vigor, and stamina in the life thrust of these characters, and indeed in Cain himself, who is still writing novels at seventy-eight. Even though a plan may underlie the characters' conduct, their lives are almost totally spontaneous. Reading a Cain novel, we have a sense that we are in the midst of shifting schemes. The characters start out with one scheme, and we delight in the shifts that are enforced by chance, coincidence, gamble, and countergamble, upon the original scheme. The characters spontaneously respond to such shifts and often turn them to advantage, so that the exploit at which we marvel is a composite of intentions and reversals. As we read, our impression—an impression which Cain strives to create—is that the author's technique also is a spontaneous phenomenon.

Cain dramatizes the aggressive arrogance of the reckless, audacious amateur, who, lacking a regulated skill, must make his way on the uncertainty of improvisation, thus risking the inglorious failure of the amateur. Cain himself, as a writer, reveals the arrogance of the expert, the craftsman certain of his ability. His characters exhibit a genuine sense of earned pride; but this pride often accelerates their downfall. Cain and his characters admire skill, and delight in seeing it exhibited; and in their own actions they celebrate the beauty and exhilaration of skill well employed. Thus, the American mystique of talent is conveyed in Cain; his characters often have several talents, ready to respond to opportunity. They achieve power and profit just as often through sheer talent as through violence. They are almost as self-centered and conceited as Ayn Rand's characters. They know they have talent, are envied and admired for having it, and they like to be where others are showing it.

When Cain's heroes are engaged in some endeavor in which quality is required, they strive to achieve the very best. It is, of course, a trait in the author himself, who in his life and work is keenly conscious of quality. Cain has a blistering hatred of the phony; we see this hatred in his essays; we sense it in his fiction. His heroes and tough women are always spotting it, stamping on it, refusing to tolerate it; indeed, most of Cain's protagonists take pride in preferring the genuine article, act, or talent to the bogus.

The qualities of audacity, improvisation, practicality, and ingenuity that characterized the American's conquest of the wilderness enable a Cain protagonist to accomplish various feats and solve problems. The unprogrammed possibility of failure in audacious enterprises introduces the element of challenge that is very appealing to the American. Jack is the best example of the audacious, improvising hero as he moves over America during the depression. Audacity gets him over obstacles, and improvisation serves him when he lacks the expert knowledge required to control a situation. The Cain character fully accepts certain risks as part of the dictates of the situation and revels in a sense of competition; he surrounds his ambitiousness with a mystique.

Part of the composite masculine image is that the Cain hero be a man of honor. Clay is hesitant about killing a man with whom he has shaken hands and to whom he has offered the hospitality of his place of business, though he has already made love to the man's wife. Loyalty to country is an important lever of action in *Dishonor* and *Mignon*. Loyalty to family is the most frequent form of fealty demonstrated by the women. Generally, the major figures lack blood ties, but in several novels Cain seems fascinated by the demands and the consequences in character and action of kinship.

There is also in the hero's response to life a sense of rectitude, of which Cain himself has a highly developed sense. Although his men seldom go into agonies of guilt over acts of violence, there are strictly defined areas of behavior in which conscience is always alert and in which remorse follows the violation of rules connected with relatively minor social modes of conduct. Cain's class consciousness resembles F. Scott Fitzgerald's; for, while he may sneer at pretensions, he is basically sensitive to class levels, betraying a certain respect, awe, and envy of superior upper-class qualities.

Perhaps Cain asserts these "heroic" American traits through exceptional characters in reaction to the puny spectacle of the American in the 1930's; for Cain is himself the archetype of the aggressive, self-confident American who is uncomfortable in the midst of failure, timidity, and small-scale ambitions. We sense Cain's pure delight in the spectacle of triumph.

The behavior of the Cain hero may be summed up as "impulsive," and as often lacking in conscience. The woman is less impulsive; in fact, she often plans the adventure. The hero impulsively responds to both girl and plan in the same instant of heedless commitment. The adventure requires such passionate involvement with the girl that we can hardly expect prudence or rational assessment from the hero, although periodically he may attempt to examine his behavior; but something happens quite soon to plunge him deeper and more mindlessly into the action. Clay's comment on himself and Cain's third-person remarks in *The Ma-*

gician's Wife apply to most Cain characters, and perhaps to Cain himself:

> "You know you have to have her, and this is the way you get her —and the only way. So get going. So do it. And see that you do it right." That vanity was his trouble, inflamed by obsessive desire; that his great source of strength, the element in his nature that drove him ahead in business, riding all obstacles down, could also be his weakness; that this giddy twin sister of pride could have a soft underbelly, loving praise above everything else, especially this girl's praise, and dreading her phony scorn—none of this could he have thought of or believed if he had thought of it. To him, it centered on love and a Jabberwock to be slain.

The Cain hero moves from praise to condemnation several times. If he cannot gain recognition in that for which he is temperamentally and by training suited, he will respond to the opportunity to earn it elsewhere, as when bridge-builder Borland, idle during the depression, responds to the proposition that he become a singer. Condemnation, especially if it comes from a woman, sometimes immobilizes the hero. More than prison or physical harm he fears shame, as detrimental to action, that medium in which he thrives. But Cain's men never experience anxiety, for all their fears are nameable; they never expend their energies upon the objectless spiritual traumas that engulf the heroes of so much modern fiction. They know that their immobility is temporary, until chance provides another opportunity for the audacious response that will lift them out of the slough of despond.

Some of Cain's characters are confidence men, either in the criminal sense or as a part of their everyday personalities. As Frank works a "con" on Nick when he first meets him, Cain suggests the complicity of the victim in the process of getting "conned." Sometimes the hero "cons" himself; however, the dialectics of self-deception in Cain are only potentially profound. But in every novel he suggests the "con" and the "self-con" as a dominant trait in the American character, and as the normal mode of everyday relationships—one especially visible in mass communications techniques used for political or economic ends.

An aura of deceit and fear hangs over most Cain novels. His characters are afraid, partly because they cannot separate reality from illusion. One trap is their sense, often, of being the creator and controller of a little world of their own which thus appears real and knowable. But a hovering atmosphere of fear, deception, and treachery produces a cynicism in Cain's characters. Side by side with this cynicism persists the famous American tough optimism that all problems can be solved if we just get tough with ourselves and with others; and this view applies particularly to the weak who are inclined to give up.

II   Cain the Inside-Dopester

The acquisition of inside knowledge and of "good old American knowhow" is a vital process in the shaping of American character. Cain knows that the American would like to acquit himself as superbly as Cain's characters do; failing this actual talent, most American males delight in witnessing an exhibition of official, expert, inside knowledge and perfect "knowhow." The reader may feel that he is learning something from the man who knows: first from the character, but always from the greater figure of authority in the background—Cain. Thus, each Cain novel provides blocs of inside knowledge and dramatic demonstrations of "knowhow"; and the range throughout the novels is impressive.

Cain is a teacher who wants to give his readers expert information, to show them how a thing is properly done. He has the American awe of, respect and voracious appetite for, the hard facts that fill in the full picture. Cain in his essays (like his characters in the stories) often conducts himself with the charming arrogance of the American in possession of the facts; he assumes he speaks on behalf of those who know *to* those who don't, exclusively; he never assumes that the reader already knows half of what *he* knows. Curiously, Cain's heroes often know better than their women what a woman should wear, and they advise them on fine points of fashion and appropriateness.

As the man who was there, Cain immerses himself in the actual; he lives his backgrounds to authenticate the particulars of his imagination: "Yes, I have actually mined coal, and distilled liquor, as well as seen a girl in a pink dress, and seen her take it off" (preface, *Butterfly*). But, as a journalist with acquired habits of exhaustive research, he also substantiates his experiences by a scrutiny of official documents and other library sources. John Farralley was one of several reviewers who charged that there were anachronisms in the speech and in other aspects of *Past All Dishonor:* "If Mr. Cain intended a little study in antiquity, he has achieved a major blunder in anachronism." But Cain insists that he fully researches all his books: "That my integrity would be doubted, that it would be assumed that I got all this from picture sets, I confess astonished me."

The burden of authenticated, documented raw material threatens several other novels, particularly *The Moth* and *Mignon.* Two pages of acknowledgments at the back cite all the "authorities" who advised and instructed him in his gargantuan effect to research *The Moth's* areas of special knowledge. He also pays tribute to the hoboes among whom he lived for a time to ensure authenticity, thanking them "for initiation, sometimes painful, into the life of jungles, box cars, missions, and flop joints." Cain goes directly to men who know, listens to them, and absorbs the knowledge of his sources. In *Mignon,* Cain is so immersed in his exhaustively researched background that historical accuracy impedes the development of human drama. Cain read or consulted four hundred books and traveled hundreds of miles of the novel's settings. Cain *can* become obsessively preoccupied with pedestrian matters.

The major area of inside knowledge in Cain's novels is music. As early as *Career,* Dawn Powell noted "Cain's musical obsession." *Mildred,* in which Veda studies piano and voice, offers much detailed talk of music. Music is used as an ironic motif in *Postman.* In *The Moth,* it once more has a prominent place, at least in the early section, for Jack is a child prodigy who loses his singing voice. Cain's heroes immerse themselves in sudden hard work over a short period, but there is no year-after-year drudgery in the working toward a singing career; the character usually knows or is suddenly told that he or she has a great gift. In all the novels, some form of music is presented; and it is seldom merely incidental.

Some of the most interesting passages in *Serenade,* and indeed in all of the Cain novels, are the ones on music, particularly singing: "I was as good as they come," says Sharp in *Serenade.* "I ought to be, seeing it was all I ever did, my whole life. . . . I had a hell of a good voice . . . and I had worked on it, lived for it, and let it be a part of me until it was a lot more than just something to make a living with." And, when he lost his voice, something in Sharp had "died." (This passage indirectly expresses the central role of music in Cain's own life.) In a Mexican café, Sharp and the Irish opera-lover Captain Conners engage in a near-violent argument about singers and composers. Later, aboard ship, Sharp and Conners instruct each other on the relative merits of Rossini and Beethoven—seven pages of fine talk about music, made vivid, immediate, and tough by the situation: these two tough guys talk, while the ship smuggles Sharp and Juana, wanted by the police, out of Mexico. Sharp's talking of music in his tough diction does not sound incongruous. His lengthy comments, coming in the midst of an otherwise melodramatic narrative, are very absorbing.

In Guatemala, Sharp has to stop singing or fugitive Juana will be discovered and sent to the electric chair: "Then I began to get this ache across the bridge of my nose. . . . A voice is a physical thing, and if you've got it, it's like any other physical thing. It's in you, and it's got to come out. The only thing I can compare it with is when you haven't been with a woman for a long time, and you get so you think that if you don't find one soon, you'll go insane." The premise of the novel associates sex and singing—no singing when the sexual impulse is perverted or suppressed, great singing when mother-earth Juana provides inspiration. The ending is all the more ironic; feeling responsible for her death, Sharp vows to the priest who conducts her funeral service that he will never sing again; it was she who influenced him to stop singing "like a priest" in that very church months before.

In 1935, a year after *Postman* appeared, Cain published the essay "Close Harmony" in *The American Mercury*. Like "Them Ducks," it is a "how-to" piece, full of inside knowledge, opinions, and judgments, presented in his tough-guy manner, about how to organize an informal singing group in one's home. Cain also conveys a vivid sense of what music means to him: "It is rather hard, perhaps, if you have never taken part in such a rite, to understand the excitement that takes hold of you when you do good music, the sense of accomplishment that you get when you have mastered it, the feeling that comes to you after a whole evening of it, of having stood in the shadows of great edifices, of having identified yourself with something that was pointed at the stars." Cain believes that one must actually participate in music to get its fullest emotional impact—his typical action-versus-theory approach to life.

It is strange to encounter so much serious concern with music in a body of fiction that is often passed over as being simply very good "commercial stuff"; and Cain himself has remarked that:

> It is true I write about singers, but not, you will notice, swooning over their voices. But Real dramatization is focussed on their minds, their skill at reading music, and improvising to cover emergency, at comprehension (Borland was hooked when he found that music had structure, "like a bridge has.") This, I suspect, is all a bouquet on the grave of my mother. She had a beautiful voice, a big hot lyric endlessly trained by teachers and equal to any music ever written for soprano. But what held me under the spell was her prodigious musical gift. She could read anything.

Cain's greatest disappointment was his failure to measure up to his own and to professional standards of excellence in singing. In the issue of *The American Magazine* which carries "Two Can Sing," there is a sepia-tone picture of Cain, looking very debonair, craggy, and sophisticated in front of some klieg lights on a stage set. He is labeled a Theorist, and the caption emphatically draws the conclusion that Cain's novella is a compensation for his failure as a singer. The wish did not come true. Inside knowledge failed to produce know-how.

Like Hemingway, Cain likes to reveal—usually in dialogue, one character explaining to another—inside knowledge in various fields. Many reviewers early became aware of the "specified knowledge that he draws on in all of his novels." Fadiman noted in *Mildred* "the firm mastery of the intricacies of the restaurant trade" which is examined also in *Postman, Root of His Evil, Galatea, The Magician's Wife,* and "The Baby in the Icebox." Cain, like the readers he has in mind, is fascinated by the intricacies of the law, as in the courtroom scenes in *Postman, Galatea, Mignon,* and in Frank's dialogue with Katz and with Sackett, the district attorney. In *Counterfeit,* Cain probably tells less about organized crime, politics, and gambling than he knows. In *Career,* there is, along with opera, the construction business and bridge-building, and more of the same in *Mignon.*

Newsweek observed that *Embezzler* and *Indemnity* "are also remarkable examples of the art with which Cain makes unfamiliar readers feel at home in such worlds as banking and insurance, the skill with which he uses business routines to build suspense." Dawn Powell observed that in *Indemnity* "the unfamiliar background of insurance intricacies provides protection against charges of implausibility." Reviewing *The Moth*, Merle Miller testifies to "some quite exciting and authentic-sounding scenes in an oil field (sometimes I had the feeling I knew a little too much about the operating end of the oil business)." Safe-cracking and many other mechanical matters, fruit picking, voice and chest control for singers, elementary education for backward children— *The Moth* offers these as well.

Other areas of special knowledge are: real estate in *Mildred;* mining, spying, and guns in *Dishonor;* moonshining and mines in *Butterfly;* hoboing, the machinist's trade, and the frozen foods industry in *The Moth;* boxing and dieting in *Galatea;* the meatpacking and food-packaging industries in *Magician's Wife.* Many other, minor inside-knowledge angles are repeated among the books, stories, and essays: football (there are few sports in Cain), food, movies, labor unions, stocks, tigers, wine-drinking, and observations on land, character, and culture.

To get out of a predicament or deliberately to put himself in a position to gain, the Cain hero must have real know-how. Sharp sums up the Cain hero, symbolically, when he says: "There's not many instruments I can't play, some kind of way, but I can really knock hell out of a guitar . . . and any other instrument in my practically unlimited repertoire." The *mariachies* do not do it well enough, so he does it better, and draws an admiring crowd—a typical Cain hero gesture. Sharp tells Juana, a whore, what a whorehouse should have. They do not need her mother to cook; Sharp learned how in Paris. He speaks Italian like a Neapolitan. In *Don Giovanni*, he departs from the usual practice and plays a real, instead of a prop, guitar. Sharp sings at the Hollywood Bowl without practice; he goes into radio and movies and tells everyone how to do his job. Faced with the problem of persuading Conners to smuggle him and Juana out of Mexico, Sharp wins his aid by singing for him. More than in any other book, except *The Moth*, *Serenade* presents some such instances of know-how in every chapter.

Cain's heroes, always involved in one deal or another, conducted with absolute expertise, give the impression of being in command; and they reinforce our sense of Cain's also being fully in command of our responses—or at least we admire his effort to achieve that aim. Bennett audaciously offers to repay a man's embezzled debt in order to justify taking the man's wife; Huff goes for the highest stakes in an insurance-murder swindle, thinking up the perfect murder-accident; Mildred steps into a waitress's job, suddenly goes into business, and Veda suddenly becomes a famous singer; Ben Grace, a punk, takes over after the big dog has been kicked out of town, goes into the pinball racket, and takes over the town; Roger suddenly becomes a big shot in the mines; Jess suddenly goes into the moonshining racket to keep Kady with him; and Duke undertakes the task of working layers of fat off Holly.

Inside knowledge must produce know-how. This aspect of Cain's work is best suggested by one of his essays, "Them Ducks." We would think that the least likely subject on which a tough writer could well demonstrate his tone, style, and sense of authority would be the subject of how to prepare a pressed duck dinner. But Cain's use of the tough tone in the role of gourmet or bon vivant is not feigned; it is natural and convincing. "Them Ducks" (*Esquire*, 1936) is a remarkable tour de force. Cain's purpose is simply to tell us, in complete detail, *how to do it*. What gives to even his most trivial essays a sense of authority is the forceful, absolute confidence of the "I" essayist, a force also characteristic of his tough fictional "I." Cain always has an immediate awareness of his audience, over whom he seems certain he is exerting his control. He conveys at once a marvelous arrogance, conceit, and exuberant amiability: "The first thing you must get through your head, if you are plotting a wild duck dinner, is that there is something silly about the whole rite." He leaves his reader with a big brotherly pat on the back, assuming that any red-blooded American can do a job well if he gets the right expert advice. Though witty and charming, this piece generates a sense of urgency, frightening and encouraging the reader. In his other two "how-to" food essays, Cain uses the same tough technique, one worthy of James Cagney in *Public Enemy*.

Cain actually excites the pulse as he describes the do's and don't's of getting a duck properly before guests. And what makes it just as exciting as any other action in Cain's works is a pure sense of the reality of the thing for its own sake. One dimension of the experience of attaining, possessing, and demonstrating know-how and inside knowledge is as pure as drinking a cold glass of beer at high noon in August heat. It *means* only what it is—the satisfaction of a secondary appetite. It is one part of the American character to respond to certain phenomena for their own sake; another aspect, based on a multisource guilt, is the compulsion to make sense of the response, which is often like trying to find some mystical significance in the simplicity of Winslow Homer's seascapes. In a sense, a duck dinner is no less important than many other events in a man's life; hosting it can consume a man's immediate consciousness, his emotional presence in time, as thoroughly as Frank's murder of Nick. On one very real level, all human experience, even intellectual activity, is a physical experience which it is absurd to discuss in terms of values, especially comparative ones. Perhaps the essence of all man's endeavors is *play*.

III   *The Impulse to Self-Dramatization*

Cain presents his protagonists' tendency toward self-dramatization as a particularly American characteristic. His heroes' acts are performances, arias of action, often solo; and his novels are themselves exhibitions, "performances." There is something of the aural and visual dramatic immediacy of opera about Cain's melodramatic plots and characters: the loving inattention to character detail and motivation, to plot nuances, and the sense the reader has of beholding magical and hypnotic gestures that sometimes seem to signify more than they do. In his essays, Cain often explicitly states what is always implicit in his fiction—that what interests him is the show of drama for its own sake, rather than its thematic significance.

The phenomenon of life imitating cheap art fascinates Cain. In his essay "West Virginia: A Mine-field Melodrama," he speaks of the lure of the props on the scene: "You are drawn close to these big inanimate things," he says, referring to the locomotives. He suggests the universal appeal of such shows: "To see it is to get the feeling of it." Not the *meaning* of it, but "the feeling" of it. This line expresses part of his implicit credo as a writer: that the feeling of a thing is an intense human experience just as valid as the understanding of it.

In "American Portraits III, The Editorial Writer," Cain argues that the repulsiveness of the editorial writer lies in his lack of luster and drama. The editorial writer must defy the newspaper reader's natural interest in the mere show of events by laboring to derive some intellectual and spiritual nourishment from hollow sources. With an "almost pathological fear of being bored," most people refrain from reading the editorial page. What they read must be "interesting on its own account," not just "in relation to some practical problem that stands at the moment in need of solution." Having written with equal awareness of his audience on the editorial page, Cain the novelist imagines himself writing to the opposite sort of reader. The three essays on editorials help to explain the nature of his fiction and its lack of explicit editorializing.

To get across this main theme of the impulse to drama in human behavior, Cain went straight to the theater for his effects; thus, in the dramatic dialogue, he enhances his theme by the very mode of presentation. In "Theological Interlude," he shows how *play* enhances belief, and how belief sanctifies play. In "Politician: Female" and "High Dignitaries of State," Cain, the "connoisseur of show," argues that service "won't develop; it won't orchestrate." It can be "effective dramatically only when it costs something to perform it," and service costs the politician and the do-gooder nothing. In "The Pathology of Service," Cain argues that, even when the opposite may appear to be true, the desire to dramatize oneself is a basic element in the American character. For instance, those legions of "servists" in America *appear* to be selfless, self-effacing, drab people because of their manner of crusading and serving. But, though their show may appear depressing to others—particularly to people whose own life roles are inherently dramatic—the servists are satisfying within themselves a powerful craving for drama. To "usefulness," or "service," Cain opposes the "glamour," "glitter," and "hypnotic lure" of the statesmen of the past—"the way they look and sound, their effectiveness as dramatic figures." Missing today are the pyrotechnics of power, which Cain and, he believes, most men, love to view. The great dramatic figures in history—Napoleon, Alexander, Frederick, Charlemagne—show that "there can be no real magnificence without a foot on somebody's neck."

Many of Cain's fictive characters are somewhat conscious of their love of drama, with themselves on center stage. In his first published short story, "Pastorale" (1928), Cain attempts—without analysis, letting *show* tell all—to illustrate the urge to self-dramatization in dull people. "Pastorale" is told in first-person dialect by an unspecified townsman of the main character, Burbie. Cain is interested in the spectacle, witnessed by the townsman, of a man who fails to keep the dramatic instinct under control, to subordinate it to larger concerns, even to the preservation of freedom and life. The narrator himself cannot resist perpetuating the sense of drama in the manner of his own telling. Cain as author offers no moral; but the narrator, in character, halfheartedly tacks one on: "And if he hadn't felt so smart, he would of been a free man yet." Cain, though, is simply showing how the dramatic process works. The narrator is ignorant of the true point of his story; but, by telling it, he demonstrates the power of the impulse to dramatize; as the man with the story—a story about a man whose impulse to dramatize led to his death—he dramatizes himself.

In 1936, two years after *Postman* made Cain the famous dean of hard-boiled writers, Cain's nostalgic, charming story "The Birthday Party" appeared in *The Ladies' Home Journal*. Considering the life and reputation of its author, it is a remarkable story that somewhat softens the Cain image. It is one of the best tests of sentimentality in Cain, for it is narrated in the third person; and sentimentality erupts almost exclusively in his third-person fictional voice. Although Cain the author intrudes with a little editorializing on the behavior of the young hero, Burwell Hope, the story is one of genuine sweetness; and although the story deals with characters, situations, and sentiments traditionally exploited sentimentally in such women's magazines, the tone is perfectly controlled. (A similar story, "Everything But the Truth," appeared in *Liberty* in 1937; and the early chapters of *The Moth* capture something of the mood common to both stories. Only in these three instances does Cain focus on the experiences of children.) "The Birthday Party" is a careful and authentic delineation of the pyschology of self-dramatization in childhood and of the consequences of this impulse when mingled with false values and when acted upon without full awareness of the nature of one's behavior. Cain seldom again looks so intimately at the origins, the dialectics of human conduct. Enhancing the effect of dramatization, melodramatic characters and action and surface sensationalism often occur within a context of banality. Cain shows us that seemingly trivial and banal aspects of our lives conceal malevolence or some element of fascination. He raises the given banality of life to the level of drama.

IV   *The American Dream as Nightmare*

One of the central themes in American literature is the relationship of American land and character to the American Dream. Just as Cain's life and work have spread over the American scene in time, they cover much of the landscape itself. What Farrell says of *Mildred* reflects the observations of many critics and is generally true of Cain's works: "Cain has empirically grasped some important details of the modern American scene." While Cain concentrates consciously on California, he is interested in the Southwest (especially Reno, Nevada); in New York, West Virginia, the Southeast; and in the open road itself. Mexico and Guatemala also fascinate him. Cain's travel over the country stimulated him to set a novel or story in almost every region; thus, if we include his articles, essays, and newspaper work, America becomes the locale of the Cain canon. The novels exhibit, however, only a tendency to capture the look of the American scene. Still, we feel a sense of place keenly because Cain's incidental evocations of landscapes and cityscapes linger in our minds.

That Cain is keenly aware of the potential impact of certain locales is intimated in his notes which appear at the front of his books. Although it was a convention in the 1940's to disclaim any similarity between real and fictive persons and events, few writers called attention to locale. A typical Cain note reads: "The locale of this book is California, and the Californian will find much in it that is familiar to him." California is the general locale of seven Cain novels; Glendale is the scene of four—as a representative middle-class residential area in *Indemnity* and *Embezzler*, and as a consciously examined little cosmos in *Mildred* (Cain's Glendale is similar to O'Hara's Gibbsville, Pennsylvania). Sharp's descriptions of Hollywood and movie-making, with its previews in Glendale, are powerfully expressive. "The Baby in the Icebox" describes the garish highway restaurant-filling station-zoo combination to be seen all over the country today.

The tough novelists and screenwriters produced images of an area of the American scene that had little prominence in fiction before: California. Hammett focused on San Francisco. Chandler

was a master of lingering description; for him Los Angeles repre-
sented the American scene as "the Great Wrong Place." Lawrence
Clark Powell, in his foreword to *The Raymond Chandler Omnibus*, lists *Postman* as one of the most memorable novels ever
written about Los Angeles. The California evoked by Cain, Hammett, Chandler, and McCoy stays with us in the way that the
movies of the late 1930's and early 1940's do—particularly the
movies made from their novels. Their scenes, giving off the cold
gloss of movie stills, belong with the California writings of more
"serious" writers. The Hollywood novel is a special genre: Nathanael West's *Day of the Locust* and Huxley's *After Many a
Summer Dies the Swan* (1939); Budd Schulberg's *What Makes
Sammy Run?* and F. Scott Fitzgerald's *The Last Tycoon* (1941);
Evelyn Waugh's *The Loved One* (1948). The tough Hollywood
novel is a subgenre: McCoy's *They Shoot Horses, Don't They?*
(1935) and *I Should Have Stayed Home* (1938), and Chandler's
The Little Sister (1949). Like these writers, Cain is interested in
the way the high hopes of the westward movement collapsed on
the Pacific shore in the vacant glare of a sunlight that gilds the
cheapest artifacts of transient American technology.

Cain's simplest American Dream fable is *The Postman*. Frank
and Cora represent in broad outline the young men and women of
their economic level during the depression. Their extreme insecu-
rity accounts in part for their lack of conscience. Frank, the drifter
lost in a land of promise, no longer seeks the dream; and he is
compelled to enact the nightmare when he can no longer elude it.
In the background, Frank and Cora pursue separate dreams
which mock the shared realization of the immediate wish. Cora,
who came to Hollywood from a small Iowa town, is bemused by
the dream many girls of the 1930's cherished: to become a movie
star. She failed. Basically, her values are middle-class ones; for
above all, she wants respectability, even if murder is the pre-
requisite: "I want to work and be something, that's all. But you
can't do it without love." She *can* do it without ethics. After the
murder, "she looked," Frank says, despite all her pretensions to
respectability, "like the great grandmother of every whore in the
world."

Though Frank has a certain skill as a garage mechanic, he is an
anachronism in the age of technology. He dreams a very male and
American dream of continuing to walk, a free man, down the

open road; but his immediate desire for Cora restrains him. After they first make love, he suggests that they "blow": "I'm not talking about the hash house. I'm talking about the road. It's fun, Cora. And nobody knows it better than I do. I know every twist and turn it's got. And I know how to work it, too. Isn't that what we want? Just to be a pair of tramps, like we really are?" For a moment, but only for a moment, Cora shares his idyllic vision. After the failure of their first attempt to murder Nick, they set out together for a life of wandering—like Charlie Chaplin, the tramp, and Paulette Goddard, the girl next door turned gypsy, who, abjuring modern times, strike out upon the open road, unfettered, into the sunset. When cars pass Frank and Cora by, Cora gives up after a quarter of a mile. Her perverse middle-class female pride is expressed in her allegiance to superficial values: ashamed to be seen in daylight hitching a ride, she is not ashamed to steal Nick's car or to use it to kill him in the dark.

At the height of passion or danger, Cora is *with* Frank; but, when things settle, she is always the bourgeois grabber. Like Mildred, she wants to earn money in a business she knows. After the murder, she insists on turning the restaurant into a big enterprise. When Frank resists, she asks, "Frank, don't you ever want to *be* something?" Then she repeats what she had said in the beginning: "You're a bum, that's all. That's what you were when you came here, and that's what you are now." She declares that she will not let him make a bum of her as he has tried to do from the start. With sex, she wins him over; to maintain a foothold in respectability, she will exert female cunning over brute violence. When she has a gun pointed at Kennedy, the blackmailer, Frank tells her to shoot if he gives her the sign: "She leaned back and an awful smile flickered around the corner of her mouth. I think that smile scared Kennedy worse than anything I had done."

In the criminal affair of these lovers, these deliberate outsiders, the two central dreams of the American experience—unrestrained mobility and respectable sedentariness—and two views of the American landscapes—the open road and the mortgaged house—collide. As the dreams betray them, they begin, ironically, to turn on each other, for basically, what Frank wants is Cora, the sexual dynamo; and what Cora wants is an instrument to be used to gain her ends—money and respectability. And, though she may convince herself that the right man, instead of a fat foreigner, is a necessary part of her aspirations, *this* man would soon wake up in the wrong dream. Frank and Cora lie down in "the great American dream bed" only to wake up in a living nightmare.

Sometimes the protagonist pursues two general, conflicting dreams. Sharp's general dream is to be a great opera singer, but the more sophisticated his successful world becomes, the less inhabitable it is for Juana, who is his specific dream. Mildred's general dream is to fulfill herself, specifically through her daughter Veda, but the two aspects of this composite dream-wish conflict. Trying for both dreams, Sharp and Mildred realize neither.

By depicting desperate people who grab for the future in a very immediate present that ignores the past, Cain offers one perspective on the American Dream. In his essay "The Pathology of Service," he analyzes the problem even more specifically. The American Dream as it verges on nightmare directly stimulates the impulse to self-dramatization. Americans need "more artificial bolstering up of personal roles" than other men, says Cain, because, where all men are politically and philosophically equal, "all men must justify their existence." Thus, Americans are frantic to succeed; in the nature of things success is not possible for all men; but "the national imperative being as it is, this sets them to brooding and self-castigation." "Lowly" men seek the appearances of success, some way "to induce other men to look at them with respect, envy, and maybe a little fear."

In the early days of America, this craving for drama was just as strong; but "the despair of those days discharged itself in a great national adventure which has now come to an end. This was the adventure of winning the West. . . . That great region over the horizon came to be the symbol of romance and opportunity." A land of destiny, it evoked epic, mystic poetry. "Giving up that glamorous frontier was a wrench." Then about 1900 "the idea of Progress" seemed a reprieve for the death of drama. So the dull people plunged. Cain went to the scene of the last-ditch stand of western romance—the shores of the Pacific—to deal in broken American dreams. On this landscape of decaying dramatic scenery, he continued to depict man's innate desire for the drama which life seems to deny the average man.

CHAPTER 5

Cain's Craft

MOST critics first write Cain off as a popular novelist and then proceed to reproach him for failing to rise to the level of artistic achievement toward which they have felt him striving. Frohock's response to Cain is typical: "*The Postman* is Cain's book almost in the same sense that *Don Quixote* is Cervantes' book: nothing he wrote later could break down the association—he could neither live it down nor live up to it. The obvious ingredients of its success have often been enumerated, but every time we run down the list we discover something new about Cain and about ourselves," and we conclude, he argues, that Cain's technique is fraudulent. "Cain calculated his effects," and "grimly . . . schooled himself to supercharge every sentence and jolt the reader anew on every page. He was one of the few writers then practicing in America who were really sure-handed in the manipulation of their materials." He gave the public what he knew it wanted, and made a living from his art much in the way Sharp, the opera singer "so far down on his luck that he turned 'Professor' for a cathouse," played "the kind of piano the customers wanted."

But Lerner felt that "more than any other contemporary writer, Cain has become the novelist laureate of the crime of passion in America," that he takes his task seriously, that he strives to get his characters caught in the same grip of fatality that the Greek tragedians did but that "formula defeats him." Farrell and Wilson lament the fact that Cain's special technique and style sometimes defeat his often promising thematic purposes. Wilson sums up a general critical attitude about Cain's technique: "*Serenade* is a definite improvement on *The Postman*. It, too, has its trashy aspect, its movie foreshortenings and its too-well oiled action; but it establishes a surer illusion. *The Postman* was always in danger of becoming unintentionally funny. Yet even there brilliant moments of insight redeemed the unconscious burlesque; and there

is enough of the real poet in Cain—both in writing and in imagination—to make one hope for something better than either."

I   *Dubious Influences: Literary and Cinematic*

Cain's own comments on his work reveal a conscious attention
to craft and a clear understanding of his intentions. In his preface
to *Three of a Kind*, he says that the novels make "an interesting
commentary on my own development as a novelist, and as I am
probably the most mis-read, mis-reviewed, and misunderstood
novelist now writing, this may be a good place to say a word
about myself, my literary ideals, and my method of composition. I
have had, since I began writing, the greatest difficulties with . . .
fictive technique." His first three novels were so bad he disposed
of them; ten years later, at about forty, he tried again: "I had at
least learned it is no easy trick, despite a large body of opinion to
the contrary." (One wonders where he encountered that "body of
opinion.")

At a time when Cain was meditating a great deal on problems
of style he "fell under the spell" of Vincent Lawrence, whose
banner was, as we have seen, *technique:* "Until then I had been
somewhat suspicious of technique. Not that I didn't take pains
with what I wrote, but I felt that good writing was gestative
rather than fabricative, and that technique for its own sake probably anagramed into formula, and perhaps into hoke." Until he
met Lawrence, Cain's "ideal of writing . . . was that the story
correspond with life, mirror it, give a picture whose main element
was truth." But Lawrence observed that "if truth were the main
object of writing, I would have a hard time competing with a $3
camera." The 1944 preface contained a declaration of departure:

Recently, I have made steady progress at the art of letting a
story secrete its own adrenalin, and I have probably written the
last of my intense tales of the type that these represent. The trouble with that approach is that you have to have a 'natural,' . . .
and a natural is not to be had every day. If what you start with
is less, if you shoot at passion and miss by ever so little, you hit
lust, which isn't pretty, or even interesting. Again, the whole
method, if the least touch of feebleness gets into it, lends itself to
what is perilously close to an étude in eroticism. . . . Having got

past the stymie of style that bothered me for so many years, I want to tell tales of a little wider implication than those which deal exclusively with one man's relation to one woman.

In *Mildred Pierce* Cain had already made such a departure; and *The Moth* was an even grander try at wider implications: "In the future, what was valid in the technical organization of my first few novels will be synthesized, I hope, into a somewhat larger technique." Cain is always trying to break away from what he does well; from a raw material angle, his historical novels are such a break; from a technical angle, the use of third person is the most disastrous. But Cain still stressed in 1949 in *Three of Hearts* the importance of holding a reader's acute attention: "The worst offense of narrative, in my belief, is tepidity, and in my work, God willing, you will never find it, whether I write of past, present, or future."

Cain does not seem, according to the evidence, to be the sort of man who is generally open to literary influences. He is somewhat aware of popular writers; but, except for a few, he is little inclined to read them carefully enough to be influenced. Though he has appeared in the same magazines with the major writers of this century, he does not seem to have read such contemporaries as Dos Passos, Steinbeck, Faulkner, Fitzgerald, and Caldwell: "This reflects no particular disinterest in these writers, merely a disinterest in all fiction, no matter who writes it—though I can get my mind on it well enough, if I have a reason to, such as writing a review. But I don't read it for entertainment."

Cain's art sprang almost full-blown from certain basic concepts of the craft of writing that are, we might say, "in the air" for newspapermen such as Cain was (he never thinks of myself as an artist, nor even as a novelist, but as a journalist). The major effects upon his writing were observations of the tastes and interests of the American people; while he has a certain contempt for their gullibility, for their susceptibility to manipulation through cunning appeals to their tastes, he respects techniques that accomplish aims. Criticism dwells too much upon influences (which often amount to little more than supposition inspired by happy similarities) and fails to examine the phenomenon of simultaneity: ideas *are* "in the air" at a given time, and several writers often respond independently to the same mood.

Cain regards the question of influences as being more important
to critics, those "strange surrogates for God," than to novelists. A
writer cannot write a book "by peeping over his shoulder at somebody else." On behalf of all writers, Cain informs the critics that
"we don't do it that way." His tone is condescending and arrogant,
and his point, of course, shows a naïveté of which most critics are
incapable. Cain often reveals a strange concept of writers and
critics; I doubt whether he has read even a little serious criticism.
In his preface to *For Men Only*, Cain cites the story expert for one
of the big picture studios as "one of the best authorities on fiction
that I am acquainted with." If he sometimes seems obtuse about
literature, he does so because his knowledge is confined to elementary aspects and, because he knows them with such keenness,
he is able to use them objectively, effectively, and with a sense of
authority.

The simplicity of Cain's style has evoked frequent comparison
with Hemingway. He *is* like Hemingway in the sense that it is
mainly in his style that we feel his sensibility. Wilson observes
that, after *Serenade,* Cain himself had a number of imitators:
"The whole group stemmed originally from Hemingway but it
was Hemingway turned picaresque. . . . Mr. Cain remained the
best of these novelists." In 1947, Cain commented on the Hemingway comparison: "I owe no debt, beyond the pleasure his books
have given me, to Mr. Ernest Hemingway, though if I did,
I think I should admit it. . . . Just what it is I am supposed to
have got from him I have never quite made out." He sees no "similarity in manner, beyond the circumstance that each of us has an
excellent ear, and each of us shudders at the least hint of the high-
falutin, the pompous, or the literary. We have people talk as they
do talk." There is "a certain leanness in each of us, as a result of all
this skinning out of literary blubber. . . . Although for conven-
ience of expression I have thrown what appears to be a very
chummy 'we' around his neck, I intend no familiarity and claim
no equality. This, as I well know, is a Matterhorn of literature,
while my small morality tale is at best a foothill. But small though
it be, it is as good as I know how to make it. . . . But it does
strike me as a very odd notion that in setting out to make it good I
would do the one thing certain to make it bad."

Elements of terror and grotesquerie in Cain might tempt one to
compare him with Faulkner of *Sanctuary,* but Cain says, "I can't

read Faulkner, and know almost nothing about him." And, though
Cain has written stories set in the South, and though there are
superficial resemblances to Caldwell-like situations in Cain's
novels, the temptation to compare him with Erskine Caldwell
should be resisted. Caldwell's early work has received more respect than Cain's, possibly because there was some social-protest
significance to *Tobacco Road* and *God's Little Acre;* but actually
Cain has written as many *good* novels as Caldwell.

Especially in his early efforts, Cain was also bracketed with Mc-
Coy, Hammett, Chandler, and Traven: "But actually, I have yet
to read one line by McCoy, I never read Traven until a few
months ago, when I was picked to do a preface to *The Treasure of
Sierra Madre,* though I liked him so little that nothing came of it;
I have read but a few pages of *The Big Sleep,* by Chandler." Cain
deplores in his preface to *The Butterfly* the ease with which Clifton
Fadiman "can refer to my hammett-tongs style and make things
easy for himself." Cain says he has read less than twenty pages of
Hammett. Of the novels in *Three of a Kind* (*Double Indemnity,
Career, The Embezzler*) Cain prefers the latter because "the writing is much simpler, much freer from calculated effect, than . . .
the other two. And for long stretches I find the story quite free"
of what Fadiman once called Cain's "conscious muscle-flexing."
Four years later Cain made a more explicit statement: "I belong
to no school, hard-boiled or otherwise, and I believe these so-
called schools exist mainly in the imagination of critics."

Cain himself cites several writers who may have influenced his
work somewhat. Some traces of his "wonderful imitations of
Lardner" can be seen in *Our Government,* and Cain sees probable
echoes of Lardner in "Pastorale" (with "Haircut" in mind, most
likely) and "The Baby in the Icebox." He doubts that this influence was a "vivid" one, but he "purged" himself of it when he
moved to California.

Conan Doyle is a "writer never mentioned in connection with
me, but is probably a greater 'influence' than any, though I never
knew him personally." (It is typical of Cain that the men whom
he lists as influences should be almost exclusively men he knew
personally, men in the business of writing, rather than men whose
works he simply read.) In the preface to *For Men Only,* Cain
says, "I began reading him at the age of twelve. . . . I have been
reading him ever since, and expect to go on reading him until I

die. . . . He is incredible, nonsensical, and pure, unadulterated magic."

It would be difficult to prove that the theater and the movies have had a significant influence on Cain's fiction. His direct response to his raw material and his apprehension of the technique best suited to project it are a single event. For instance, given his natural sense of the dramatic, he quite appropriately expressed his satirical observations on American government, religion, and such subjects in the form of the dramatic dialogue. Certain theatrical and cinematic techniques are implicit in material that appeals to mass audiences. What Cain was doing and what theater and movies were doing paralleled each other.

In his review, Fadiman used movie terms to describe *Mildred's* positive achievement: Cain shows a "mastery of cinema-plot tricks"; the "scenario" is executed in a "devilishly skillful manner. You feel ashamed to find yourself following the fortunes of these dismal characters with breathless interest, but shame or no shame, you follow them." *Mildred* "in regulation Hollywood fashion, is soon in the money." The novel "would make a bang-up movie" if it could get past the censors, "for it is a first-rate example of the sort of tricky, cynical realism that the superior Hollywood writer likes to turn out in his more conscientious moods." [1] Fadiman seems to suggest that the proper effects of a good Cain novel are also the proper effects of a good Hollywood movie. But Van Nostrand, Wilson, Frohock, Farrell, and Lerner insisted that Cain was negatively influenced by the movies; and reviewers consistently and glibly attacked movie clichés in Cain. Farrell argued that "the consequences of the Hollywood alterations of this already Hollywoodized realism are such that [*Mildred*] becomes stupid and senseless" and confuses public taste.

Cain declares that he knew while he was writing his novels that they might have censor trouble, "yet I never toned one of them down, or made the least change to court the studio's favor. In *Past All Dishonor,* for at least four versions, the girl was not of the oldest profession; she was the niece of the lady who ran the brothel, and for four versions the story laid an egg. I then had to admit to myself that it had point only when she was a straight piece of trade goods. Putting the red light over the door, I knew, would cost me a picture sale, and so far it has; it is in there just the same, and it made all the difference in the world with the book." Wilson sees dark implications in the fact that, as Cain states on the jacket, the idea for writing the book came on a trip to Virginia City "in connection with a picture." In the novel, Wilson sees "a lot of old studio properties. . . . It used to be said about Cain's earlier novels that they sounded like movie scripts too outrageous to be produced." Wilson felt that by 1946 Cain had "been eaten alive by the movies."

In a chapter in *The Denatured Novel* called "Hollywood Pay-Off," Van Nostrand elaborates upon Wilson's charge. Having documented his thesis that Hollywood denatures the novels adapted to the movies, he says: "But not all novels so stoutly resist the 'treatment' of the scenarist. If a novel emphasizes only 'what' and 'how' to begin with, and if its conflict already resolves by a 'switcheroo,' then making a scenario is no trouble at all." Such a novel is *The Postman*, which satisfies "movie values," partly because it was written "like a movie 'continuity.'" Its sixteen chapters are comprised of scenes. Within these scenes, short units—sometimes only eight or ten lines—approximate camera shots. . . . In all its formal aspects *The Postman* was a scenario the moment it was published." But Van Nostrand's argument is based mainly on *Past All Dishonor,* which "is constructed exactly like every book" Cain sold to the movies. His breakdown of the novel, chapter by chapter, into scenario structure is an impressive demonstration of his charge. For Van Nostrand, Cain's work remains exemplary of the scenario mode of fiction. Even if he is right, he does not prove that such dramatic presentation is in itself a bad thing for the kind of fiction *Cain* writes.

The early comments of Wilson and Farrell on the movie elements in Cain sum up the typical charges. As we follow the development of Cain's plots, Wilson says, "we find ourselves more and more disconcerted at knocking up—to the destruction of illusion —against the blank and hard planes and angles of something we know all too well: the wooden old conventions of Hollywood." Wilson calls these novels, produced in Cain's time off from the movies, "a Devil's parody of the movies. Mr. Cain is the *âme damnée* of Hollywood. All the things that have been excluded by the Catholic censorship: sex, debauchery, unpunished crime, sacrilege against the Church—Mr. Cain has let them loose in these stories with a gusto as of pent-up ferocity that the reader cannot but share."

Farrell felt that the movies defeated a great talent in Cain. He is a master at playing between popular and serious fiction: "He is a literary thrill-producer who profits by the reaction against the sentimentality of the other years and, at the same time, gains from the prestige of more serious and exploratory writing. Thus James M. Cain is not an insignificant or unimportant American literary phenomenon. He has helped to perfect a form which can properly be termed movietone realism." Cain's novels at best are "literary movies." Even the more sympathetic Lerner feels that too much of Cain's writing depends, like popular movies, on terrific pace, shock, and formula writing.

Though critics overemphasize their charge of negative influence, Cain's fiction does have cinematic characteristics; and Cain himself admits that the movies taught him a few techniques. In "Camera Obscura," an important essay, well-written in the hard-boiled manner, he expressed his own practical perspective on writing for the screen and on cinematic "art" in general. In this essay, which appeared in *The American Mercury* in 1933, a year before he published *The Postman,* Cain deals with two related questions: (1) "Why is it that the movies seem unable to afford the writer the requital that he finds so quickly elsewhere; burning shame for work badly done, glowing pride in work that hits the mark?" (2) "Is this really destined to be one of the major arts, worthy of serious critical attention?"

As usual, Cain feels obliged to be fair to both sides, the writer and the producer, and to disabuse his reader of certain preconceptions about both. Outsiders and writers themselves charge that the studios want only the worst a writer can do. "No doubt they pity themselves handsomely, but I'll tell you why their effort was turned down. It was no goddamn good, and that was the beginning and the end of it." Producers want good stories, Cain argues. "But by good they mean just what *you* mean by good. That is, they mean what you mean when you have paid your money and . . . want what you paid for: that kick, that excitement, that emotion, which takes you out of the seat you are sitting in, transports you to where things are going on, and holds you there in hot suspense to see how it all comes out."

Because of the nature of the "art" of "pictures," says Cain, the writer can never really achieve satisfaction in his work. The movie writer, unlike the stage writer, must write first of all for the actor, the model. One difference between stage and screen is that a play has a literary script that is separable from the actor, but in 1933 a movie had no real script: "for the first time in the history of such things, imagination and performance go together, and there is no way to get them apart." "Imagination is free or it is not free, and here it is not free. It serves the medium instead of the medium serving it, and once that is felt, that is the end of pride, of joy." It is not surprising that in a situation where Cain could not put his hands on the master controls, he would cease to function.

The critic, "posterity's bookmaker," refrains from calling the movies art, says Cain, because he isn't going to make book on something so mechanical. Art "pays off on wings, on that imaginative vitality which can fly down the cruelly long distance through the years. Thus the critic is concerned with what, in telegraphy, is known as the phantom circuit . . . the imagination. . . ." The high-minded writer will always be disappointed with the movies because he can never be sure *whose* imagination has made a particular film good. Cain's conclusion balances with his attitude as a fiction writer: "there are worse trades than confecting entertainment, and if you realize clearly that you are at work on entertainment, something that lives tonight and tomorrow is forgotten [unlike much of Cain's own work, however,] then the suspicion that you are a prostitute of the arts loses much of its sting. . . . There is good entertainment and bad, and a chance for plenty of honest resourcefulness. . . . For my part, when I go to a movie, I am entertained best if it is unabashedly a movie, and not a piece of dull hoke posing as something else."

Aware of the realities of the cinema, as he experienced them, Cain knew that what he wanted to do could be done only in the solitude of novel writing, only in the way a novel can do things. Cain sums up his attitude about "moving pictures": "I know their technique as exhaustively as anybody knows it, I study it, but I don't feel it." Cain's worst mental anguish came with the realization that he had "flopped flat" and was being paid for something he didn't deliver: "a new sensation to me, and a disagreeable one. I was in a scramble of personal emotions, for on both lots there were men who had treated me very decently, whom I had got to like, and whom I had let down. . . . But all that involved what you might call my social conscience. My artistic conscience barely stirred." He showed in his movie career that even in mass entertainment, diligence coupled with contempt causes a short in the "phantom circuit."

It is a curious paradox that a writer famous for the theatrical and cinematic qualities in his fiction should fail as a screenwriter and as a playwright. Extremely effective curtain lines close his fiction chapters. The theatrical, musical, and operatic motifs that abound in his work derive from his thematic concern with the element of drama in human behavior. But perhaps Cain is so aware of the mechanics of drama that in his plays and in his work with films he failed to subordinate mechanics to substance. Cain is a dramatist who writes good novels; but, as a novelist who writes dramas, he is ineffective.

II   *The Reader as Accomplice, the Reader as Captive*

Although the popular and the avant-garde writer often have surprising affinities, the tough writer would violently disagree with the final declaration of a proclamation that appeared in *transition* in 1929: "The plain reader be damned." More than in most writers, a study of Cain is a study of the craft of fiction itself; and, in him, more than in most writers, a study of craft requires an awareness of the fascinating ways in which the author deliberately, and indirectly, creates a relationship between himself and his ideal reader. It is easy to understand his appeal to the average reader; for, when Cain is at his best, there is little difference between author and reader. His characters are not far removed in status or aspiration from the average reader Cain envisions. Thus, his knowledge of what his reader wants is phenomenal. But it is fallacious to call his work "popular" in the negative sense. Part of his ability lies in the way he mingles serious and popular fictive elements. Even the serious reader becomes so involved that he is unaware, until after finishing a Cain novel, of ways in which the author's achievement may be examined technically as literature. Sophisticated literary elements operate in Cain, but so "naturally" that they neither tax the popular reader's patience nor, at first, impress the sophisticated reader.

The good Cain novel is, then, neither serious nor popular; it is pure entertainment, an experience in which strong distinctions between one sort of reader and another seem superfluous. For instance, while Graham Greene's "serious" novels may discourage the popular reader, his "entertainments" bring all sorts together. If Greene is a serious novelist who writes entertainments, Cain is an entertainer who sometimes attempts or approaches "seriousness." But then, as Cain himself has asked, "What is a 'popular' novelist, and who writes these unpopular novels? The aim of art is to cast a spell on the beholder; it has no other aim—or in other words, the whole object of a novel is to get itself read."

While we might quarrel with this statement, we must allow that a novel which succeeds in purely entertaining all sorts of readers has some claim to "seriousness." Who are the popular and who are the serious readers of fiction? Many Renaissance specialists who pride themselves on their ignorance of the avant-garde have nevertheless read Cain; the scholar of contemporary literature, who bases his estimation of many writers more on the criticism he has read than on the works themselves, has *made* time to read Cain. Few are the serious writers or students of literature who have not read him, knowing full well the sort of experience they were to have. For what do they go to Cain? In what sense can we condemn what they get from him?

Both "serious" and "commercial" writers write popular books, as a glance at the best-seller lists over the years, particularly in the last decade, shows. By this one superficial criterion, Cain *is* a popular novelist. *The Postman, Serenade, Mildred Pierce,* and *The Moth* were on the list, says Cain. *Postman, Serenade,* and *Mildred Pierce* each sold nearly two million copies in hard cover. Since new paperback editions of Cain's novels appear every year, it is difficult to estimate the millions of copies each has sold. Considering the fact that cheap hard-cover reprint and soft-cover editions are readily available in any secondhand bookstore, the Cain readership over the years must be incredibly huge. *The Postman* is one of America's all-time best-sellers and has gone through a great many editions (it was in its eighth Knopf printing by May, 1946; Bantam brought it out in July, 1967). After thirty-three years, it is still widely read. Cain takes "some satisfaction in the fact" that his novels are "made well enough to reap some of the rewards mainly reserved for the small fable; it translates, so that it is known all over the world; its point is easily remembered, so that it passes easily from mouth to mouth and so lives on from year to year" (preface, *Butterfly*).

In discussing Cain's technique, we are dealing with elements

that worked when the cave man told stories; and his reader seems
to make the ancient request, "Tell me a story." And that is what
Cain does. He even turns reviewers into story listeners. While reviewers often attack Cain as though he were running for public
office and would certainly misguide the multitudes if elected, they
sometimes sound less like critics than members of a Fundamentalist congregation standing up to give a testimonial, as the following
battery of reactions suggests: "I wouldn't miss a new Cain novel
any more than the Mayor would miss a fire," says Fadiman. Walter Havighurst testifies, "What I will remember from 'The Butterfly' is the kind of thing you can't any more forget than you can
forget the wreckage of a car in the roadside with the glass shat-
tered and the steel top crushed like a kicked-in derby and the
upturned wheels still spinning." For Merle Miller, Cain, at his
best, "writes like an angel—a slightly malicious, dyspeptic, and
ribald angel with a lust for gore."

But reviewers were almost always aware that the novels suc-
ceeded despite certain elements. Dawn Powell, reviewing *Three
of a Kind*, said: "Validity in art is recognized by the after-effect,
and the after-effect of a Cain book is a half-angry feeling of having been gypped, of . . . having cried over 'Mother Machree.'"
Still, Cain's work is "important in its own peculiar way"; it is not
"mere hammock reading." His "special trick" is that he creates an
"intensity of suspense" that "successfully anaesthetizes all other
senses and might even induce a trance." Reviewing *Past All Dishonor*, Jay Adams sums up the attitude of the "faithful": "To be
sure, Cain has not written an important book. If we are lucky, he
never will. He will continue to agree with Somerset Maugham
who . . . dared to say that the purpose of a novelist was to be a
'story-teller.' Cain is a superb story-teller; his pages breathe excitement rather than life, but, for a pleasurable evening, that's
enough."

Quite early, reviewers were dealing not only with each new
Cain novel as a phenomenon but with the author's reputation as
one. This reputation is based on the rightness of such early observations as Benét's: "You can't lay [*The Postman*] down, for all its
brutality and ugliness." He predicted: "so long as writers can tell
their stories as well as Mr. Cain does, and make a murder almost
as deeply shocking as the Ruth Snyder–Judd Gray affair so vivid in
detail, we will continue to read them." The second novel satisfied

his expectations: "You may not like *Serenade*, but I defy you to lay it down. . . . Mr. Cain is a real writer who can construct and tell an exciting story with dazzling swiftness—one of our hard-boiled novelists whose work has a fast rhythm that is art." The *Time* reviewer reviews the audience as well: "It is popularly supposed that people go right on reading the thrillers of James M. Cain . . . through five-alarm fires." He envisions Cain's multitudes hanging on his "hypnotic typewriter."

Most reviewers, critics, and other serious readers, feeling some obligation to absolute standards, charge that at least some of Cain is trash. Frohock notes the relative trash of "serious" writers. We think of Hemingway's *To Have and Have Not*, Faulkner's *Mosquitoes*, Caldwell's *Tragic Ground*, much of Steinbeck. But, if there was excellence among the other fiction of these writers, "with Cain there is no choice—you take trash or you don't get Cain. Moreover, you get what Cain intends you to get." However, Cain does not control his reader in order to deliver trash; and Frohock—who says many things about Cain's novels that cannot be said about trash—knows it. Even *Newsweek* discerns that "Cain's writing is too proficient and disciplined to be classed as pulp, too intelligent to be classed as trash, and some of it certainly ranks with the classics of shock fiction." Only in *Sinful Woman* does Cain seem to be writing down to the sort of audience that sustained the massive body of formula writing (he has never written for the "pulps"). In a review of Cain's most recent novel, *Time* summed up the element of trash and formula in Cain: "For thirty years, Novelist James M. Cain has worked a literary lode bordering a trash heap. Even his best works . . . reeked of their neighborhood." But, in *The Magician's Wife*, he achieved a breakthrough—it is "pure trash."

Cain makes so many apt assumptions about his readers that we are palpably aware of the author's intimacy with the reader-community he has visualized for his work. Commenting on his novels, he reveals himself as a man who writes as a community act, within the context of middle-class society, rather than as a writer among writers and critics. Cain has an enormous respect for his reader that comes from a particular kind of egotism: his standards and those of his ideal reader are similar; his fear of boring his reader comes from a refusal to be bored himself. Cain makes the reader feel terror, and every device of the novel that

will heighten that experience is made to work. His magical
technique can make the reader forget that, beyond the stark tensions of their predicament, his characters are often not fully
drawn. But he is primarily a novelist of simple theme and action;
between his characters and the action there is, in his best work, an
absolute congruity; over his characters and the action, and thus
over the reader, he has absolute control.

Since his heroes are very clever, it is appropriate that Cain himself should exhibit great cleverness in depicting his characters in
action. He is a performer aware of his audience, one which wants
to see him *do it again;* and he often uses this expectation by playing against it, reversing it. His awareness of the way stock responses operate enables him to manipulate the reader; he often
sets up a stock situation and reverses it, to get a more intense
response. One way in which Cain persuades the reader to identify
with his characters is to appeal to the reader's natural interest in
the amateur. Borland, the bridge-builder, is an outsider to opera,
then an observer, then a participant; via these stages we are
drawn in to experience the vicarious thrill of singing as well as the
professional and the fear that as an amateur we will fail and get
the "bird." Cain reverses this natural appeal by depicting Sharp,
the opera singer, as a tough guy. Having made initial stock responses, the reader finds these turnabouts appealing; and Cain
makes him feel he is *in* on the narrator's overwhelmingly confident
and knowledgeable feats.

In the openings of his novels, so much happens so fast that the
reader either immediately rejects everything or submits to Cain's
will; he does not necessarily *willingly* suspend his disbelief and his
"finer instincts." Cain has never done more to his reader than in
The Postman; for, as Frohock observes, the reader is "never quite
prepared for what happens. . . . In boxing this trick is known as
feinting a lead to pull your opponent off balance. . . . It is clear
that Cain's opponent is his reader; he feints us into position and
hits us before we can get our feet untangled." I see this as a
positive value. "The significant fact about this trickery is that if we
did not happen to think twice, Cain would be getting away with it
completely." We wonder *when* Frohock thought twice—while
reading the book, or after his intellect resumed control? Frohock
answers: "Only after a considerable number of readings does one
even realize what a piece of ham Cain has persuaded him to swal-

low at this point!" That is, of course, a fallacious procedure; though we may enjoy rereading several of his novels, Cain is not meant to be read as one reads James Joyce. Cain discovers, caters to (some say debauches), and ultimately creates popular taste. Frohock convicts Cain of manipulating the reader, a talent I think essential to pure entertainment: "Cain worked on the assumption, justified by the facts, of course, that he could do just about what he liked with the reader. The latter was a sort of victim, with weaknesses to be exploited." As in the church scene in *Serenade,* Cain exploits "simultaneously our prurience, our instinctive fascination with sacrilege, and our curiosity about the ways of the unknown and hence glamorous savage."

Frohock is right in some ways, but there are indications that Cain is interested in the consequences of such prurience, fascination, and curiosity, so that he achieves not so much the reader's ideological as his emotional commitment. Cain is fascinated by such things himself, in his own way, and by the ways in which his ideal reader is fascinated. In much popular fiction, the reader so totally identifies with the hero that he is unaware of the author. But Cain's pure entertainment provides a unique value in contemporary literature: the reader, sensing the way Cain is controlling everything, identifies more with him than he empathizes with Frank; for he wants to be able to control as Cain does. The serious reader experiences yet another dimension: he observes Cain manipulating his concept of the popular reader; and, in the process, he becomes a captive himself.

But Frohock contends that Cain's appeal to his reader "was not legitimate, for a book like *The Postman* is thoroughly immoral—immoral not so much because of the unpraiseworthy behavior of the characters as because of the unpraiseworthy behavior of the reader." Certainly, Frohock, Farrell, and others commit the affective fallacy quite readily in discussing Cain. "Everything in the book conspires to excite the reader to hope that somehow Frank will get away with murder, keep Cora, and elude the police. Frank Chambers does not deserve such sympathy. The reader is tricked into taking the position of a potential accomplice." The reader as accomplice becomes the reader as captive of Cain's control.

But we should permit Cain (who has not read Frohock) to have the last word: "Making the reader an 'accomplice' of Chambers

and Cora somehow seems to say it is up to me to act as an
indignant commentator on what they are up to. Their crime gets
its punishment and consequent comment in the end, but if the
idea of the story is to sit with the criminal, hear his account of
what he did and why, and suffer and sweat and fear as he suffers
and sweats and fears, how can we do that and at the same time
stand apart, taking no interest in what he does? If we feel his danger, we *care* how he feels; we can't help it." One reviewer complained that there were no "admirable characters" in Cain's novel.
"Our national curse, if so perfect a land can have such a thing, is
the 'sympathetic character,'" said Cain, in his introduction to *For
Men Only* (1944). "The world's great literature is peopled by
thorough-going heels, and in this book you will find a beautiful
bevy of them, with scarce a character among them you would let
in the front door."

III *Getting a Story Well Told*

Cain's approach to and his attitude toward his raw material are
seldom governed by a genuine conception. Wright Morris, in *The
Territory Ahead*, defines raw material as "that comparatively
crude ore that has not been processed by the imagination—what
we refer to as life, or as experience, in contrast to art. . . . Technique and raw material are dramatized at the moment that the
shaping imagination is aware of itself. . . . It is conceptual
power, not style or sensibility, that indicates genius." [2] Of course,
Cain measures up to none of these high standards; he is the man
who was there, who returns to give the reader a realistic report of
what happened. Well read in nonfiction, Cain is often more interested in the lived or researched raw material for its own sake than
in the reimagined event. He gives us the raw material of his
novels straight and produces a sense of the authenticity of it all,
but seldom awe—for awe as a reader's response is generated by
the heat of imagination. Cain's imagination does not process in
terms of a conception and thus transform his raw material; rather,
with basic fictional techniques, he expertly manipulates and controls all the elements for calculated effects. Thus, we might with
greater justification speak of Cain's inventive powers and his
structuring mind—which is indeed "aware of itself" and of the
mind of the reader—rather than his "shaping imagination." Cain's

imagination and his talent remain *tools;* conception never puts them to use in the service of high art.

So, in studying Cain's technique, we don't deal with profound concepts of the creative process but with such simple matters as plot, in the service not of something esthetically, ideologically, or thematically higher, but simply of getting a good story well told. Craft rather than conception is Cain's genius; and we should look then at what he really is: a superb technician.

In Cain, obviously, plot is extremely important. The charge is often made that his plots are too melodramatic, at the expense of character. But reviewing *Serenade,* Dawn Powell argues the opposite: "Mr. Cain's secret lies not so much in what he tells or in his prose as in a brilliant manipulation of story and a dexterous staggering of terror effects. . . . His words are simple but inflated with horror; the story grows in memory; its minor implications will roam through your dreams for days to come. There is nightmare material here for a whole winter." Economy gave Miss Powell the impression of abundance of material. Except for *The Moth* and *Mildred,* each of which *does* contain plot enough for three novels, all Cain's novels are very clearly constructed.

What we follow in Cain's novels is the spine of surface narrative action ("positive action" is Cain's phrase). The hero usually meets the woman in the first few paragraphs; the whole problem is set, usually, in Cain's first chapter; and the transitions, the turning points, the narrative shifts from one chapter to the next are swift, pointed, and carefully controlled; everything is kept strictly to the essentials. The characters, for instance, exist only for the immediate action; there is almost no exposition as such. The narrative is made up of clearly delineated incidents and episodes, each of which has its own integrity, with endings that propel the reader inevitably on into the next.

It is most relevant to look at Cain's plots mechanically—in terms of openings, scene building, endings, and general length. Cain uses three types of opening (or "narrative hooks," as such an opening is called in "hack" writing): (1) the introduction of the girl in the first few lines; (2) the delayed introduction of the girl for several pages, but with the immediacy of the first person; and (3) the third-person, leisurely introduction to the story, with little emphasis on the girl. In the first category, *Butterfly*'s opening is similar to *Serenade*'s, *Embezzler*'s, and *Dishonor*'s: "She was sit-

ting on the stoop when I came in from the fields, her suitcase
beside her and one foot on the other knee, where she was shaking
a shoe out that seemed to have sand in it. When she saw me she
laughed, and I felt my face get hot, that she had caught me looking at her. . . ."

In the second category, the immediacy of the first-person
opening of *Indemnity* draws us in: "I drove out to Glendale to put
three new truck drivers on a brewery company bond, and then I
remembered this renewal over in Hollywood." But then Cain, im-
patiently, sinks a "hook" that will be symptomatic of lack of control in later novels, though not quite in this one: "I decided to run
over there. That was how I came to this House of Death, that
you've been reading about in the papers." Several pages later,
Cain's introduction of Phyllis suggests a certain banality about the
lust and evil to come: "A woman was standing there. I had never
seen her before. She was maybe thirty-one or two, with a sweet
face, light blue eyes, and dusty blond hair. She was small, and had
on a suit of blue house pajamas. She had a washed-out look."
Twenty years later, another insurance man, Ed Horner, begins his
story, *Jealous Woman,* in a similar manner; but somehow the volt-
age is low, as it is in *Career* and *Evil.*

In the third category, most of the third-person novels begin
woodenly. *Mildred* begins: "In the spring of 1931, on a lawn in
Glendale, California, a man was bracing trees. . . . The living
room he stepped into corresponded to the lawn he left." The
woman the man encounters in the house is his wife; the third
person dilutes her impact: "his wife was icing a cake. She was a
small woman, considerably younger than himself. . . . A pair of
rather voluptuous legs . . . showed between smock and shoes."
Love's Lovely Counterfeit, Sinful Woman, and *The Magician's
Wife* open with routine descriptions of the main character's enter-
ing or leaving a building. In these novels, it makes little difference
whether the girl is introduced in the first line or on page eighteen;
the style does not generate interest, and sometimes it is embarrassingly bad. However, the opening description of the movie star in
Sinful Woman does become rather interesting: she is like "a nude
descending perpetual public staircases; thus she moved as though
withdrawn into herself, with an abstracted, Godivanian saunter
that was aware of nothing nearer than the sky."

If the appearance of the girl, well timed in most cases, is essential very early, Cain also introduces interesting characters later on, thus revitalizing the plot. In *The Postman* two fascinating characters, the lawyer and the district attorney, appear in the middle of the novel; Madge Allen, toward the end. Cain often introduces another girl to give added thrust to his plot, as in *Indemnity;* a second girl also enters *Love's Lovely Counterfeit,* as though to salvage a sinking narrative; and in the episodic *The Moth,* Jack constantly encounters new women.

Cain also keeps the reader constantly expectant with temporary balances: the hero reaches a condition of triumph that will often produce new trouble in the next chapter. Offsetting the balances are the many thematic and/or structural ironic reversals; whether negative or positive in their effect upon the lovers' goals, they always advance the action. In some instances, there is a double reversal, as in *The Butterfly* when the birthmark reveals the solution to the complex mystery of progeny.

In the cyclical or circular plots, Cain creates a deep sense of the restoration of balance. For instance, we meet Sharp when his fears of homosexual tendencies have reduced him to singing like a priest. Juana, the supersexed whore, whom he meets on page one, constantly reminds him in one way or another of his sexual dilemma, which is a mystery to him until she blurts it out when Hawes re-enters his life midway in the novel. Until then, Cain makes a suspenseful mystery of Sharp's condition and Juana's response to it, each chapter ending on that note until she puts the *toro* into his voice in the lovemaking in the church. Until Hawes enters, Cain continues to end even those chapters focusing on Sharp's rise as a singer with a strong stress on Juana. With the homosexual threat posed once more, Juana again immerses Sharp in sex and, as a final solution, kills Hawes. They flee to Guatemala; unable to sing, Sharp fears he will respond to boys; he goes with whores; Juana leaves him and returns to Mexico City. There, taunted by the bullfighter whose girl (Juana) he had stolen, Sharp succumbs to his masculine pride and sings, thus betraying who he is and who she is to the police; Juana is killed by the police, and Sharp gives up sex and singing. *Mildred, Moth,* and *Career* also follow circular plots, but they move more slowly; the charm of *Mildred* is that we move with her in a comic cycle from banality through tormented glamor back to banality.

As we have seen in other contexts, Cain's ability to build a scene is extraordinary. Some of the finest are the murder scenes in *Post-man* and *Indemnity;* the lovemaking and eating scenes in the church, and the "faggot" party at which Juana stabs Hawes in *Serenade;* the many electrifying scenes between Mildred and Veda in *Mildred Pierce;* the singing scenes in *Career;* the spider and vault scene in *Embezzler;* the scenes in the mines in *Dishonor* and in *Butterfly;* the death of Belle in *Butterfly;* the hobo scenes in *The Moth;* the scenes between Duke and Holly in *Galatea* as he tries to persuade her to reduce. Even the "bad" novels have re-deeming moments: the confrontations in *The Root of His Evil* between Carrie and Grant's sisters and Carrie and Grant's mother; the dives Ben and June make into an isolated lake, looking for a body, in *Love's Lovely Counterfeit;* the gambling casino fire in *Sinful Woman.*

The effectiveness Cain exhibits in his openings is dynamically sustained in the structure of individual chapters, and the endings confirm what the beginnings claim. Some of them are "punchy trick endings," but others end on a downbeat. Several end simi-larly. *Postman:* "No stay. Here they come. . . ." *Indemnity:* "I didn't hear the stateroom door open, but she's beside me now while I'm writing. I can feel her." *Dishonor:* "I'm cut off. Ed Blue is out there and. . . ." *The Magician's Wife* is more explicit: "After a glance at the ground, to make sure no one was there, he vaulted and went hurtling down on the parking lot, twenty-two stories below." With the girl dead, Sharp in *Serenade* is haunted by a sign: "As they lowered her down, an iguana jumped out of it [the grave] and went running over the rocks." Bill is in a similar predicament at the end of *Mignon:* "So, the hoodoo passed me by at Red River but didn't forget me, at all. He sleeps in the other bed." The endings of several other novels are cute, coy, corny, or face-achingly sentimental.

The length of Cain's novels determines the effectiveness of their plots. Of the sixteen novels, ten are between one hundred-fifty and two hundred regular pages. *Serenade, Evil, Mignon, Magi-cian's Wife, Mildred,* and *The Moth* are (in ascending order) longer books. The extended *Mildred* has certain atypical qualities that give it impact anyway; unity is partly achieved by the use of a single locale, while the multiplicity of characters and the long time-span give the novel an epic dimension. *Serenade* is broken up into three somewhat distinct adventures (each of novella length): the Mexican, the Californian, the New York. Several of Cain's novels are rogues' tales of a sort, and are to that extent picaresque. *The Moth* covers a great number of years, much territory, many episodes, and studies the manners of a multiplicity of people and many aspects of human nature. An obvious attempt at a serious theme, this novel flits too much; details weigh it down; it is too long—a failure of style and technique on the whole, although not in all its parts. Most of Cain's stories, being concerned with a few characters over a short period of time in a single locale, lend themselves to brevity.

If we look closer at the narrative structure of *The Postman* we will see more clearly some of these technical elements at work; to do this we must recapitulate some of what has already been said. The novel falls into three parts, developing the wish and love-rack theme: Frank and Cora meet and wish to be together; they go on the love-rack as they attempt to fulfill their wish in the two attempts to kill Nick; after Nick's murder, they suffer on the love-rack.

"They threw me off the hay truck about noon," Frank begins. ". . . That was when I hit this Twin Oaks Tavern." A few pages later: "Then I saw her." Twenty pages later, Frank and Cora have made love and planned the murder. The compression, the swift execution of the basic situation in these pages is typical of the entire novel; each development, each scene, is controlled with the same narrative skill; inherent in each episode is the inevitability of the next. Frank's character, of course, justifies the economy of style, the nerve-end adherence to the spine of the action. "As the dreadful venture became more and more inevitable," says Cain, "I strove for a rising coefficient of intensity, and even hoped that somewhere along the line I would graze passion. The whole thing corresponded to a definition of tragedy I found later in some of my father's writings: that it was the 'force of circumstances driving the protagonists to the commission of a dreadful act.'"

Cain often begins a scene at a high point, then ends even higher, and picks up the next scene well into a new shift in the narrative. Thus, before the reader can absorb sufficiently what happens in the first twenty-four pages to question it, Cain thrusts him into the actual attempt to murder in the fourth chapter. "Got any hot water?" it begins. Not until after five lines of seemingly innocent dialogue do we realize that Frank and Cora are within minutes of the attempt. Then: "We played it just like we would tell it." The first murder attempt is compressed into three pages in which a great deal happens, and the climax is a surprise to reader and character in the same instant. We think the cat is introduced as a cliché interruption of the action, to promote suspense; but then it "blows a fuse" and wrecks the murder attempt. Because a cop saw Frank on watch outside, Frank and Cora have to get Nick to a hospital. The question, "Did Nick see Cora 'sap' him?" sustains suspense through the end of the first movement of the plot. The structure of Cain's best novels is similar. One of his worst is a flabby, mangled version of the same basic structure, *The Magician's Wife*.

The ironies of action in *The Postman* are stunningly executed. Frank's "conning" Nick out of a free meal backfires when Nick "cons" Frank into operating his service station; thus Frank initiates a situation that ultimately leaves all three of them dead. As he approaches his death, Nick, appropriately, is full of ironic statements: "You go plenty slow. Maybe all get killed." Cora does not die in the ocean, testing Frank's love, in a mock accident of her own devising; she dies in a real accident (in contrast to the fake car accident that covered the murder of Nick; that fake accident became a real accident for Frank and almost killed him). Since a truck brought Frank to the tavern, it is appropriate that a truck causes the accident in which Cora is killed. The note Cora left in the cash register refers to their having killed the Greek for his money. From the note, the police deduce that Frank engineered the wreck so he could have all the money; since he can't be tried twice for killing the Greek, they convict him of murdering Cora. A careful pattern of minor ironies contributes to the impact of the major ones. The novel is as loaded page by page with irony as *Oedipus Rex* is line by line. Van Nostrand dissents: "The novel has no theme, no attitude toward its subject. It simply tells how the murderers ironically escaped until they were ironically punished."

IV *The Objective Eye*

Cain's world is a man's world; and it is through the eyes of the male, usually, that the reader views that world. It seems that the first person is most appropriate to the tough-guy novel; though

McCoy seldom uses it, Traven, Chandler, and Hammett often do; all but Chandler occasionally use also the third person. Objectivity is a virtue in hard-boiled novels; paradoxically, Cain achieves it most forcibly in the assumed "I" of his fiction. All but four of Cain's sixteen novels are in the first person. Most of his sixteen short stories, oddly enough, are in third person.

There are interesting differences among the narrating voices. As we go from Frank to Sharp, for instance, the style changes; the more complex sentences are appropriate to the more sophisticated Sharp; we get more detailed descriptions of mental states and of the external world; yet Sharp's tone is sometimes tougher than Frank's. Among Huff, Borland, Dave Bennett, and Ed Horner there exist few stylistic differences in speech patterns. Though Jess retains a little of the flavor of speakers in Cain's either dialect pieces, such as "Pastorale," he differs from Frank only in modulations. Jack, like Sharp, is educated, artistic, sophisticated; but he is less consistently tough-sounding (as though Cain were trying to change his signature). The three strongest and steadiest voices are Frank's, Sharp's, and Jess's.

The four third-person novels seem to be periodic attempts to depart from a mode that Cain knew was almost too easy for him. *Mildred* was a challenge whose success encouraged Cain to try others in the third person; although it is one of Cain's four most significant books, its language, despite moments of brilliance, is generally undistinguished (very little is distinguished about the style of *Love's Lovely Counterfeit* or *Sinful Woman,* in which Cain most awkwardly indulges in the omniscience of the third-person narrator). How *Mildred* might have told her own story is suggested by Carrie's narration in *The Root of His Evil,* written two years earlier. But Cain conveys a sense of a woman's perspective more convincingly in the third-person *Mildred.* Bill's first-person narration in *Mignon* suggests a meshing of the faults of Cain's third person with his usually effective first person. Sometimes muscular and economical, the telling is generally soggy and sentimental. Somehow the forced rhetoric of Cain's third-person novels gets into Bill's first-person telling.

During the ten years in which Cain resigned himself to the conviction that he could not write a novel, he discovered that "what had made the novel so hopeless was that I didn't seem to have the least idea where I was going with it, or even which paragraph should follow which. But my short stories, which were put into the mouth of some character, marched right along, for if I in the third-person faltered and stumbled, my characters in the first-person knew perfectly well what they had to say" (preface, *Three of a Kind*). Just before beginning *The Postman* he got another perspective on this problem. He had spent most of his life writing newspaper editorials, "speaking for the corporate awfulness of a newspaper," stories in the first person, and sketches in dialogue— pretending to be somebody else. He knew what he was doing; he had a sure, light touch, a definite style. But writing a weekly column under his own byline, he began to detect a self-consciousness that surprised him; and writing fiction in the third person, again being himself, he had the same problem.

The discovery affected his whole literary output. *The Postman* started out in third person; but, when Cain found Frank's voice, the novel moved and rang true. In the last few years, however, his thinking on this point has changed. Ironically, my discussion in an essay of Cain's point-of-view strategies led him to recast the book he was finishing, *The Magician's Wife*, into the third person (an effect that does *not* delight me).[3] "I'm letting myself be me, and don't have anything like the compulsion I used to have, to put it in somebody's mouth. I can still do the garrulous punk, with my eyes shut, of course. But isn't it time for a change?"

It is Cain's first-person language that generates much of the excitement in the explosive character relationships, presented in incendiary situations. The first-person narrative is made immediate by the fact that the character often writes his story as a kind of confession, from a social or quasi-religious motive or from a compulsion rooted in sex or love. Although the narrator usually writes down his story, he sounds as though he is telling it; usually we do not know that he is writing until the end.

Frank writes his story in his death cell to let the world know he didn't kill Cora, but not because he wants his fellow man to have a better opinion of him; it is not to obtain forgiveness for taking Nick's wife and killing him that Frank wants men to intercede in heaven for him. He has a romantic notion that in the eyes of the world it should be known that he loves Cora, for that knowledge will lend purity to their love. Society must witness his death, his innocence, his love.

Van Nostrand and Frohock object to this gimmicky device. I do not entirely disagree with them; but, if a man like Frank should ever attempt to write his story, Cain shows exactly the way he would have done it. Cain himself is far from satisfied with this method. He denies that his characters confess or tell their stories for any "large emotional, mystical reasons." It is never "a valid, internal thing, springing from an obscure compulsion of the character, though I have always tried to make it appear so." Repeatedly, he has imagined the reader is asking, immediately or at the end, why this man would confess. More than any other single phase of his writing, the justification for the telling posed problems. The device of having Mignon come back as an apparition, "giving Cresap some kind of compulsion to write things down" was, Cain confesses, "a pretty thin stratagem."

Despite Cain's disclaimer of intention in the matter of narration as confession, with social or religious significance, certain effects are achieved. The reader's interest in criminal behavior is associated with confession, and there is a natural interest in confession itself; the person who falsely confesses to a sensational crime testifies to man's impulse to self-dramatization. Confession lends a tone of importance to the narrative and offers character revelation. The ordinary person's impulse, when in the presence of a writer, to say, "I could tell you a story . . ." is felt in the confessionals of Cain's characters, who are often very similar to such ordinary people.

Apparently, Sharp (*Serenade*), Borland (*Career in C Major*), and Bennett (*The Embezzler*) are telling their stories to no one in particular, as though Cain were quite naturally responding to literary convention. The confessional aspect comes in only when the story ends unhappily. In the end, when Sharp tells the priest that he will never sing again, he says, "I knew, then, I had made a confession, and received an absolution, and some kind of gray peace came over me." Huff writes a report of his crime, as he would of any insurance investigation, at Keyes's request; but he also puts it all down because he wants Lola, Phyllis' stepdaughter, for whom he has a "pure" love, to "see it sometime, and not think so bad of me after she understands how it all was." His motive is love, not a desire to benefit society. But Roger Duval writes his story partly so that other men may benefit from his errors by understanding "how it came about that a boy that went to St. Anne's in Annapolis, and believed what he heard there, should turn into a traitor, a killer, and a thief." Van Nostrand reacts: "These tailor-made rationalizations would fit only a robot."

In *The Butterfly*, Jess Tyler, sitting like Duval in a cabin waiting to be killed, tells his story so that men will know his side of it, for Kady may tell hers. "I've got to tell it too, because I didn't do anything but what I thought was right." Van Nostrand declares that, except for *The Butterfly*, all of Cain's novels are the same: "a narrative without an attitude becomes a confession without a theme." I agree with his eloquently stated position on *The Butterfly*. It is the best of Cain's novels because, as Van Nostrand says, "the hero has believably fooled himself about his trespasses. . . . This novel is more persistently sordid than any of the others, involving multiple possibilities of incest, bastardy, cuckolding and murder. But when this hero dies, with the usual confession, he is believable because he has agonized all along over his impossible compromise with God." Cain regards *The Butterfly* as his best novel.

Even in Cain's short stories, we find the confessional or socially oriented motive for first-person narrative. In "Dead Man," in which nineteen-year-old hobo "Lucky" kills a railroad detective, Cain depicts Lucky's guilt in relation to the community. Having gone through intricate preparations for avoiding detection, and learning in the end that the man was believed to have died in an accident, Lucky feels left out of the society of men: "He recognized the feeling now; it was the old Sunday night feeling that he used to have back home, when the bells would ring and he would have to stop playing hide in the twilight, go to church, and hear about the necessity for being saved. It shot through his mind, the time he had played hooky from church, and hid in the livery stable; and how lonely he had felt, because there was nobody to play hide with; and how he had sneaked into the church, and stood in the rear to listen to the necessity for being saved." He turns himself in. Here, quite clearly, Cain is interested in the theme itself of the compulsion to confess.

Both Frohock and Wayne C. Booth (*Rhetoric of Fiction*) see moral implications in the first-person, unreliable narrator; for, as the reader's guide, he is like the purblind leading the purblind, a false agent of irony and ambiguity. But that criticism is valid only if we accept the moral imperative. It is true that language refuses to permit pure objectivity, and the inclination of any human being to *mean* something whenever he speaks is irrepressible. But, if the writer strives for objectivity and approaches "pure" art, then the unreliable narrator may be an agent whose deliberate function is to keep specific meanings at a distance. For instance, we cannot for a moment rely on Frank to act as filter for Cain's moral intentions. The technique forcibly, deliberately, and continually turns us back to the experience itself.

V Style "Like the Metal of an Automatic"

There is remarkable compatibility between Cain's raw material and his terse diction: "I moved to California and heard the Western roughneck: the boy who is just as elemental inside as his Eastern colleague, but who has been to high school, completes his sentences, and uses reasonably good grammar. Once my ear had put this on wax, so that I had it, I began to wonder if *that* wouldn't be the medium I could use to write novels. This is the origin of the style that is usually associated with me." It is a style, says Benét, "like the metal of an automatic."

Cain remarks that, like all writers, he thinks about style. "Yet I confess I usually read comments on this style with some surprise, for I make no conscious effort to be tough, or hard-boiled, or grim, or any of the things I am usually called. I merely try to write as the character would write, and I never forget that the average man, from the fields, the streets, the bars, the offices, and even the gutters of his country, has acquired a vividness of speech that goes beyond anything I could invent, and that if I stick to this heritage, this *logos* of the American countryside, I shall attain a maximum of effectiveness with very little effort." Even when a character is writing his story, the prose has the sound and pattern of natural speech. "In general my style is rural rather than urban; my ears seem to like fields better than streets. I am glad of this, for I think language loses a bit of its bounce the moment its heels touch concrete" (preface, *Three of a Kind*). A certain southern tone leavens the coarseness of the speech he cultivates. Though the Elizabethan speech of West Virginians fascinated Cain, he made no attempt at strict fidelity in *The Butterfly;* "for in my observation too much concern with local speech usually results in distraction from the tale, to which all dialogue and action, in my belief, should be subservient."

The texture of Cain's prose is tight but, except for certain passages in *Mildred* and *The Moth*, not dense. His syntax is extremely simple, though he often strains for complexity in the third-person novels and in *Mignon*. He achieves his descriptive effects with little use of adjectives or figurative language. The hospital sequence in *Postman* consists of six short, separated paragraphs that achieve a subtlety through simplicity reminiscent of the Hemingway's Nick Adams vignettes between stories in *In Our Time*. Adjectives would only dilute the effect of the homecoming scene, following the trial and the funeral: "It was all just like we left it, even to the glasses in the sink that we had drunk the wine out of, and the Greek's guitar, that hadn't been put away yet because he was so drunk. She put the guitar in the case, and washed the glasses, and then went upstairs." Stylistically, some of Cain's finest passages appear not in his fiction but in his essays.

Although he uses such basic devices as repetition, he does not seem to strive to use all the resources of rhetoric. But, if we use the term "rhetoric" as Booth uses it in *The Rhetoric of Fiction*—as standing for the ways, stylistic and other, that a writer deliberately attempts to control the responses of his readers from moment to moment—Cain is indeed a master of rhetoric in his use of description, dialogue, clichés, profanity, and the techniques of selectivity and compression.

Encountering the prevalence of clichés—of situation, theme, character, and style—in Cain, we may wonder whether he uses at least some of them intentionally. Cain testifies that he does: "My clichés are more or less deliberate. I hate narrative that is one hundred percent distinguished, like Cabell's. To me, it evokes utter unreality. Many of life's most moving things are banal—what more banal than a steak? What more beautiful, when you're hungry? I try in using a cliché, to set it up so perhaps it gains its own awkward, pathetic eloquence." Sometimes Cain, like Wright Morris, though without his especial success, consciously sets out to resurrect, control, and transform the cliché for expressive use.[4]

Halford Luccock seems to have been listening to voices not of the author's creation when he charges Cain with a bad-boy delight in the use of "bad words."[5] Contrasting himself to Hemingway, Cain says: "He uses four-letter words (that is, those dealing with bodily function); I have never written one." There is much free-wheeling profanity in Chandler and McCoy but relatively little in Cain.

We find little evidence of mannerism in Cain's style. Chandler could never say of Cain what he said of Hammett, that the latter's style at its worse was "as formalized as a page of Marius the Epicurean." But certain recognizable Cain touches, often fitting similar occasions, recur throughout the novels: "I'm on the end of the plank"; "Who walked in the door was Juana"; "and that was all I knew for a while"; "I'm up tight"; and the repeated use of "then" to string very brief episodes together. But it takes more than the repetition of such phrases to constitute mannerism. Though Thurber managed to parody Cain's style, we would have more difficulty recognizing it than Hemingway's, Faulkner's, or even Chandler's.

The failures of Cain's style are seen mainly in the third-person works, in which he is sometimes as bad as a writer can be. Sometimes even in the first-person narratives, the neat phrase turns into embarrassing cuteness, particularly in *Mignon*. A few purple passages mar the essays slightly, but they are rampant in the third-person novels, particularly in *Love's Lovely Counterfeit* and in *Sinful Woman*. He seems to be consciously trying, with style alone, to appeal to the reader in terms of artificial and separable tools of rhetoric. Sheer verbosity is another problem in the third person. Cain has more control over himself when he is pretending to be Frank Chambers or Howard Sharp than when he is pretending, as in the third person, to be a literary creator.

The sense of authority we feel in Cain is in large measure a triumph of style. Style seems to flow from an absolute command of all the elements which style should serve. Though sometimes his style sounds more impressive than what it expresses, and thus "hoodwinks" him, Cain manages usually to infuse every moment with apparent urgency.

The dialogue sketches in *Our Government* were not conceived as plays and certainly are not stageworthy. But the effectiveness of Cain's fiction dialogue may be traced in part to these early exercises (including several straight plays in *The American Mercury*), in which he had nothing else to concentrate upon except authentic and significant speech. Cain's sense of reader response to the dramatic immediacy of dialogue enables him to space it

effectively throughout each novel; indeed, the shorter novels are
about fifty percent dialogue. Part of the effectiveness of Cain's
technique is the omission of artificial dialogue tags. Cain claims
that he goes further than Hemingway in cutting "down to a
minimum the *he-saids* and *she-replied-laughinglys*." While there
is relatively little sustained dialogue in *Serenade,* the dynamic
thrust of Sharp's narrating voice sustains dramatic tension; long
stretches without dialogue in *The Moth,* however, retard the pace.
In his last two novels, *Mignon* and *The Magician's Wife,* the
dialogue is very talky, often strained, but sometimes glitters with
a slick wit.

Frohock admires the effectiveness of Cain's deceptively simple
dialogue, which performs the functions of analysis and description, thus insuring "the great rapidity of the story's tempo." He
comments on the dialogue between Frank and Cora on their return to the restaurant after the failure of their first attempt to kill
Nick: "In eight lines we have passed from the admission of the
first defeat to the sure knowledge that the couple will again attempt murder. This is dialogue that really moves! Its effectiveness
depends on the reader's ability to catch allusions, to know why
Frank and Cora do not answer each other's questions, to see what
is behind what they say."

Many of the characteristics of Cain's dialogue may be seen at
work in the following passages from seven pages of *Double Indemnity.* When Phyllis says she will pay for her husband's insurance and not let him know she has taken out a policy, Huff knows
that she intends to murder him. Impulsively, he makes love to her.
Later, their conversation is superficially banal and innocent; but it
is monstrous considering the context. That night she comes to his
apartment. After much dialogue between Phyllis and Huff, Huff
finally brings the unstated to the surface and hits her with it. She
declares she loves her husband, "More here lately, than ever."

> "Why 'here lately'?"
> "Oh—worry."
> "You means that down in the oil fields, some rainy night, a
> crown block is going to fall on him?"
> "Please don't talk like that."
> "But that's the idea."
> "Yes."

"I can understand that. Especially with this set-up."
". . . I don't quite know what you mean. What set-up?"
"Why—a crown block will."
"Will what?"
"Fall on him."
"Please, Mr. Huff, I asked you not to talk like that. It's not a laughing matter. It's got me worried sick. . . . What makes you say that?"
" You're going to drop a crown block *on* him."

After a few more swift exchanges, she says:

"I'll not stay here and listen to such things."
"O.K."
"I'm going."
"O.K."
"I'm going this minute."
"O.K."

She returns the next night, and he tells her he will help her do it. Sometimes Cain's dialogue, typographically, has the impact of a graph:

"What would you do this for?"
"You, for one thing."
"What else?"
"Money."

The scene ends a few pages later:

"But we're going to do it."
"Yes, we're going to do it."
"Straight down the line."
"Straight down the line."

The kind of dialogue repetition seen in the last passage is used in all the novels; often a reader's own response to a situation is echoed in repeated phrases. The novel moves from beginning to end, from page to page at a pace set and sustained by such dialogue. We can readily see its similarity to sharp, staccato, tough-movie dialogue, with the movie use of incremental progression; the next line of dialogue takes its key from the other character's previous line. And key words regarding future action and attitude

at the end of one scene are picked up and developed in the next
with almost mathematical precision.

Cain's dialogue is sometimes sophisticated, witty, scintillating;
and it is sometimes deliberately banal as in the dialogue between
Frank and the motorcyle cop; the clichés and the underplaying
heighten the tension of the attempt at murder. Cain's dialogue
keeps undercurrents flowing. In dialogue between a man and a
woman, the pace builds with the swift rhythm of sexual passion to
a climax. When Mildred and Monty are reunited, their banal
banter exchange conceals sexual desire. Cain "grips" the reader
with dialogue that twists and turns, shifts, and reverses. Frank
seems to be directing the dialogue with Sackett, when suddenly it
turns against him, as Sackett lays the evidence against him on the
line, presenting the whole picture of the crime in a sustained mon-
ologue. Dialogues or monologues about the mysteries of insurance
and other such matters are almost always engrossing.

Character is often revealed almost entirely through dialogue.
Sackett is characterized by a speech tag: "As the fellow says."
Katz repeats at opportune moments: "I'm handling this, and that
means I'm handling it. You got that?" Certain dialogue "bits" run
through all Cain's novels: "You like it?" "I love it." "Then O.K."

Frohock notes the American novel's heavy reliance upon dialogue in recent years: "only Hemingway did as much as Cain with
as few words; and Hemingway's dialogue was frequently so concerned with the revelation of the psychology of his characters that
he could not, as Cain could, entrust to it the job of keeping the
story moving without third-person intervention." Wyndham
Lewis advised a young writer who had sent him a novel in manuscript to read both Cain's *The Postman* and Hemingway's *The
Sun Also Rises* to learn how to write convincing dialogue.[6] "Cain's
dialogue was lifelike only to the extent that it prevented us from
saying (as we sometimes did of Farrell) that people simply did
not talk like that," says Frohock. "Once we were convinced and
the illusion was established, Cain's problem was only to give us
what dialogue the story required."

The always brisk pace is seldom impeded by unnecessary description. When Cain gives a physical description of a character,
as he seems to feel obliged to do in a third-person story, he obviously does not care. He discovered that most of his first-person
heroes in *Three of a Kind* are six feet tall (resembling his own

physique) and have curly blond hair and blue eyes: "This bothers me much less than you might think. I care almost nothing for what my characters look like, being almost exclusively concerned with their insides." This statement left him wide open for a below-the-belt blow from Van Nostrand: "By 'insides' Cain obviously means those inner motives and responses which make a character vital. But his characters are almost never vital. They almost never have any 'insides' except the literal kind which occasionally and violently spill out." This wit lies, for the guts of none of Cain's characters "spill out."

When a number of people complained that they had to read half of *Serenade* before they discovered what Sharp looked like, Cain decided to throw in a brief, neat description of his hero so his reader would "stop worrying about it." Thus, Cain's "choice of what a character looks like is completely phoney," and Cain himself has not the vaguest image of him. His women's figures are "more vivid than their faces, but this doesn't bother me either. In women's appearance I take some interest, but I pay much more attention to their figures than I do their faces—in real life, I mean. Their faces are masks, more or less consciously controlled. But their bodies, the way they walk, sit. hold their heads, gesticulate, and eat, betray them" (preface, *Three of a Kind*). He often points out that the woman is not really a raving beauty (Phyllis has slightly buck teeth), suggesting that, if she lacks beauty as an instant charge, she must have unusual sensual powers to transmit. Cain suggests that the movie writer's description of a character's externals—a "Clark Gable type"—is sufficient for his purposes, and he invites his readers to cast movie stars in the parts as they read.

We remember the atmosphere of Nick's roadside hamburger joint, of the coal mines, the hobo jungles, the opera world; but we look in vain for passages in Cain's novels that *set out* to achieve atmosphere. We remember the mood of sexual and physical violence in *The Postman;* but there are few explicit sexual scenes, and only two directly depict violence. It is not extended descriptions of the people and their landscape that create a pastoral mood in *The Butterfly*. Except for *The Moth*, which occasionally conveys an elegiac mood, there are no lyrical passages in Cain, though "The Birthday Party" is suffused with nostalgia. In his best novels, he achieves, however, the *illusion* of full description.

Nor does Cain create this illusion through an accumulation of associative images. Cain's vivid images come in the first-person narrative as a product of the character's immediate response to the constant *now;* they are usually graphic and brief, as when Frank attempts to get Nick, unconscious, out of the tub: "I had a hell of a time. He was slippery with soap, and I had to stand in the water before I could raise him at all." The kernel of a Sharp wisecrack is an image: "The room froze like a stop-camera shot." Juana's new red Ford "shone like a boil on a sailor's neck." The guitar "had a tone you could eat with a spoon." Cain's epiphanies for the main characters are crude, though the secondary characters get more deliberate treatment. About Katz we are told only that "he might be asleep, but even asleep he looked like he knew more than most guys awake, and a kind of a lump came up in my throat."

Several contemporary writers, such as Wright Morris, write of the necessity of stripping down to the essentials in our lives; D. H. Lawrence preached this idea long ago. Cain, like Hemingway, demonstrates in his technique itself how life, stripped down, feels. He has a facility for stripping without killing an experience; at worst, he is facile. Because of the success of this stripping process, we feel the appropriateness of the details he does present; yet his work has the density of real experience. Van Nostrand argues that "what is 'stripped' is the subjective existence of the characters, the thought and feeling which fashions all response and gives it significance." He indicts Cain for failing to write to his (Van Nostrand's) conception of fiction.

Looking back, we see that Cain has achieved effects by skillful omission and suggestion. As we have seen, he consciously strives but does not strain to achieve understatement, to evoke the unspoken; usually, *what* he understates is clear. But some writers believe, as Booth laments in *The Rhetoric of Fiction,* that the writer should show more than he tells. Cain almost never tells, almost never slows down the showing to analyze. Consequently, some accuse him of mere show. Others cite this technique as the cause of the success of his novels as tours de force. In his essays, Cain seems to have satisfied his desire to tell. What Cain offers his reader is a story with "terrific punch," a phrase Frohock feels appropriate to the dignity of a story that doles out violence without moral seriousness. Had he given us a true novel of destiny, Frohock claims, "We would have had to talk about 'impact' and 'concentration of effect' rather than of 'punch.' But the books he did write did not make the grade."

As we have seen, Cain's work is most aptly discussed in terms of compression, condensation, and concentration of effect—all poetic terms, describing what Grigson, Wilson, and others perhaps meant when they spoke of the savage poetry of Cain at his best. As for "impact," what is that but a euphemism for "punch"? The reader revels in the spectacle of sheer efficiency in Cain's writing. Execution often seems the best word for what he does: he *executes* his moves, cleanly, sharply, thrusting ahead.

VI   *The Device: A Major Literary Tool*

Devices, the stock in trade of "hack" writers, are employed as substitutes for the imagination when it fails. But Cain's use of devices, though it sometimes suggests the hack writer, elevates the device to the status of a major literary tool. Since such writers as Joyce and James use them, devices are contemptible only when they are employed mechanically for obvious effect. Though Cain's devices are often transparent, the reader somehow still accepts them: for instance, the device of having his narrators confess in some way is obvious; but what Cain regarded as a device to get the story well told may affect the reader as a vital experience.

Exposition is a tiresome burden the reader normally must accept as he reads a novel, watches a play or movie; but it is seldom a problem in Cain because he relies so little upon what precedes the present action. Cain's characters move as spontaneous creatures of action out of an immediate present into a future they specifically intend (though it may turn out the reverse); it is their own future, often unrelated to society's. All we know about Frank is that he is a mechanic of sorts, born in San Francisco; we learn in a few references that he has bummed all over the country. The rest of Frank is what we observe line by line, and he ceases to exist pretty much in the last line of his story. Cora's life is just as tersely presented. Only in *The Moth* does Cain present a hero's background with any fullness. So it is on the present that Cain focuses—usually, the one he himself happens to be living in at the time of writing.

In *The Postman*, Cain makes effective use of the reverse of exposition—recapitulation, as when Cora confesses: "She told it all. She went back to the beginning, and told how she met me, how we first began going together, how we tried to knock off the Greek once, but missed." This brief passage makes the whole story thus far rush into the reader's mind, so that he keeps it in full view as the second half of the story unfolds. Cain also uses the device of anticipation. In *Serenade*, the sword with which Juana kills Hawes is introduced quite casually as one item in her baggage when they leave Mexico. She wears her bullfighter's cape to the performance of *Carmen* in the Hollywood Bowl; Sharp uses it when he impulsively takes a singer's place in the opera, and thus attracts Hawes's attention. Five pages before the killing, Sharp says: "I almost got stuck in the duel scene." Then, wearing the cape, Juana plunges the sword into Hawes. Paradoxically, when the reader catches Cain preparing an action, the plant often seems so right and so appropriately a product of the action that it fascinates rather than annoys. But often Cain fools both narrator and reader. The narrator reaches a turning point; neither he (at the time) nor we know what is going to happen; he reviews, with us, all the possible ways his complicated intrigue can go wrong. Then, something totally unanticipated happens, and the reversal delights us.

We watch Cain the plot carpenter construct complications of action and character relationships; and, simultaneously, the characters themselves plot and execute intrigues—a visible, double fascination. But sometimes, complications defeat Cain; for instance, the reader just cannot follow the intricacies of the insurance schemes and counterschemes that proliferate in *Jealous Woman*.

Cain's suspense techniques sometimes operate within a few pages. Frank is in the car, ready to sound the horn if someone approaches: "I looked in the kitchen. She was still there." A paragraph of possible problems follows; then: "I looked in the kitchen again, and she wasn't there. A light went on in the bedroom. Then, all of a sudden, I saw something move, back by the porch. I almost hit the horn, but then I saw it was a cat." Immediately, the motorcycle cop happens by, and the intensity of suspense rises.

To facilitate the smooth-flowing progression of these and other devices, transitions are swiftly executed and turning points are strategically spaced to keep reader interest high. The reader experiences just enough of a scene; he is given indirect information about what is to come; then suddenly he finds himself midway into, or at the end of, the anticipated action. Coincidence sometimes acts as a pivot to turn the intrigue in another direction. This swift transition-making creates even more a sense of complication and intrigue, and generates tension.

For every character and action element there is a technical corollary. For instance, Cain, an adroit builder of crises, often creates a crisis in the actual construction of his story that parallels the crisis of the characters in the action. "Where do I go from here?" he asks. This double crisis partially explains the unusual sense of *pure* excitement the reader experiences.

One winces at failures of technique in Cain more painfully than in "serious" fiction because there is not much more to Cain than skillful execution of technique. Sometimes stock suspense devices mar the novels: the telltale note in the wastebasket, the lovely decoy, obvious foreshadowings, movie alibis (in four novels), clumsy coincidences—all found in his two latest novels, *Mignon* and *The Magician's Wife*. However, it should be pointed out that these same devices are used effectively sometimes as absurd false helps to the man who thinks he is scoring against the way things are. Devices are technical expressions of Cain's point of view on life.

Frohock and others, of course, condemn Cain mainly for his use of devices, but few critics point out enough instances to support the charge of cynical manipulation. "Out of context," says Frohock in agreeing with Edmund Wilson's attack on the famous echo device, "there is no way to defend such paragraphs as the one following the actual killing of Nick. The cheapness of the effect is staggering." The question is, is it effective *in* context? Yes. Then, why "cheap"? In Proust, it would be cheap; in Cain, it is not. If we look more closely at that scene, we find, first, that the effect is carefully prepared. When car lights hit Nick, who is throwing up, Frank laughs so that the passing driver will remember that both men were alive. Nick calls attention to the echo of Frank's laugh. Nick feels good after vomiting; he repeats high notes to get the echoes, "pleased as a gorilla that seen his face in the mirror." Frank hits Nick with the wrench, and the echo of Nick's voice comes back. Cain simply wants an effect of eerie otherness. The echo is realistic. To Frank, it seems a year before Nick is still, while the echo indicates how little time has elapsed. Cain consciously sets up parallels to this echo effect: the gurgle of the wine bottle; the gurgle of the gas in the car just after the lovers have made love; after Cora's death, her blood dripping on the car hood. These novels cannot be judged in terms foreign to their apparent purpose: to tell a story well, to entertain.

The technique of repetition and refrain is characteristic of a number of tough-guy novels. One would not expect Cain to take time to pattern out motifs in his lean, fast-paced narratives; but such patterns act in each novel as agents of unity. A pattern of animal and smell motifs runs through several of the novels. Frank smells the clear air of the country around the restaurant; then he smells Cora's body after she has worked all day, mingled with the odor of food and of grease on her uniform. When she snarls at him, he begins to smell her again. "You look . . . like a hell cat," he says. In the newspapers, it is the cat, electrocuted because it was tracking some scent, that gets the focus: symbolically, the cat is Cora, so the focus is right. While Frank is with Madge in Nicaragua puma-hunting, Madge's puma back home has kittens. Not knowing about Cora, Madge brings a kitten to the restaurant to give to Frank as a remembrance. The electrocution of the cat anticipates Frank's execution. As an objectification of Cora, the cat, ironically, fouls up the murder try by chance, and also anticipates other real cats that hinder Frank and Cora. Cain used the puma in an early story, "The Baby in the Icebox"; in his latest published story, "The Visitor," he uses a runaway tiger, and in a novel on which he was working in 1967 a little girl raises a tiger. Cain feels that cats conjure up responses that grasp reader attention.

Although Cain is adept, and seemingly quite conscious, in his use of motif, his use of symbolism is unconscious and crude, though sometimes effectively simple. What Pound says about symbolism in the "imagist manifesto" applies to Cain's use, for in purity of impact his stories are simple image-constructs. "I believe that the proper and perfect symbol is the natural object," said Pound. He favors the "direct treatment of the 'thing' whether subjective or objective. . . . Use absolutely no word that does not contribute to the presentation. . . . An 'Image' is that which presents an intellectual and emotional complex in an instant of time. . . . Go in fear of abstractions." He wants poetry to be "austere, direct, free from emotional slither." [7] Having listened to Pound (as Cain certainly never did), let us now listen to Cain:

> My symbolism, if I have any, is never conscious, and in fact symbolism is one of the things Phil Goodman warned me off of, like poison. He felt it intolerably literary, as I do—and easy. Who can't think of symbols? And yet I may have some instinctive thrust toward suitability, or whatever you call it. Once, discussing with my wife the end of *Past All Dishonor*, I said: "Why the snow, I can't tell you. But for some reason it wanted in—the thing wasn't complete without the picture of that girl, all dressed up in her finery, wearing priceless jewels, smiling there in the snow, dead." She seemed utterly startled. "But don't you *know?*" Florence exclaimed. "I got it at once. It was symbolic, don't you see, of Morina's obsession that here now at last, by blood and theft and brilliantly managed escape, she was purged of all evil, becoming at last pure . . . and the snow makes you feel it. She, of course, as a former opera singer thinks in such terms, where I merely feel in them. So perhaps lurking in me unconsciously is the compulsion to some sort of symbolism.

Sometimes there is symbolic impact where the author perhaps intends none. For instance, a temporary impotence caused by the depression is symbolized in Jack's loss of sexual desire during his year of wandering as a hobo in *The Moth*.

Cain uses certain signs and symbols for character flaws to evoke an aura of evil and the unknown. The shark as a general symbol of evil and violent death first appears in *Indemnity* when Walter sees a shark near the end: "I tried not to look, but couldn't help it. I saw a flash of dirty white down in the green." Phyllis, who makes a cult of evil and death, wants a suicide ceremony in which they wed themselves to the devil and submit themselves to the sharks. In *Serenade*, this ugly, devouring thing from the deep becomes a manifestation of Sharp's fear of homosexuality. When Juana shouts that he is a homosexual, he tries to shut her off: "But one thing kept slicing up at me, no matter what I did. It was the fin of that shark." The big, incredibly ugly iguana that Sharp catches and eats is symbolic of the dark primitive in man. In the end of the novel, primitive Juana is being buried near where the iguana was caught: "As they lowered her down, an iguana jumped out of it and went running over the rocks," suggesting that the primitive part of man's nature, to which the woman seems always to remain closer than the man, continues to live. In *The Butterfly*, even something so delicate as the butterfly mark on Kady's child's stomach becomes a sign of evil; it focuses the mystery of progeny which causes several murders. Cain uses it to put a chill in the reader, as though it were a snake or a deadly spider.

Cain is often charged with using extreme methods. The general expression of extremes in his work suggests that a certain amount of expressionism is involved, at least in the shorter novels; for certainly Cain distorts reality to achieve an effect. Most expressionistic effects are achieved by the omission of realistic connectives; thus, *The Waste Land* is expressionistic; if we put in all the logical connectives, it would make immediate sense. Omission can give the *effect* of distortion without any essential or basic distortion in form. Thus, there is a sense in which *Postman* is an expressionistic construct; the impression of extremes and of distortion (unsympathetically called "hoke" or "movietone realism") comes from the omission of ninety percent of the usual novelistic detail that realism dictates. If we take away ninety percent of the commentary and extended description in Dreiser's *An American Tragedy*, we may have a work that is more expressionistic than naturalistic. Enhancing this expressionistic effect are Cain's frequent "objective correlatives." He almost never *tells* what a man's inner state is; he objectifies it, as when the shark stands for the homosexuality submerged in Sharp that frightens him as does the literal fin of a shark. *Postman* is one sustained fabrication of objective correlatives.

What keeps the technical and fictional elements discussed above working effectively is Cain's most brilliant achievement—his *theatrical* and *cinematic* pace. (Even Frohock eagerly testifies that "the pace of *The Postman* was properly advertised as 'terrific!' ") Pace, a vital element in the lives of the characters, is itself a comment on the aspect of life that Cain has focused upon in his field of vision. Violence and sexual passion are thrust ahead at a phenomenal pace that is itself part of the reader's felt experience. Frank, tramp on the road, and Cora, tramp in the home, meet on the fifth page, make love on the fifteenth, plot to kill Nick on the twenty-third, and their wish comes true on the sixty-seventh. Cain quietly builds the first sexual encounter of Nick and Cora. Frank persuades Nick in about fifty lines to go to Los Angeles to get a new sign: "Los Angeles wasn't but twenty miles away, but he shined himself up like he was going to Paris, and right after lunch, he went. Soon as he was gone, I locked the front door. I picked up a plate that a guy had left, and went on back in the kitchen with it. She was there." Fifty lines of banal dialogue follow, the sex unspoken but palpable, climaxed by "Bite me!" "I took her in my arms and mashed my mouth up against hers. . . . I bit her. I sunk my teeth into her lips so deep I could feel the blood spurt into my mouth. It was running down her neck when I carried her upstairs." Next chapter: a brief scene between Frank and Nick; then a very brief scene between Frank and Cora. Next scene: Nick has just jumped into his car to investigate a rumor of gas price undercutting. "I was in my room when he drove off, and I turned around to dive down in the kitchen. But she was already there, standing in the door." Her lip is sore: soft kisses. Sudden transition, same page: "Look out, Frank. You'll break a spring leaf." He has pulled over into a eucalyptus grove, in the dark. Nick had sent them to the market for some steaks. In one line, Cain depicts their lovemaking. Now dialogue pace takes over, climaxed with their decision to kill the Greek. Such is the speed of Cain's best novels.

Pace contributes to the sense of inevitability that the reader feels about the events. Pace excites psychological tension and sustains narrative tension. Some critics, of course, claim that Cain's masterful use of pace is at the expense of content. When Lerner charges that "phoney tensions" defeat Cain, Cain answers: "I try to test all tensions for their soundness, and if they're phoney, to my knowledge, I throw them out or work them over." Because of early fiascoes, Cain "acquired . . . such a morbid fear of boring a reader that I certainly got the habit"—and developed the technique—"of needling a story at the least hint of a letdown."

When Benét says that *Serenade* "races along like a motorcycle," he is perhaps talking about movement more than pace: pace cannot maintain a uniform speed; it has to vary; but we ought to have the *impression* that the whole novel is moving ahead fast, at an even speed. There is also some difference between pace and rhythm. An affective rhythm is what makes pace seem natural, rather than mechanical. The over-all structure of Cain's best work is rhythmic. We have but to read one of Cain's best (and perhaps along with it, one of his worst) novels to see why he is the acknowledged master of pace.

CHAPTER 6

Cain and the "Pure" Novel

C AIN seldom obtrudes upon his narratives to make thematic points, and most of his characters are loath to elevate judgment above the surface of life. But as early as *Serenade*, Captain Conners does talk philosophically: "True beauty has *terror* in it." He is speaking of Beethoven's music, of the blue sea (full of sharks), of Juana (full of Mexico), and Mexico (full of dark forces like Juana and sharks). The shark "cleared up for me what I've been trying to say to you. Sit here, now, and look. The water, the surf, the colors on the shore. You think they make the beauty of the tropical sea, aye, lad? They do not. 'Tis the knowledge of what lurks below the surface of it, that awful-looking thing, as you call it, that carries death with every move that it makes. So it is, so it is with all beauty. . . . I hope you never forget it." Insofar as the fragmentary evidence in his work will allow us to piece one together, Cain's philosophical point of view does stress such attitudes as Conners'; for, although Cain operates mainly within the realm of terror, he strives in almost every novel to convey at the height of terror a sense of the beautiful—relative to everything else in the novel.

The philosophical *implications* of Cain's themes are not gratuitous. We know from his essays that Cain has strong opinions, if not profound insights or convictions, about such basic, immediate, practical areas of human concern as politics, religion, and economics. His general attitude is irreverent and iconoclastic. Though some of his novels end happily, we get the general impression that the world is not a safe place for men and women who enter it with the mark of Cain. But, rather than praise, tolerate, or attack various human institutions, Cain gives the impression that he accepts the given, and uses it as material for storytelling.

His approach to *the given* partly explains the harsh light he is able to throw on certain traits in American character, certain aspects of the American scene. There it is; now, how does it look, sound, and feel to move among American artifacts, to maneuver among the intricacies of human systems while asserting one's will? But Cain's characters never resign themselves to given conditions; they seldom fight them either: they *use* them; they incorporate what is *given* into their own willed action.

They are not in revolt against absurd codes of civilization, nor are they even examples of the failure of these codes: they are explicitly amoral; they simply live their lives; they seldom declare the moral value of what they do. The emphasis is less on their brains than on their bodies, on their amoral, animal-like behavior; Cain depicts biological man in ecological terms that are always implied though seldom fully described. Cain's works exhibit a fullness of human folly and ugliness; in almost every novel, someone violates one or more of the seven deadly sins and the Ten Commandments, and does so with very few subtle ambiguities of motive, act, or aftermath. Character and reader move in a realm of the forbidden, encountering and violating taboos in a swift series of actions. In our wishes, our various cravings are satisfied —healthy animal ones, made obscene by social taboos, as well as abnormal ones. Normally, neither character nor reader ventures into such territory; but, for the duration of the novel, that is where they happen to be.

Using primary elements, Cain shows, with primitive impact, through primitive emotions in primitive situations, the primitive in men. If he lacks the sophisticated awareness revealed in a highly artificial style such as Hemingway's and a complex philosophical context such as Conrad's, he, no less than Hemingway and Conrad, shows the cohabitation of the primitive and the civilized man in the same skull and skin. For all three writers, the irreducible statement remains the same: primitive man is the contemporary of each of us. Cain simplifies this truism—primarily in action. He does not *say* that the civilized man has primitive drives and instincts that long for pure expression; he so affects the reader that the reader's own kinetic response is itself the thematic assertion.

If Cain were to convey, through whatever means, a moral attitude of his own about the behavior of the lovers on the rack, that distance would destroy the tension between empathy (being on the rack with the narrator) and sympathetic witnessing. If we are to make a moral judgment, we are forced to make it on our own; we have not so wallowed in detailed orgies that we are robbed of objectivity, as we are in some recent, frankly sexual novels, for instance. But Cain's refusal to moralize does not license readers and critics to attribute condonement or exploitation to him. In his own limited way, his intentions appear to be as objective as those of Flaubert, for whom the experience itself was its own reason for being shown. In Cain, pure experience is primary. In one sense the Pandora myth, as Cain presents it, is as purely exemplary as the original, but the moral is so obvious that we experience it preconsciously in the form and immediacy of the story as it happens. We might stress the lesson we learn as we watch characters do what we (and *they*) know so clearly they should not. But people go back again and again to the same stories, fully aware of their teachings, less for the reiteration of the moral than for the mere re-experiencing of the pattern and essence of events. The tribesman spent many winter evenings listening to the saga of Beowulf because it thrilled him long after it had ceased to instruct him.

Farrell, among others, indicts Cain for producing thrills. Against such a charge there is no defense, for it is difficult to prove in literature (on whatever moral or esthetic grounds) the goodness or badness of such a quality as thrills; thrills just are. As Cain builds to the moment of terror, depicts it, and then begins building the next, there is nothing to say about thrills and terror, except that he certainly creates them, just as he creates horror and shock, with all the dedication to purity of impact as the *Grand Guignol*. He does not recognize the need to create a "significant" context for these emotions, nor to interpret them after he has aroused them. The absence of the usual *reasons* (theme- and character-based) for the employment of such elements forces us to experience them in relative purity of consciousness.

If we ask what excites Cain himself, we find little evidence that his characters and what they do greatly excite him. But there are many indications that the development of character and action in technical terms *is* exciting to him. On reflection, we can accept little of what has happened in a Cain novel; but his technique prevents reflections during the experience. Cain, then, is attending to technique, while the reader seems attendant upon character and action; but, actually, in the best of Cain, both author and reader are fascinated and excited by the dynamics of technical control.

While Cain never attempts to fulfill artificial standards of moral significance in literature, Farrell and Frohock are among those critics who feel a compulsion to rate writers according to their degree of moral seriousness. "Cain writes of people who are cruel, violent, self-centered, and who have a minimum of awareness," says Farrell. "In his world there is neither good nor bad and there is little love. The values of these people . . . are described in such a way that no concept of experience worthy of the name can be implied to the author. . . . If the wicked are punished it is purely fortuitous: punishment is the result of the needs of the story, and not of the stern hand of Providence or of the pitiless forging of a chain of necessities." Frohock declares that "if, instead of being a mere dose of unattenuated and immoral violence . . . Cain had produced a book of some moral seriousness, he would have given us a typical 'novel of destiny.' "

We have first to ascertain what Cain really sets out to do, not what Farrell and Frohock think he ought to have attempted. Though his characters received their values from the society in which they malfunction, Cain does not stress the question of blame, on either side. Usually, Cain's characters, clinging dogmatically to a fragmentary set of values, plunge into situations from which they emerge their own punishers. Cain believes that a man deserves the lot he has; whether a man stays with it or tries to rise above it—he is responsible. Perhaps Cain's is a hard-boiled attitude.

Though one of Cain's major themes is guilt, he is not interested in the spiritual and moral anguish of the guilty. Rather, he strives to depict actions that are ordinarily believed to result in gu·lt. What fascinates Cain most is the person who feels no *social* guilt; and he is aware that this sort of person fascinates readers. Roger Duval worries awhile over being a traitor; but, by the end, having experienced most of man's sins, he feels an obligation only to Morina. When a character does come to the point of deciding guilt, he always accepts responsibility for his own actions. And the moral courage in this attitude must be taken into account when we judge Cain's characters. They refuse to regard themselves as victims of obscure psychological forces within or of social forces without. Cain's characters want always to be their own masters, even when others have mastered them. Cain deals mainly in immediate surfaces because, for his characters, that is where all the action, physical and ethical, is. And, though he shows them in many ways out of control, he allows them to insist by word and deed upon the nobility of individual volition.

Cain is so far removed from the question of tragedy that one wonders why Frohock insists on even raising it: "The elements of a Cain novel added up to a sort of bogus tragedy, in which ill luck took the place of fate." Frohock concludes that Cain's novels fail to strike a tragic note "because the violence in them is not endowed with any sort of moral significance. We are aware of his violence, not as something which we must accept because it is part of Man's Fate, but as something for a clever writer to play tricks with. Cain's books, then, do not have the tragic quality of [Faulkner's] *Light in August* or [Hemingway's] *For Whom the Bell Tolls,* but they employ the same techniques." Cain's violence merely "exploits the sensibility which informs the serious novel of violence," says Frohock. "Even Harry Morgan, the bloody hero of *To Have and Have Not* . . . does his killing because having to kill is at times a part of being a man."

This statement offers very questionable grounds for conferring moral or tragic stature upon a character. Frohock goes on to say that "this glimmering suspicion that the fact of pulling the trigger in some way identifies the individual's personal destiny with Man's Fate imparts to many Hemingway characters at least a touch of the tragic hero." Is it really a shortcoming in Cain that he does not provide critics with yet another opportunity for such metaphysical sentimentality? Also, are Hemingway's characters *really* tragic? If so, by what definition of tragedy?

It is more appropriate to speak of Cain's *attitude* toward life than of his philosophical point of view, since the former is everywhere manifested in his writing, and the latter is elusive. Essentially, he reveals himself to be the romantic American male with both the weaknesses and the strengths of that attitude under control. We find his satire almost solely in the nonfiction, especially in *Our Government;* we see his cynicism in his attitude toward the little man in a democracy, who struts his illusions of power and importance upon a stage full of trap doors, in a plot rigged to drop "tragedy," on cue, into farce. But generally, both Cain and his characters respond simply to life moment by moment in a hard-boiled manner, with a tough optimism.

But, if we ask what very general philosophical point of view may be *derived* from Cain's works, apart from his own apparent intentions, it is by no means far-fetched to claim that it is basically existential. Observations already made support this claim: for instance, the hero's conscious insistence upon claiming responsibility for his actions, even though other forces may legitimately, in some sense, be blamed. The elements of chance, coincidence, luck, gamble and countergamble, risk, audacity, and improvisation—clearly discernible in his work—readily argue an existential attitude (again, as opposed to "philosophy," for his kinship is not with the systematic Sartre but with the more intuitive Camus). The themes of the love-rack and of the wish-that-comes-true with terrifying results also suggest a clear, consistent absurdist attitude about human existence. But Frohock insists that Cain should be more deliberate in expressing this attitude.

To some critics, the plot and the hero's exploits are absurd in a different sense. Hamilton Basso calls Cain a master of the comic strip. He does deal in heroes, but the fact is that such men *do* exist. Though antiheroes overpopulate contemporary literature, Cain shows that not just victims but even heroes live in an absurd world; thus, he provides another perspective on the absurd. Today, we see the absurd mainly through the eyes of victims, whiners, metaphysical piddlers; Cain shows it to us through the eyes of men on top of the dungheap—men triumphant, for a while. But some critics and readers who are willing to wallow with victims find the heroic antics of Cain's men at the top sordid. Those who repeatedly complain about the bestiality of Cain's characters seem at times almost contemptuous of the characters' refusal to elevate whining to the level of sophisticated rationalization that we encounter in many fashionable novels.

The discussion of Cain's craft in the preceding chapter and of theme in this chapter suggests that, in his best novels, he has written what Georges Simenon, discussing his own work, has sketchily described as the "pure" novel. "And the beginning will always be the same," says Simenon in a *Paris Review* interview; "it is almost a geometrical question: I have such a man, such a woman, in such surroundings. What can happen to them to oblige them to go to their limits? That's the question. It will be sometimes a very simple incident, anything which will change their lives." A popular writer like Cain, Simenon considers himself a creator, not a "moralist" like Gide (one of many "serious" writers who respected Simenon's novels): "I would like to carve my novel in a piece of wood." (Reviewing *Serenade,* Benét was prompted to recall that Joseph Hergesheimer wanted to "write a novel as compact and deadly as an automatic. Cain has—twice.")

Simenon continues: "The 'pure' novel will do only what the novel can do. I mean that it doesn't have to do any teaching or any work of journalism. In a pure novel you wouldn't take sixty pages to describe the South or Arizona. . . . Just the drama, with only what is absolutely part of this drama. What I think about novels today is almost a translation of the rules of tragedy into the novel." Simenon believes that the novel, like tragedy, should be short enough to enable a reader to absorb it in one sitting.[1] It should be, we might add, as brief as a movie and as unified in its effects and impressions as a poem.

Cain's comments on his own writing (quoted earlier) may be interpreted as notes on his variation of the "pure" novel; though he was not familiar with the concept until I brought it to his attention, he agrees that what he is trying to do approximates the "pure" novel. His credo is that narrative and action, not philosophy, are the most important elements in a novel. Cain has a story to tell; all his creative energy is directed toward getting the story told as briefly and as forcibly as possible; and it is its own reason for being. The novel should raise and answer its own necessary questions and depend as little as possible upon anything beyond the bounds of its own immediacy. All fictive elements should effect one clean, simple thrust, as do the first twenty-three pages of *The Postman,* Cain's nearest realization of the "pure" novel.

Charges that Cain writes to a formula that often defeats him must be evaluated in terms of the nature of the "pure" novel, for he strives to achieve as much as is artistically possible within the compass of the "formula." In responding to the description of his novels as "pure" ones, Cain turned immediately to an analogy in music:

Beethoven, Mendelssohn, Puccini, Mascagni, Bizet, and such men are my favorites, all different emotionally, but similar in the logic of their musical approach. Wagner, Richard Strauss, Debussy, and such men, who depend on an overpowering gush of tone, harmony, and color, tend to bore me. It even carries over to the popular side, for Vincent Youmans interests me more than any American composer. "Tea for Two" is a thematic building of tune out of three notes treated as theme. It, therefore, to my imagination, is exciting, all the more so because of its leanness, and the avoidance of any surplus, even to one grace note.

Like a piece of music, then, a "pure" novel should be an experience that has rhythm, tempo, style, movement, pattern, motif; it is generated by time or pace, following (to use a term from drama) a "spine."

While the novelist, by the very nature of his medium, cannot entirely avoid making moral and social value judgments, writers in one tradition have tried since Flaubert, Valéry, and Verlaine to make the novel or the poem as "pure" a work of art as a statue. For instance, in Rodin's sculpture we find subject and treatment; but form and space provide the most exciting aspects of the experience. Stephen quotes Aquinas in Joyce's *Portrait of the Artist as a Young Man:* "That is beautiful the apprehension of which pleases." Necessary to esthetic stasis are wholeness, harmony, and radiance. Is it possible for a novel to possess any of these qualities to the extent that the plastic arts—and also those forms devoid of apparent subject matter, music and architecture—do? Stephen argues that "art necessarily divides itself into three forms, progressing from one to the next"—the lyrical, the epical, and the dramatic, "the form wherein [the artist] presents his image in immediate relation to others." [2] It is to this last, and finest, form that the "pure" novel belongs. "Pure" means to the novel what "nonobjective" means to painting. To paraphrase Archibald MacLeish, a pure novel should not *mean* but *be.*

Esthetic or psychic distance is achieved and sustained in Cain partly because of his obsessively objective, neutral, dispassionate attitude toward the basic elements of his novels. Flaubert wanted in literature the same impersonality one attributes to Greek sculpture, and Cain would agree with Flaubert that "the illusion . . . arises . . . from the impersonality of the work. It is one of my principles that one must not *write oneself in.* The artist must stand to his work as God to his creation, invisible and all-powerful; he must be everywhere felt but nowhere seen." [3] Stephen Dedalus echoes this concept in his esthetic discourse: "The artist, like the

God of the creation, remains within and behind or beyond or above his handiwork, invisible, refined out of existence, indifferent, paring his fingernails" (213–15). Cain's apparent lack of personal involvement in moral and other such considerations enables him to achieve this impersonality.

Some may say that in reading Cain one has a kinetic ("impure"), rather than an esthetic experience, that causes one to feel desire or loathing, depending on one's moral attitudes. But Cain's characters, themes, and situations are so simple and exaggerated that we must simply exercise a "willing suspension of disbelief" for esthetic remuneration. In 1929, *transition: An International Quarterly for Creative Experiment* published a proclamation, several tenets of which are descriptive of tough novels as well as of the esoteric contents of that magazine: "We are not concerned with the propagation of sociological ideas, except to emancipate the creative elements from the present ideology. . . . The writer expresses. He does not communicate." [4] It is absurd to bring Joyce, Aquinas, Flaubert, and avant-garde manifestoes into a discussion of the special quality of Cain's best novels only if we insist on overemphasizing the problem of meaning in them. The serious reader returns to *The Postman* not for its meaning, or even for its characters, but to experience *again* an esthetic emotion. He regards thought and content as seriously as he would if he were looking at a loaded gun on a table.

It is not my intention here to formulate criteria for the "pure" novel. The genre has intriguing possibilities, and I merely wish to indicate that we may begin a study of this difficult problem with Cain. His best novels, at least, take us in the direction of "pure" form and technique. [5]

CHAPTER 7

Impact of Cain and the Tough Guys

THE recent reissue of the novels of Cain, Hammett, Chandler, McCoy, and Traven and the appearance of critical essays and books about them raises the question: Why reread the novels of Cain and other tough-guy writers? Above all, today's readers will agree with readers of former decades that they are excellent entertainment, they are interesting as a genre, and they are sometimes art in a pure state. And for those who insist on thematic relevance, tough fiction undeniably expresses a dominant trait in American sensibility. With a special purity of vision unimpaired by ideology, tough writers directly aroused the fears and nightmare images of America in the 1930's; depicting the surface of American violence, they showed that, in a civilization resolutely committed to goals that create as a by-product the conditions for it, violence is always close to the surface.

I *Revelations of Social Disorder*

Either the lives or the novels (sometimes both) of the big five tough writers show some aspect of social concern or involvement. For instance, Hammett was president of the League of American Writers, and after World War II he devoted much of his time to the left-wing political groups in which he had long been interested. Having been a seaman and a laborer himself, Traven has always defended the underdog. His *Government* (1931), "a sociological study in depth," was so full of "angry digressions on government dictators" that the Third Reich renewed its ban on all Traven's books. Many of his novels attack the injustices of the economic ruling class; according to legend, Traven was a successful Wobbly organizer; and he is perhaps more a proletarian than a tough-guy writer. While all Chandler's novels convey dissatisfaction with American social, cultural, political, and economic conditions in the 1930's, he never became personally involved in social causes. McCoy's *I Should Have Stayed Home* is an exposé of dehumanizing conditions among Hollywood extras: *No Pockets in a Shroud* is an exposé of corrupt Dallas government, resembling Hammett's *Red Harvest* and Cain's *Counterfeit,* as well as many of Chandler's depictions of the process by which crooked laws, politics, and unemployment make criminals of men.

A study of all types of popular fiction should tell us much about ordinary people in a way that "serious" fiction, aimed at an intelligent esthetically inclined minority, cannot. The image may be false, but so, in a sense, are Faulkner's and Fitzgerald's—for instance, when examined as reflections of society *as it is*—from this or that point of view. For society "as it is" is society not only as men live it, but as they desire to see it; and, seeing it so, they assimilate it into the so-called *actual* pattern. In this sense, the Europeans were right to believe that any man on any corner in America ran the risk of being machine-gunned, and to cherish the impression that buffaloes, Indians, and cowboys still roamed the plains. Many critics have argued since the 1930's that the hard-boiled crime story made a special contribution to our understanding of the society that produced it.

William O. Aydelotte claimed that tough fiction deserves study because it reveals social psychology: "A knowledge of people's daydreams may enable us to progress to an understanding of their desires . . . may reveal popular attitudes which shed a flood of light on the motivation behind political, social, and economic history"; for tough fiction deals in its own way "with the most essential and urgent problems of the human situation." Tough novels, says Harry Levin, are "psychological myths" without psychological analysis; they are "social documents." [1] But Fiedler in *Love and Death in the American Novel,* is skeptical of this view of the "proletarian thriller. . . . Lower-middle-brow Americans find it possible to countenance bared breasts and bellies in their literature only when violence is threatening, or when somewhere in the outer darkness a gangster plots his kill. . . . Such readers relish thinking that the sadist fantasies in which they find masturbatory pleasures are revelations of social disorder, first steps toward making a better world" (476).

But Wilson insists that reading what "the people" are reading is *one* way of understanding society. He observed in the works of

the tough writers "the socialist diagnosis and the socialist hope,"
placing them in the tradition of radical writing which Californians
like Otto Storm and Steinbeck were carrying on from Frank Norris, Jack London, and Upton Sinclair. "Cain himself," Wilson says,
"is particularly ingenious at tracing from their first beginnings the
tangles that gradually tighten around the necks of the people involved in those bizarre and brutal crimes that figure in the
American papers; and is capable even of tackling—in *Serenade*, at
any rate—the larger tangles of social interest from which these
deadly little knots derive. Such a subject might provide a great
novel: in *An American Tragedy*, such a subject did."

Though Cain writes out of the social and literary milieu that
produced the deliberate attacks of the proletarian novelists, Cain
never deals directly, as we have noted, with society's ills. While in
several novels the relevance of Cain's characters to a larger social
context is fairly intimate, his most effective social criticism
emerges from his treatment of another interest—character por-
trayal, handled statically in the essays; dramatically, in the dialogues; narratively, in the novels. But, in all three genres, it is the
dramatic thrust of characters in action that intrigues him; and
they add up to an impressive gallery of American public types.

Few of Cain's fictional characters serve society, not even in
Philip Marlowe's oblique manner. In *Love's Lovely Counterfeit*,
Cain is less interested in exposing corrupt practices and gangster-
ism in small-town politics than in telling a good story; and the
story is weak to the extent that exposé *is* one intention. His characters are less interested in public service than in self-service or,
in June's case, in family-centered rather than community-oriented
idealism. When Ben asks her why she works for Jansen, the good-
guy politician, she replies that she needs money to buy her sister
out of trouble. " 'Listen,' " Ben says, " 'if it was just idealism, I
might give you tips, but I'd be plenty worried. I don't believe in
that stuff, and I don't believe in people that do believe in it. Now
I know it's the old do-re-mi, that's different. O.K., June. We can
do business.' "

Roger and Bill of the two historical novels *Past All Dishonor*
and *Mignon* have a sense of duty to country, but they sell out
temporarily or permanently for the sake of women. Most of Cain's
heroes are self-seeking, antigroup, anticommunity, and Cain is
less interested in the murderer's relation to society than in his rela-

tion to himself or to the woman he loves. But, while Cain denies that the compulsion to confess is anything but a device to explain why the character is writing his story, the development from *Postman* to *Mignon* of the narrator's motive for writing indicates that some of the characters feel a sense of obligation to society or a desire to connect with it. One reason the narrator *writes* his story is that he hardly knows anyone to *tell* it to. Frank and Cora are completely cut off from society by their personalities and by the nature of their relationship. Even when she aspires to "be somebody," she is thinking of money and abstract status, not of friends and social intercourse. Always, to be together is the fervent desire of lovers like Frank and Cora, Sharp and Juana. On the other hand, Roger's, Jess's, and Duke's motives are almost entirely social; no longer are both the relationship and the writing isolated from society. Carrie Selden's purpose is solely social—she wants to correct the public's false impression of her relationship with her husband.

One of the most persuasive arguments for the importance of studying Cain and other tough writers as reflectors of the condition of literature and society is presented, oddly enough, by Frohock: "The historical importance of books like *The Postman* is that they were the ultimate exploitation of the climate of sensibility that also produced the best novels of Faulkner, Hemingway, Wolfe, Steinbeck, Farrell, and Dos Passos." Thus, a study of Cain sets in stark relief a study of the more "serious" writers. Frohock treats *Postman* as a thing—something like a murder weapon, with Cain as the killer. Cain's "knowledge of what the public wants" makes him "both a literary and a sociological phenomenon, of a kind remarkably useful to our understanding of what has gone on in America in our lifetime. For a pertinent comment on *The Postman* cannot help but be a pertinent comment on the time which took Cain and his best-known book to its bosom." Tough novels have "become part of our patrimony." Their manner of dealing with the universals of sex, money, and violence presents a somewhat expressionistic picture of American society and culture in the 1930's and 1940's and provides insights into the American Dream-turned-nightmare and into the all-American boy-turned-tough guy.

II *Effect upon American and European Literature*

Critics are somewhat split in their estimation of the contribution of the hard-boiled technique and of Cain's special version of it to American prose. Whether its influence—one everywhere obvious in popular culture and discernible in "serious" fiction—is good or bad is difficult to assess. Even before Hammett won fame, a few movies and novels struck the tough-guy pose. Carl Van Doren credits W. R. Burnett's *Little Caesar* (1929) with setting the romantic, tough gangster as a new fashion.

George Snell in *The Shapers of American Fiction,* noting writers who were imitative of, similar to, or tributary to Hemingway, said, "The corruptions of a John O'Hara or a James M. Cain could not, however, be regarded seriously, and no imitator has yet produced a fiction that has the greatness of the originals." [2] Even assuming that the charge of corruption is just, Cain's failure to be superior to Hemingway on the latter's own ground is no basis for deciding that Cain must not be taken seriously. In *The Shape of Books to Come,* J. Donald Adams deplores the influence even of Hemingway's work among younger writers, though he admits it had a "vitalizing effect." "The 'hard-boiled' tradition which he established brought nothing to the illumination of life" in America or anywhere, "for it excluded too much." Writers "who took elements from his work calculated to have a purely sensational appeal produced the synthetic shockers of a James M. Cain." Though struck in the name of virility, "the attitude itself was sterile." [3]

In 1937, Herbert J. Muller rejected the hard-boiled school, "a peculiarly American product," as deserving "only brief notice"; for its insidious influence appeared to be negative. This school is "another sign of disintegration and revaluation." "As a whole, the hard-boiled school has simply swollen the flood of slovenly, downright bad writing on the market today" (402–3). In *On Native Grounds* (1942) Alfred Kazin, too, rejected the tough guys on moral grounds. The exploitation of Hemingway's "nihilism" resulted in titillation, use of forbidden subjects, and avoidance of common problems of experience: "In a writer like James M. Cain this practice was indirectly a pandering to the same taste which enjoyed the synthetic violence of the murder mystery."

But Kazin's dislike did not so dull his perceptions that he failed to see a correlation between the tough and the proletarian writers: "The violence of the left-wing writing all through the thirties, its need of demonstrative terror and brutality, relates that writing to the slick, hard-boiled novel, which, in the hands of writers like John O'Hara, James M. Cain, Jerome Weidman, and many others, became a distinctive contemporary fashion." [4] Paul West, an English critic, also describes the lack of ethical judgment in the tough guys: "Avoid, disrupt, deny: these are the aims and reflexes which endear, say, Faulkner to the intellectually feuding French; which account for American pre-eminence in the unjudging thriller and crime novel (Hammett, Chandler, Spillane)." He concludes that "our power to stop a body from existing in time . . . develops into a Hemingway mystique, a Steinbeck main theme and, in the novels of James M. Cain, a meretricious obsession." [5]

Despite their moral limitations, most critics agree there is no carelessness of technique in the hard-boiled novel. Its writers, says Alexander Cowie in *The Rise of the American Novel*, "have made a serious contribution to modern American prose." [6] Carl Van Doren's conclusion speaks for the majority today: "The thirties saw toughness by itself developed into a standard fashion, which reached what may be called its high point" in Cain's *Postman*.[7]

Muller, in the course of a discussion of Hemingway, wrestled with the problem of studying the tough guys seriously: "This 'cult of the simple' appears in various forms in the modern world: the 'hard-boiled school,' the movement back to the farm, the interest in primitive people, the craze for primitive art. It is usually a symptom of surface restlessness, a craving for novelty or thrill—the popularity among the sophisticated readers of novelists like Dashiell Hammett is more a fad than a portent. But it also represents a serious effort by some intellectuals to find happiness in the mere being or doing of the great mass of common people; and as a means of salvation, a cult, its futility is obvious" (398).

Kenneth Rexroth, on the other hand, makes the extravagant claim that "the only significant fiction in America is popular fiction. Nobody realizes this better than the French. To them our later-born imitators of Henry James and E. M. Forster are just *chiens qui fument*." Rexroth anticipates the current interest in tough action when he says that "the connection between the genuine, highbrow writers and the genuinely popular is very close. Hemingway had hardly started to write before his style had been reduced to a formula in *Black Mask*, the first hard-boiled detective magazine. In no time at all he had produced two first-class popular writers, Raymond Chandler and Dashiell Hammett. Van Vechten, their middle-brow contemporary, is forgotten. It is from Chandler and Hammett and Hemingway that the best modern fiction derives" (34–35).

Traces of tough characteristics, used quite naturally and intentionally, may be seen in certain works of "serious" writers (the following novels appeared during the same decade in which most of the work of the big five tough writers was published): Faulkner's *Sanctuary* (1931); Dos Passos' *U.S.A.*, Steinbeck's *Of Mice and Men*, and Hemingway's *To Have and Have Not* (1937); Dorothy Baker's *Young Man with a Horn* (1938). In the 1940's, Robert Penn Warren's *All the King's Men* (1946) was one of many novels which made partial use of the tough-guy vernacular and attitude. And, of course, even as Cain, McCoy, Chandler, and Burnett continued to publish into the 1940's and early 1950's, other tough novelists, ranging from popular to "serious," continued to appear. Cain himself saw his own touch in Jay Dratler's *Ducks in Thunder* (1940). *I, the Jury* (1947) began the spate of Spillane books. James Gunn's *Deadlier than the Male* (1942), David Goodis' *Dark Passage* (1946), and Eleazar Lipsky's *Kiss of Death* (1947), kept the gangster novel in vogue. But the reigning vogue was the environmental or juvenile delinquent novel: Willard Motley's *Knock on Any Door* and Irving Shulman's *The Amboy Dukes* (1947); Charles O. Gorham's *The Future Mister Dolan* (1948); Leonard Bishop's *Down All Your Streets* (1952).

In the war novel, Robert Lowry's *Casualty* (1946) and Norman Mailer's *The Naked and the Dead* (1948), showed the influence of the hard-boiled school. As late as 1952, Jim Thompson's *The Killer Inside Me* and John D. MacDonald's *The Damned* were recognizable "pure" tough novels. The hard-boiled, unethical struggle for success was seen in Budd Schulberg's *What Makes Sammy Run?* (1941), William Lindsay Gresham's *Nightmare Alley* (1946), and Charles O. Gorham's *The Gilded Hearse* (1948). Among women writers Maritta Wolff turned out *Whistle Stop* (1941). In 1946, Chester Himes was already writing the tough Negro novel, *If He Hollers Let Him Go*. In much of the "beat" poetry and fiction we see lucid evidence of the reading habits in tough fiction of young men who grew up in the late 1930's and early 1940's. At the very least, we can be certain that Cain has influenced those writers who have created the shallower parts in the stream of American fiction.

American literature first made an impact on Europe through the tough novel. The United States has given the world three native modes of expression: in music, jazz; in movies, the Western as pure escape; and in both literature and the movies, the detective and the tough guy as creatures who move in an ambiguous world, where primitive fantasy and stark reality clash. If the effect of the tough writers upon American literature of the past three decades and on the writing of the present remains to be fully assessed, its impact on English and especially European literature was clearly revolutionary.

A French writer, reviewing the years before the war, declared that the 1930's was an American decade; the same works were appreciated simultaneously in Moscow, Paris, Berlin, Buenos Aires. Bookstore successes were: Pearl Buck's *The Good Earth*, Hervey Allen's *Anthony Adverse*, Kenneth Roberts' *Northwest Passage*, Margaret Mitchell's *Gone with the Wind*, Steinbeck's *Grapes of Wrath*. Americans were "astonished at how a literature such as *Gone With the Wind* or works of James Cain which they considered chiefly commercial were winning the respect of intellectual Europeans." [8] Cain and Hammett were accepted on a level with Faulkner, Hemingway, Dos Passos, Caldwell, Steinbeck, and Henry Miller. Literary histories of European countries and of England point out this curious phenomenon.

Frohock claims that English writers refrained from imitating the tough guys, but Robert E. Spiller reports that in 1945 Peter Cheyney, a young Englishman, was included in a French anthology of American writing because his style was so American. James Hadley Chase, in *No Orchids for Miss Blandish* (1948), is another example of a writer who assimilated the tough-guy style so well that the French mistook him for an American. And, while in Hollywood, Richard Hallas (Eric Knight) wrote *You Play the Black and the Red Comes Up* (1937). Spiller calls Graham Greene an English disciple of Hammett, though he has "a psychological depth lacking in his American precursors, except Hemingway." [9] Greene's *This Gun for Hire,* one of his finest "entertainments," appeared in 1936, a great year for tough novels; thus, he was probably affected by the literary atmosphere, whether or not he was directly influenced by Hammett and Cain. In 1954, a special edition of the *Times Literary Supplement* (later published as *American Writing Today*) spoke of "the rumors and alarms of Caldwell and Cain," suggesting that Cain, by distracting from "good" American writing, had some impact in England.[10]

Sergio Pacifici's description in *A Guide to Contemporary Italian Literature* of the influence of tough writers on Italians is succinct: "At the end of the last war, several prominent Italian intellectuals readily confessed that their encounter with American literature had been one of their most significant and rewarding experiences. Strange as it may seem, the violence and deep pessimism of Faulkner, Cain, Caldwell, and Steinbeck, whose works were widely read in Italy in the Thirties, had actually given them the measure of hope and courage they needed to continue living and writing. Through the fiction of the American, they kept in touch with the free world, and were delivered from the sterile conventionality of Fascist 'culture.'" We begin to understand, in part, the appearance in the late 1940's of the tough realism of Italian movies, *Paisan, Bitter Rice, Open City.* "The effects achieved by such novelists as Cain and Steinbeck, Hemingway and Saroyan, were eventually first imitated then thoroughly assimilated by Pavese, Vittorini, and, through their example, Berto and Calvino." [11]

In Spanish literature, Camilo J. Cela's *Pascual Duarte's Family* (1942) resembles both *The Postman* and *The Stranger;* the killer priest writes in prison about his crimes. And, according to the chief librarian of the Royal Swedish Library, "The 'hard-boiled' literature plays an important role for younger authors. . . . No literature has during the last decade [forties] been more important and more read here than the American" (Spiller, 1383).

But the greatest impact was felt in France. Céline's fiction early anticipated the tough attitude. Muller groups Céline's *Journey to the End of the Night* (1932) with Faulkner's *Sanctuary* (1931) and certain works of Hemingway, Aldous Huxley, and Julian Green as depicting "a superior savagery . . . the apotheosis of downright disgust with life" (29). On Malraux's recommendation, Gide read Faulkner and Hammett, with equal seriousness. Traces of the tough manner and substance may be seen in Simenon. "French critics," says Wallace Fowlie in *A Guide to Contemporary French Literature,* "in many cases paid earlier and more sophisticated attention to contributions of American art than American critics." [12] Steeped in a decade of tough fiction, Americans were perhaps too close to see the originality of *The Postman.* In 1946, Horace McCoy was hailed in Paris as the first American existentialist and as the peer, in England as well, many said, of Hemingway and Steinbeck. Harry Levin perceives the existential immediacy of McCoy's best novel: "And if, as Camus . . . suggests, the human condition is that of Sisyphus, going through his motions eternally and ineffectually, it is easy to understand French admiration for a novel about an American dance-marathon: Horace McCoy's *They Shoot Horses, Don't They?*" (246). In 1946, Marcel Duhamel started *Série noire* in Paris, bringing out three books a month (150 by 1955); these were nothing more than hard-boiled American, or *style americain,* detective books. Peter Cheyney, James Hadley Chase, and others imitated Cain, Chandler, McCoy, Burnett, Hammett, Raoul Whitfield, Don Tracy, P. J. Wolfson. Other publishers copied this formula for success.

Richard Lehan reports that "when *L'Étranger* was first translated into English, a few of the reviews mentioned Camus' debt to James M. Cain." He also reports that in private conversation with Frohock, Camus acknowledged this debt.[13] In *The Novel of Violence in America,* Frohock himself says that Camus paid Cain "the compliment of imitating him." Lehan declares that "there are obvious parallels between *L'Étranger* and *The Postman Always Rings Twice,* a novel, by the way, which was extremely popular in Paris in the late Thirties." In *The Novelist as Philosopher,* John Cruikshank says that the six years after the war was "the great period, in French novel-writing, of trial and experiment based on American models. In *L'Étranger* . . . Camus proved a forerunner in the use he made of devices borrowed from Hemingway and James M. Cain." [14] A very brief look at a few of the many similarities, contrasts, and parallels between *The Stranger* and *The Postman* will suffice to suggest the intricacy of the relationship.

Frank threatens society by what he does; Meursault by what he is. Frank's defense against life's pressures is physical: violence. Meursault's defense is mental: indifference. Neither has a past, except as it functions directly in the progression of the present. Both are "passive heroes who respond to immediate stimuli" automatically and very physically; though both kill, both generally "react rather than act" (Lehan). Both simply satisfy their animal needs: they eat, drink, smoke, and fornicate. Frohock says that "A Cain character, like a good existentialist, *is* what he does"; but from the shooting on to the end, Meursault, unlike Frank, becomes increasingly articulate about his relationship with society and his place in the universe.

Both Cain and Camus employ retrospective narration, and Frank and Meursault narrate in much the same manner, without reflection. Frank's blunt narration does violence mainly to the reader's emotions; Meursault's does violence to the reader's normal mode of response—stock attitudes. Cain's technique of understatement enhances the stark *situation;* Camus' suggests a philosophical attitude about life. Both novels progress with rapid pace along a similar plot line, except that *The Stranger's* action is philosophical while *The Postman's* is pure narrative. The climax of both novels is a murder, followed by a trial and a waiting for execution in the death cell. Each killing occurs almost exactly in the middle of the novel, and both novels are almost exactly the same length.

In both novels the locale is simple, the time-span brief. The lovers in both novels go twice to the beach, and the scenes there are very similar. The beach is the scene of the crime, and later the sea provides a kind of rejuvenation.

A "perfect," premeditated murder in *The Postman* becomes a gratuitous, spontaneous, impulsive, irrational killing in *The Stranger.* Nick stands between Frank and continued sexual gratification; the Arab stands between Meursault and animal pleasure— shade, relief from the sun. Both kill unhesitatingly. Frank marks off the event with a sexual climax, Meursault with a philosophical, rhetorical one.

Both writers proceed from certain assumptions about the reader. Cain assumes that he will sympathize with the killer, Camus that he will be repelled by Meursault's attitudes, but gradually won over to sympathy after the killing. Camus' novel is deliberately *about* attitudes and assumptions, worked out through Meursault's relationship with society; Meursault's attitudes would shock even Frank. Cora and Meursault are quite similar in their responses to their mothers' funerals. Assumptions about masculine fraternity are examined in both novels in the relationships between Frank and Nick and between Meursault and Raymond. Sackett's interrogation of Frank is similar to the magistrate's interrogation of Meursault. Cain's brief satirical cuts at the conduct of justice may have suggested to Camus the possibilities for a whole sequence of ironies.

Each is to die, ironically, for a crime other than the one he really committed—Frank for killing Cora, Meursault for failing to weep at his mother's funeral. Both Frank and Meursault insist on taking responsibility for their crimes. Both novels conclude in a death cell; many things in *Postman* parallel the much longer death cell section in *The Stranger*. While Frank knows his execution date, Meursault's predicament is more like the daily predicament of all men: he does not know exactly when they will come for him, though it will be in the night, softly. In the death cell, Cora is more important to Frank than God's love and forgiveness; he merely suspects that Father O'Connell will doublecross him; but Meursault's violent rejection of the priest and his certainties is his first move toward interacting with other human beings; this assault is the prelude to the moment when he exposes his heart to "the benign indifference of the universe."

Both novels project a prophetic sense of doom and anticipate in many ways the hero's fate. Chance and coincidence help to create this aura of inevitability. Meursault's gratuitous act is a profoundly existential equivalent of Frank's premeditated act. If Cain moves toward the pure novel, Camus, with his philosophical concerns, moves toward the antinovel. Cain, too, though less intentionally, develops his novel out of some awareness of the basic absurdity of life. But whether Cain is aware of it or not, the persistence of this theme is real enough in his work forcibly to show that he feels the truth of the concept, but does not feel compelled to preach it. Almost everything Camus takes, or seems to take, from Cain he transforms into something better. Using a tough-guy novel of action as a model, Camus wrote a serious novel of character and the human predicament. In *The Magician's Wife*, we have seen what happens when Cain himself takes *Postman* as a model and rewrites it.

But Cruikshank reports that Camus regretted "the widespread influence of the 'tough' school . . . on his French contempo-

raries," and even the influence of Hemingway. He felt that the
French novel was being "diverted from its traditional path and
severely impoverished." Ultimately, the Cain-like methods which
he used in *The Stranger* do more harm than good in novels; such
methods produce one-dimensional, cinematographic characters
who are very animated but lack human substance and flesh.
Camus apparently felt that there was little point in writing more
than one novel using this method; Cain's feeling was similar when
he observed that there were few naturals like *The Postman;* yet
he wrote *The Magician's Wife,* following the pattern of *The Postman.* Camus' method and style became more complex and dense;
so did Cain's, off and on, though with strikingly less success.

Apparently, the French preferred the tough guys' picture of
America to Fitzgerald's or Wolfe's, for instance. These books, like
the tough movies, were taken to be true of American life. Sartre
testifies to the attraction of the picaresque hero: "What fascinated
us all really—petty bourgeois that we were, sons of peasants se-
curely attached to the earth of our farms, intellectuals entrenched
in Paris for life—was the constant flow of men across a whole continent . . . the blind and criminal love in the novels of James
Cain" (*Transatlantic,* 43). Gide seemed to believe what he read:
"The American cities and countryside must offer a foretaste of
hell" (Spiller, 1380). Levin quotes French critic Maurice Nadeau:
"What gives American literature the glamour it has for us today is
not that it is more talented than ours, but that it expresses more
faithfully, more sincerely, and more brutally the despair of our
time" (246). Fowlie sums up the tough guy's appeal to the
French: "In a very special way, they have heeded the Hemingway
myth of the man aggressively virile, opposed on all sides by society or fate" (133).

With deep pessimism, these novels showed the European the
futility of the wish-come-true in an absurd world. The crime novel
dealt with fundamental drives and reflexes. It was at this level
during the depression, the war, and afterward that Europeans
were living their lives. To such a life, the Jamesian temperament
offered little. Europeans recognized the world of violence as their
own, and the tough characters reflected facets of themselves. To
deal with the world, they aspired to the tough-mindedness of the
American hero as outsider. Tough writers seemed to deny the validity of established institutions and attitudes, and they refused to

judge violent behavior in a world made absurd by individual and state violence. Though they probably were looking for the picture of America they preferred to believe, Europeans were also responding to reflections of their own world—or they would not have modeled their own serious writing on the tough guys.

In view of the suggestiveness of the preceding testimonials and in view of the translation history of Cain's books, we should expect an accurate survey in foreign countries to disclose that Cain's influence has indeed been great. As of 1960, twelve of his novels had appeared in the United Kingdom, and translations had appeared as follows: Argentina (1), Denmark (8), France (7), Germany (4), Hungary (2), Israel (1), Italy (11), Japan (4), Mexico (1), Portugal (1), South Africa (5), Spain (2), Sweden (2), Turkey (1), Yugoslavia (1). As part of the tough school, dealing with universals set in a neutral frame, Cain contributed to the essential restructuring of European fiction.

III *Conclusion: A Just Estimation*

I have attempted to suggest some aspects of Cain's novels which indicate that he deserves more careful study than a first glance at his work or at his rather strange reputation may reveal. From one point of view, some may charge that an admiration of Cain is an act of "camp," perhaps low "camp" at that.[15] Perhaps this is the first book of "camp" criticism, though Philip Durham's study of Chandler may deserve that distinction. We can force quite a bit of juice, if not blood, out of a turnip; but Cain, while there seems to be no serious intention nor artistic conception at the heart of any of his sixteen novels, does exhibit in his work a strange mingling of serious and of popular elements which he has made his own; and he has always, in his own way, been serious about craft. A writer of unfortunate faults, he is an interesting example of the author who often lets his journalistic temperament blur his creative field of vision. But, if his vision of life never becomes sharply focused, controlled, or conceptualized, it is obviously heightened and exaggerated to create effects that are often poetically compressed. While Cain seldom rises above certain commercial elements and never seems quite to step over the threshold into novelistic art, as it is normally conceived, his novels are valuable illustrations of the concept of the "pure" novel.

Certainly Cain's art, more than anything else, moves even the serious reader to almost complete emotional commitment to the traumatic experiences Cain renders; and this artistic control convinces me that without his finest novels—*The Postman, Serenade, Mildred Pierce,* and *The Butterfly*—the cream of our twentieth-century fiction would be thinner. Straddling realism and expressionism, he often gives us a vivid account of life on the American scene as he has observed and experienced it; and, in his best moments, he provides the finer vibrations afforded by the esthetic experience. Cain the entertainer may fail to say anything truly important about life, but he takes us through experiences whose special quality is found in no other writer's work.

A survey of the criticism on Cain reveals that at least half of the critics (Wilson, Lerner, Benét) accept him for what he is and give him his due, while another half (Farrell, Frohock, Van Nostrand) have condemned him for being commercial and for failing to be "significant," but have also grudgingly conceded that he is good at what he intends to do. But few histories of American literature and of the modern literature of other countries lack a fair-sized note, at least, on Cain and his influence; and nearly all biographical encyclopedias of authors write him up (while often omitting Hammett, Traven, McCoy, and Chandler). His place in American literature—touching the traditions of naturalistic and realistic novels and of proletarian and tough novels—makes him important to world literature as it is influenced by these American strains. But "even in America Cain enjoys a special status," says Frohock. Cain's is indeed a unique sensibility.

In his preface to *The Butterfly,* Cain himself suggests the kind of question that perhaps needs to be asked about his work. "I don't lack for at least as much recognition as I deserve." Looking at him in his own field of vision and in the light of his best work, this book has implicitly asked: How much recognition *does* James M. Cain deserve?—what *is* a just estimation? By asking that question, one which embraces the whole tough-guy school, and by offering some answers, this book has attempted to reopen an important chapter in American literature.

Notes and References

Chapter One

1. For a more detailed discussion of Hammett, McCoy, Chandler, and other tough writers see *Tough Guy Writers of the Thirties,* and for a discussion of Traven and other proletarian writers see *Proletarian Writers of the Thirties,* both edited by David Madden (Carbondale, Ill., 1968). See also Philip Durham, *Down These Mean Streets a Man Must Go: Raymond Chandler's Knight* (Chapel Hill, N.C., 1964).

2. All these novels—and indeed most of the hard-boiled and pure tough novels, as well as some of the best proletarian works—were published by Knopf; with the exception of McCoy's. Blanche Knopf was Hammett's, Cain's, and Chandler's editor.

3. Frederick Hoffman, *The Modern Novel in America* (Chicago, 1956), p. 205.

4. Herbert J. Muller, *Modern Fiction: A Study of Values* (New York, 1964 paperback edition), p. 402.

5. Kenneth Rexroth, "Disengagement: The Art of the Beat Generation," *New World Writing,* No. 11 (New York, 1957), 28–41.

6. William Aydelotte, "The Detective Story as a Historical Source," *Yale Review,* XXXIX (1949–50), 76–95. See also John Paterson, "A Cosmic View of the Private Eye," *Saturday Review,* XXXVI (August 22, 1953), 7 ff.; Ben Ray Redman, "Decline and Fall of the Whodunit," *Saturday Review,* XXXV (May 31, 1952), 8 ff.; Charles J. Rolo, "Simenon and Spillane: Metaphysics for the Millions," *New World Writing,* No. 1 (New York, 1952), 234–45. *The Art of the Mystery Story,* ed. Howard Haycraft (New York, 1947), is an excellent collection of forty-eight essays.

7. Howard Haycraft, *Murder for Pleasure* (New York, 1941), pp. 169, 171.

8. Raymond Chandler, "The Simple Art of Murder," reprinted in *The Simple Art of Murder* (New York, 1964), p. 190.

9. W. H. Auden, "The Guilty Vicarage," *The Dyer's Hand* (New York, 1962).

10. Leslie A. Fiedler, *Love and Death in the American Novel* (New York, 1960), p. 475.

11. Stanley J. Kunitz, ed., "Raymond Chandler," *Twentieth Century Authors*, First Supplement (New York, 1955), pp. 186–87.

Chapter Two

1. Mr. Cain's generous notes provided a good deal of the material for this chapter. I want to let Cain's own voice convey a sense of his life; therefore, I have used a rather unorthodox method in this chapter. With Cain's permission, I have restructured, pruned, and sometimes rephrased the autobiographical notes he sent me, and blended them with my own observations and information. To avoid a tedious and unsightly briar-patch effect of quotation marks, paraphrases, and endless footnotes, I have sometimes retained Cain's own wording, *in the descriptions of the events of his life*, without enclosing it in quotation marks. The result is a rather unusual, but I hope, effective and interesting collaboration, giving the reader a sense of Cain's life that he would not otherwise obtain. Elsewhere in this book, *all* statements drawn from Mr. Cain's letters to me are enclosed in quotation marks; and unless otherwise noted, the source of all Cain's statements are his communications with me.

2. Cain's childhood friends and acquaintances generally became men of distinction in their fields; even his small-time fictional heroes have some of their qualities.

3. We get a fuller picture of Cain's childhood in Chestertown and of his father from Cain's essay "Tribute to a Hero"; something of Cain's attitudes as a boy concerning masculinity, girls, and honor may be glimpsed in that essay; in the early pages of *The Moth* (in which Helen, Jack's nymphet beloved, skips a grade as Cain did); and in the short stories "The Birthday Party" and "Everything but the Truth."

4. Stanley J. Kunitz, ed., *Twentieth Century Authors* (New York, 1942). See also the First Supplement (1955). For another biographical sketch, see Harry R. Warfel, *American Novelists of Today* (New York, 1951), pp. 75–76.

5. In E. R. Hagemann and Philip C. Durham, "James M. Cain, 1922–1958: A Selected Checklist," *Bulletin of Bibliography*, XXIII (September–December, 1960), 57–61.

6. See Selected Bibliography for Cain's three essays about editorials.

7. Throughout, sources of quotations from reviews of Cain's novels are given in *Book Review Digest* in the volume that covers the year of each novel's appearance.

8. Several other plays of Cain's had tryouts outside New York. In 1938, one of them was postponed because Sinclair Lewis' *It Can't Happen Here* was held over. Cain was a good friend of Alexander Dean, Lewis' director, so when Lewis began attacking Dean and Cain

failed to join him, "Lewis' manner cooled toward Cain," says Mark Schorer, "and that friendship, which had been pleasant if casual for 15 years, was concluded" (*Sinclair Lewis*, p. 640).

9. Edmund Wilson, "The Boys in the Back Room," *Classics and Commercials* (New York, 1962), pp. 19–56. Hereafter, unless otherwise indicated, all Wilson quotations are from this essay.

10. For a historical and critical account of tough movies, see Lewis Jacobs, *The Rise of American Film* (New York, 1939), pp. 509–15. For a more detailed discussion of Cain and other tough writers in Hollywood, see my essay "James M. Cain and the Movies of the Thirties and Forties," *Film Heritage*, II (Summer, 1967), 9–25. For a discussion of the tough Hollywood novel, see Carolyn See, "The American Dream Cheat," *Tough Guy Writers of the Thirties* (Carbondale, Ill., 1968).

11. Parker Tyler, *The Hollywood Hallucination* (New York, 1944), pp. 100–36. For further discussions by Tyler of *Mildred Pierce* and *Double Indemnity* as movies consult the index of *Magic and Myth of the Movies* (New York, 1947). For still another perspective on the movie versions of *Mildred Pierce* and *The Postman*, consult the index of Martha Wolfenstein and Nathan Leites, *Movies: A Psychological Study* (Glencoe, Ill., 1950). For general discussions of the social implications of gangster and cowboy movies see Robert Warshow's *The Immediate Experience* (New York, 1964). John Howard Lawson offers a Marxist point of view in *Film: The Creative Process* (New York, 1964), pp. 230–42.

12. In the four years Cain spent on the movie lots, he accumulated only three fractional script credits: *Stand Up and Fight*, with Charles Bickford and Robert Taylor; *Algiers*, 1938, Metro-Goldwyn-Mayer, which made a star of Hedy Lamarr, and co-starred Charles Boyer (a feeble remake of *Pépé Le Moko*); *Gypsy Wildcat*, 1944, Universal, starring exotic hokum Maria Montez. None of Cain's full scripts reached the projection booth.

13. James M. Cain, preface, *Three of a Kind* (New York, 1943), p. xii.

14. James M. Cain, "Vincent Sargent Lawrence," *The Screen Writer*, II (January, 1947), 12, 15.

15. *The Literary Digest* (March 7, 1936) reported that critics found the play "a skilled, forceful melodrama . . . written with gravel on sheets of flint." Edith J. R. Isaacs, reviewing the play for *Theatre Arts* (April, 1936), was glad to see less of the novel's "foulness" in the play. Nevertheless, Frank and Cora "are part of the lower order of humanity. . . . But at least a portion of the audience found a degree of sympathy, rather than revulsion, for their exhibition of human baseness."

16. *Current Biography* (New York, 1947).

17. *Raymond Chandler Speaking* (Boston, 1962), eds., Dorothy Gardiner and Katherine Sorley Walker. Chandler's script of *Double Indemnity* is published in John Gassner's *Best Film Plays of 1943–1944* (New York, 1945). Compare Chandler's comments on Hollywood with Cain's.

18. *Agee on Film* (New York, 1958), pp. 176, 187. For Agee's comments on *The Postman* and on *Double Indemnity*, see index.

19. James M. Cain, preface, *The Butterfly* (New York, 1947), p. xiv.

20. Albert Van Nostrand, *The Denatured Novel* (New York, 1962), pp. 126–32, 157, 207, 211. Hereafter, all quotations from Van Nostrand come from these pages.

21. The novel's original title was *Bar-B-Q*, which Knopf hated, and which Cain decided to change to *The Postman Always Rings Twice*, which Knopf hated even more; he and others wrote to Cain, pleading for something else; the suggestion they urged was *For Love or Money*. In his preface to *Three of a Kind*, Cain relates the origin of his title. He was talking with his playwright friend Vincent Lawrence one day about Lawrence's nervousness while waiting to hear from a producer about a play. "I almost went nuts. I'd sit and watch for the postman, and then I'd think 'You got to cut this out,' and then when I left the window I'd be listening for his ring. . . . He'd always ring twice," so Lawrence would know it was the postman. Cain interrupted Lawrence's "harrowing tale" to declare that he had given him the title for his novel. "Say, he rang twice for Chambers, didn't he?" "That's the idea." "And on that second ring, Chambers had to answer, didn't he? Couldn't hide out in the backyard any more." "His number was up, I'd say." "I like it." "Then that's it."

22. Geoffrey Grigson, *The Concise Encyclopedia of Modern World Literature* (New York, 1963), p. 101.

23. James M. Cain, *Three of Hearts* (London, 1949), pp. v–x. An omnibus containing *Love's Lovely Counterfeit*, *Past All Dishonor*, and *The Butterfly*. Many critics and reviewers quote from Cain's prefaces, out of sheer delight, though sometimes with intent to ridicule.

24. Luther Nichols' interview with Cain, "Postman's Assistant," *New York Times Book Review* (May 13, 1962), p. 8.

25. Harrison Smith, "The Authority," *Saturday Review*, XXIX (September 23, 1946), 18.

26. James T. Farrell, "Do Writers Need an 'AAA'? A Debate on the Plan for an American Authors' Authority," *Saturday Review*, XXIX (November 16, 1946), 9 ff. (Ironically, Farrell's and Cain's novels were often reviewed or discussed together; Stanley Edgar Hyman, Dawn Powell, W. M. Frohock, and others observed that, though Farrell

was more "important" and "serious," Cain was more successful in *holding* his reader.)
27. "Cain Scrutiny," CIX (April 23, 1962), 99.
28. James T. Farrell, "Cain's Movietone Realism," *Literature and Morality* (New York, 1947), pp. 79–89. Hereafter, unless otherwise noted, all Farrell quotations come from this essay.

Chapter Three

1. Max Lerner, *Public Journal: Marginal Notes on Wartime America* (New York, 1945), pp. 46–48. All Lerner quotations used hereafter come from this brief essay.
2. W. M. Frohock, "James M. Cain: Tabloid Tragedy," *The Novel of Violence in America: 1920–1950* (Dallas, 1950). This and *most* of the Frohock quotations used hereafter come from the revised second edition (Boston, 1964), a paperback.
3. Edmund Fuller, *Man in Modern Fiction* (New York, 1958), pp. 84, 88.
4. Robie Macauley, "Let Me Tell You About the Rich," *Kenyon Review*, XXVII (Autumn, 1965), 671.

Chapter Five

1. See above, Chapter 2, note 7.
2. Wright Morris, *The Territory Ahead* (New York, 1958), pp. 3–17.
3. Rereading *The Postman* in July, 1967, on the occasion of its reissue by Bantam, Cain was inspired to recast into the first person an adventure tale which he had been writing in the third.
4. For a discussion of the cliché in Morris, see David Madden, *Wright Morris* (New York, 1964), pp. 121–23. Cain's interest in clichés and in words generally is suggested by Mencken in *The American Language* (New York, 1936), pp. 264, 269; *Supplement One* (1945), pp. 512, 586; *Supplement Two* (1948), p. 32.
5. Halford Luccock, *American Mirror: Social, Ethical, and Religious Aspects of American Literature, 1930–1940* (New York, 1941), p. 95.
6. *The Letters of Wyndham Lewis*, ed. W. K. Rose (Norfolk, Conn., 1963), pp. 442–43.
7. *Prose Keys to Modern Poetry*, ed. Karl Shapiro (New York, 1962), pp. 104–9.

Chapter Six

1. *Writers at Work*, First Series, ed. Malcolm Cowley (New York, 1959), pp. 151, 156.
2. James Joyce, *Portrait of the Artist as a Young Man* (New York, 1956), pp. 213–14.

3. Quoted in *Novels in the Making*, ed. William E. Buckler (Boston, 1961), p. 69. In a letter to Louise Colet, Flaubert wrote, "Poetry is as exact a science as geometry," p. 58.

4. In *Fitzgerald and the Jazz Age*, ed. Malcolm Cowley (New York, 1966), p. 108.

5. Although in *Against Interpretation* (New York, 1966), Susan Sontag formulates a severe version of the concept of the "pure" novel that goes beyond Cain's achievement, a look at her timely pronouncements on all art provides a better understanding of Cain in relation to the "pure" novel. See her chapters "Against Interpretation" and "On Style."

Chapter Seven

1. Harry Levin, *Contexts of Criticism* (Cambridge, Mass., 1957), p. 248.

2. George Snell, *The Shapers of American Fiction* (New York, 1947), p. 157.

3. J. Donald Adams, *The Shape of Books to Come* (New York, 1945), p. 112.

4. Alfred Kazin, *On Native Grounds* (New York, 1956 ed.), pp. 301, 303.

5. Paul West, *The Modern Novel* (London, 1963), pp. 311, 284.

6. Alexander Cowie, *The Rise of the American Novel* (New York, 1948), p. 750.

7. Carl Van Doren, *The American Novel, 1789–1939* (New York, 1940), p. 332.

8. Thelma M. Smith and Ward L. Miner, *Transatlantic Migration: The Contemporary American Novel in France* (Durham, N.C., 1955), p. 22.

9. Robert E. Spiller *et al.*, *Literary History of the United States* (New York, 1957), p. 1377.

10. *American Writing Today*, Allan Angoff, ed. (New York, 1957), p. 219.

11. Sergio Pacifici, *A Guide to Contemporary Italian Literature* (Cleveland, 1962), pp. 293–305.

12. Wallace Fowlie, *A Guide to Contemporary French Literature* (Cleveland, 1957), p. 133.

13. Richard Lehan, "Camus's *L'Étranger* and American Neo-Realism," *Books Abroad*, XXXVIII (Summer, 1964), 233–38. In *Modern Fiction Studies*, X (Autumn, 1964), 296, Professor Lehan elaborates briefly on a few parallels between *The Postman* and *The Stranger*. For further comment on the Cain-Camus influence, see Rayner Heppenstall, *The Fourfold Tradition* (Norfolk, Conn., 1961), p. 190, and Germaine Brée, *Camus* (New York, 1964), p. 103n, revised edition;

in a conversation with me in 1965, Professor Brée emphatically stated that Camus told her he had been influenced by Cain. For a very detailed comparison of the two novels see my essay "Cain's *The Postman Always Rings Twice* and Camus' *L'Étranger,*" *Papers on Language and Literature,* V (Fall, 1970).

14. John Cruikshank, *The Novelist as Philosopher* (New York, 1962), p. 16.

15. For an analysis of "camp" see Susan Sontag, "Notes on 'Camp,' " *Against Interpretation,* pp. 275–92.

Selected Bibliography

PRIMARY SOURCES

For a more detailed listing of reprintings of stories, plays, essays, and of editions, including foreign, see E. R. Hagemann and Philip C. Durham, "James M. Cain, 1922–1958: A Selected Checklist," *Bulletin of Bibliography*, XXIII (September–December, 1960), 57–60. Items below are arranged in chronological order.

A. Books:

Our Government. New York: Alfred A. Knopf, Inc., 1930.
The Postman Always Rings Twice. New York: Alfred A. Knopf, Inc., 1934.
Serenade. New York: Alfred A. Knopf, Inc., 1937.
Mildred Pierce. New York: Alfred A. Knopf, Inc., 1941.
Love's Lovely Counterfeit. New York: Alfred A. Knopf, Inc., 1942.
Three of a Kind. New York: Alfred A. Knopf, Inc., 1943. Contains *Career in C Major, The Embezzler*, and *Double Indemnity*, with Cain's preface.
Past All Dishonor. New York: Alfred A. Knopf, Inc., 1946.
Sinful Woman. New York: Avon Editions, Inc., 1947.
The Butterfly. New York: Alfred A. Knopf, Inc., 1947, with Cain's preface.
The Moth. New York: Alfred A. Knopf, Inc., 1948.
Jealous Woman. New York: Avon Book Co., 1950.
The Root of His Evil. New York: Avon Book Co., 1951.
Galatea. New York: Alfred A. Knopf, Inc., 1953.
Mignon. New York: The Dial Press, 1962.
The Magician's Wife. New York: The Dial Press, 1965.
Cain X 3. New York: Alfred A. Knopf, Inc., 1969. Contains *The Postman Always Rings Twice, Mildred Pierce, Double Indemnity*.

B. Short Stories:

"Pastorale," *The American Mercury*, XIII (March, 1928), 291–95. First-person narrator, "we" point of view. Set in the South. Story pattern of *The Postman*. Cain's best short story.

"The Taking of Monfaucon," *The American Mercury*, XVII (June, 1929), 136–43. Humorous first-person, autobiographical tale, based on an incident in World War I, told in illiterate Southern vernacular. Included in *Our Government;* reprinted twice in *The Infantry Journal.* Although the Civil War is the background for his two historical novels, there is no contemporary war in Cain's fiction.

"The Baby in the Icebox," *The American Mercury*, XXVIII (January, 1933), 7–17. First-person, imaginative, improbable, entertaining tale, with many similarities to *The Postman*, which appeared a year later. Set in California. A study in American exhibitionist masculinity. Reprinted five times in the 1940's.

"Come-back," *Redbook*, XXXVIII (June, 1934).

"Dead Man," *The American Mercury*, XXXVII (March, 1936), 326–31. One of Cain's best works in the third person, and one of his best stories (reprinted six times, including *O. Henry* collection). Set in California. Similarities to *The Moth* and "The Girl in the Storm."

"Hip, Hip, the Hippo," *Redbook*, XL (March, 1936).

"The Birthday Party," *Ladies' Home Journal*, LII (May, 1936), 30–31, 59–60. Cain's best third-person story. One of two about childhood, it involves a boy and a girl. Theme of masculine self-dramatization.

"Brush Fire," *Liberty*, XIII (December 5, 1936), 16–20. Third person; set in California. Ironic tale of a man who saves a bum from a brush fire in the morning and kills him in the afternoon because the bum seduces his wife.

"Coal Black," *Liberty*, XIV (April 3, 1937), 20–22, 24. One of Cain's least effective stories in third person; set in eastern Kentucky. Nineteen-year-old miner and a sixteen-year-old girl are briefly trapped in a haunted mine, one of Cain's favorite sex situations.

"Everything But the Truth," *Liberty*, XV (July 17, 1937), 14–17. Less successful third-person voice than in "The Birthday Party." Set in Annapolis. A variant of "The Birthday Party" situation; a little boy's masculine boasting gets him into trouble, and, in this story, a girl named Phyllis rescues him from the scorn of his peers: they deceive their juvenile society into thinking that he is more of a hero than he is.

"The Girl in the Storm," *Liberty*, XVII (January 6, 1940), 6–9. One of Cain's best third-person stories. Set in California. Similar to "Dead Man." A nineteen-year-old hitchhiker and a girl take refuge from a flood in a deserted supermarket. Reprinted twice.

"Pay-off Girl," *Esquire*, XXXVIII (August, 1952), 30, 108–9. First person. Set in Maryland, near Washington, D.C. The narrator, a

twenty-five-year-old code clerk, meets a payoff girl for bookies
and frees her from her boss. One of Cain's worst stories.
"Cigarette Girl," *Manhunt*, I (May, 1953), 85–89.
"Two O'Clock Blonde," *Manhunt*, I (August, 1953), 84–91.
"Death on the Beach," *Jack London's Adventure Magazine*, I (October, 1958), 93–101.
"The Visitor," *Esquire*, LVI (September, 1961), 93–95. Third-person
tale of a suburbanite who wakes in the night to find a runaway
tiger staring into his eyes; the hero subdues the tiger with a
plastic bag. Humorous, a sense of the absurd; embarrassingly
contrived ending.

C. Plays (With the exception of three, only those plays not included
in *Our Government* are listed here):
"Trial by Jury," *The American Mercury*, XIII (January, 1928), 30–34.
Chapter VII in *Our Government;* and in Lawrence E. Spivak and
Charles Angoff, eds., *The American Mercury Reader* (Philadelphia: The Blakiston Co., 1944).
"Theological Interlude," *The American Mercury*, XIV (July, 1928),
325–31. Theme of the dramatic appeal and sexual excitement of
Fundamentalist religion; play enhances belief, and belief sanctifies
play.
"The Will of the People," *The American Mercury*, XVI (April, 1929),
394–98. In *Our Government*, Chapter IV; and in Robert N. Linscott, ed., *Best American Humorous Short Stories* (New York:
The Modern Library, 1945), as "The Legislature."
"Citizenship," *The American Mercury*, XVIII (December, 1929), 403–8.
"The Governor," Chapter III in *Our Government;* and in *A Subtreasury
of American Humor*, E. B. White and Katharine S. White, eds.
(New York: Coward-McCann, 1941), pp. 224–34.
"Don't Monkey with Uncle Sam," *Vanity Fair*, XL (April, 1933), 39.

D. Essays and Articles (Arranged to suggest concentrations of Cain's
interests as a journalist):
I. The American Character
"American Portraits. I. The Labor Leader," *The American Mercury*,
I (February, 1924), 196–200. Rather cynical, mocking in tone,
written in the coarse language of the subject, starting off with
witty impressions. Cain's description of the change in the man
who slugs his way into the presidency of the union (changes in
clothes, house, popular-culture tastes) evokes a picture of the
upper-lower-class working man and his environment.

"American Portraits. I. The Editorial Writer," *The American Mercury*,
I (April, 1924), 433–38. A witty, biting description of the evolu-
tion of a reporter's cynicism into idealism when he becomes an
editorial writer. Compares the reporter's with the editorial writer's
treatment of the same news event. Analysis of clichés.

"The World Hits the Trail," *The Nation*, CXX (March 4, 1925), 233.
As editorial writer for the *World*, Cain ridicules his colleagues on
the *World* for attacking immorality in *Desire Under the Elms*.

"Are Editorials Worth Reading?" *The Saturday Evening Post*, CC
(December 24, 1927), 21, 38. A balanced discussion of the positive and negative aspects of editorial writing in the United States,
with anecdotes out of his own experience. *The New Yorker* reprinted his editorial on Battling Siki, a boxer, which, "it is said,
almost got the Pulitzer Prize for the year 1925."

"Pedagogue: Old Style," *The American Mercury*, II (May, 1924),
109–12. Exhibits the merciless invective of Sinclair Lewis lacer-
ating a go-getter. Written when Cain himself was teaching, the
essay describes the pedagogue's "incurable hankering for the
posture of wisdom." Mimicking a typical faculty meeting, he lets
the clichés roll. One of his finest essays.

"Politician: Female," *The American Mercury*, II (November, 1924),
275–78. Some of the wit sounds merely "cute" today, but it is
here that Cain overtly expresses a number of his attitudes about
women.

"High Dignitaries of State," *The American Mercury*, III (December,
1924), 438–42. "It is clear that politics under democracy, on its
visible levels, is an impossible trade for heroes. The man who
seeks romance there is doomed to disappointment."

"The Pastor," *The American Mercury*, V (May, 1925), 30–34. To Cain
the American pastor is ridiculous and contemptible; and his role
is dramatically impossible. He lacks a sense of poetry, beauty,
and imagination in his conception of religion and places of wor-
ship. One of Cain's wittiest and most vicious essays.

"The Pathology of Service," *The American Mercury*, VI (November,
1925), 257–64. "I propose herein to isolate the bacillus of Service," says Cain, "the itch to make the world better." Its specific
cause is the idea of Progress, its roots are in the appetite of dull
people for drama. This brilliant, scornful, antialtruistic essay contributes to our understanding of the reformist element in American society. It summarizes a dominant strain in all the essays that
focus on the American character.

"The Man Merriwell," *The Saturday Evening Post*, CXCIX (June 11,
1927), 12–13, 126, 129, 132. It is not surprising that Cain should
find William Patton, the creator of Frank Merriwell, hero of 204

novels for boys, fascinating. They are both magnificent showoffs. Patton dealt with the basic sources of the interest which the American male has in masculine drama. The essay is both a straightforward history of pulp fiction and a tribute to a one-man drama industry (about one book a week for ten years). As for the problem of "bad" fiction, Cain betrays no awareness that it exists.

"Tribute to a Hero," *The American Mercury*, XXX (November, 1933), 280–88. Nostalgic memoir of Cain's childhood in Chestertown, focusing on a football hero who had a "yellow streak." One of Cain's finest essays.

II. The American Scene

"Treason—To Coal Operators," *The Nation*, CXV (October 4, 1922), 333–34. First of three on the drama of coal in West Virginia. Extremely competent, tight, straightforward journalistic prose; reports on the farcical trial in Charles Town of Walter Allen, a miner accused of declaring war on the state of West Virginia; Cain condemns management's tyranny and attacks the conduct of the judiciary. (Forms the basis for "The Governor" in *Our Government*.)

"The Battleground of Coal," *The Atlantic Monthly*, CXXX (October, 1922), 433–40. Well-written account of the condition of the coal industry, of the miners, repeating the story of Allen against a broader and longer presentation of the history of the industry; he also analyzes the problem and offers a few solutions.

"West Virginia: A Mine-field Melodrama," *The Nation*, CXVI (June 27, 1923), 742–45. Here Cain's interest in the pure drama of events comes out; using opera motifs, he examines the common man's appetite for drama. Both labor and management look silly. The theme and the technique objectify his material.

"The Solid South," *The Bookman*, LXVIII (November, 1928), 264–69. "It is my purpose in this article," says Cain, "to discuss certain twists in the Southern mind . . . perhaps to hazard a few forecasts as to what the future may hold." He attempts to "clear up any misconceptions that may have arisen in your mind" about notions of lawlessness, intolerance, race relations, and the backwardness of the "bozarts" in the South. He feels that the best people should have certain rights which the worst cannot handle.

"Paradise," *The American Mercury*, XXVIII (March, 1933), 266–80. In his longest essay, Cain attempts "an appraisal of the civilization of Southern California" as part of the present American scene and vanguard of the future American civilization. Missing in this region is a sense of the unexpected; and a terrifying sameness withers the imagination. He demonstrates his concept of dullness as a producer of a frantic desire for drama. With his typical American tough fairness, he enumerates the good points and the factors favoring a bright future for the region. He concludes that the future is a show worth seeing. Interesting autobiographical detail.

"The Widow's Mite, or Queen of the Rancho," *Vanity Fair*, XL (August, 1933), 22–23, 54. A witty, cynical look at the history of Malibu; an explanation, an interpretation of the significance of its present image.

III. On Writing and Writers

"Camera Obscura," *The American Mercury*, XXX (October, 1933), 138–46. An important, very well-written essay about writing for the movies; an objective analysis of the medium. Cain comments on his own career and attitudes.

"Introduction," *For Men Only* (Cleveland: The World Publishing Co., 1944), pp. 5–8. A likely title. Cain's choices for the collection and his comments in the introduction on each author suggest something about his reading habits and interests. He includes stories by Irwin Cobb, Poe, Bierce, London, Alexander Woollcott, Farrell, O'Hara, John Collier, Dorothy Parker, Ben Ames Williams, Jack Boyle (Boston Blackie), Maugham, Irwin Shaw, Steinbeck, Hemingway, Fitzgerald, and Conan Doyle, along with one of his own, "The Girl in the Storm." Interesting comments on writing as well.

"The Opening Gun," *The Screen Writer*, I (May, 1946), 6–9. First of five articles about Cain's attempt to organize an American Authors' Authority.

"An American Authors' Authority," *The Screen Writer*, II (July, 1946), 1–14.

"Just What Is A. A. A.?" *The Screen Writer*, II (October, 1946), 1–4.

"Do Writers Need an 'AAA'?" *The Saturday Review of Literature*, XXIX (November 16, 1946), 9, 40–41.

"Respectfully Submitted," *The Screen Writer*, II (March, 1947), Supplement, 12–21.

"Vincent Sargent Lawrence," *The Screen Writer*, II (January, 1947), 11–15. Cain pays tribute to his mentor on the occasion of his death, using a tough tone, as though he were writing about Lawrence as he felt Lawrence would like.

"Preface," *Three of Hearts* (London: Robert Hale, 1949), pp. v–x. Cain expresses his special interest in the Southwest, in Sacramento, in ghost towns such as Virginia City and Port Tobacco, Maryland, and clears up popular misconceptions about ghost towns. For his English readers, he also describes the Middle West and the culture and dialect of West Virginia. Comments on his own approach to writing. See also the prefaces to *Three of a Kind* and *The Butterfly* for comments on California and eastern Kentucky and on writing.

IV. Miscellaneous

"How to Carve that Bird," *Esquire*, II (December, 1934), 38, 140. First of three witty "how-to" essays in the tough-guy manner, revealing Cain's interest in food, an important element in his fiction.
"Them Ducks," *Esquire*, III (January, 1935), 38, 166, 168. One of Cain's best essays.
"Oh, *les Crêpes-Suzettes*," *Esquire*, III (February, 1935), 33, 174.
"Close Harmony," *The American Mercury*, XXXVI (October, 1935), 135–42. Offers important insights into another major element in Cain's life and work—music. The theme of self-dramatization is explored here, as it is in most of the other essays and articles.

SECONDARY SOURCES

"Cain's Books Popular in All Editions," *Publishers' Weekly*, CLIII (January, 1948), 143. An account of the phenomenal publishing history and sustained popularity of Cain's novels.
"Cain Scrutiny," *Newsweek*, CIX (April 23, 1962), 99. Biographical details.
FARRELL, JAMES T. "Cain's Movietone Realism," *Literature and Morality*. New York: Vanguard, 1947. Argues that Cain's talent has been corrupted by movie techniques; focuses his discussion on *Mildred Pierce*, novel and movie.
FROHOCK, W. M. "The Tabloid Tragedy of James M. Cain," *The Novel of Violence in America: 1920–1950*. Dallas, Texas: Southern Methodist University Press, 1950. Generally unsympathetic discussion of Cain's work, emphasizing *The Postman*. Charges Cain with immorally exploiting his raw material and manipulating his audience. Although I quarrel with Frohock on many points, his excellent essay is important and very interesting.
LERNER, MAX. "Cain in the Movies," *Public Journal: Marginal Notes on Wartime America*. New York: Viking Press, 1945. Brief but very perceptive commentary on Cain's work, on the occasion of the appearance of the movie *Double Indemnity*.
MADDEN, DAVID. "Cain's *The Postman Always Rings Twice* and Camus' *L'Étranger*," *Papers on Language and Literature*, V (Fall, 1970).
———. "James M. Cain and the Movies of the Thirties and Forties," *Film Heritage*, II (Summer, 1967), 9–25.

————. "James M. Cain and the Pure Novel," *The University Review —Kansas City*, XXX (December, 1963), 143–48; continued XXX (March, 1964), 235–39. A general discussion of Cain's novels.

————. "James M. Cain and the Tough Guy Novelists of the 30s." *The Thirties*. Ed. Warren French. Deland, Florida: Everett Edwards, Inc., 1967. Cain's novels in the context of other tough-guy writers.

————. "James M. Cain: Twenty-minute Egg of the Hard-boiled School," *Journal of Popular Culture*, I (Winter, 1967), 178–92. Biographical account of Cain's career.

"Massachusetts Supreme Court Clears Cain's *Serenade*," *Publishers' Weekly*, CLVIII (September 30, 1950), 1585. Account of attempts to censor *Serenade* for depicting sexual depravity and desecrating religion.

NICHOLS, LUTHER. "Postman's Assistant," *The New York Times Book Review* (May 13, 1962), p. 8. Interview on the occasion of the publication of *Mignon*.

OATES, JOYCE CAROL. "Man Under Sentence of Death: The Novels of James M. Cain." *Tough Guy Writers of the Thirties*. Ed. David Madden. Carbondale, Illinois: Southern Illinois University Press, 1968. Miss Oates, author of two volumes of short stories and two novels, exhibiting her own tough vision of sex and violence in America, has written the best single essay on Cain's works.

SMITH, HARRISON. "The Authority" (Editorial), *The Saturday Review of Literature*, XXIX (September 23, 1946), 18. An attack on Cain's American Authors' Authority efforts.

VAN NOSTRAND, ALBERT. *The Denatured Novel*. Indianapolis: Bobbs-Merrill, 1960. Although I disagree with many of Van Nostrand's points, he presents an excellent analysis of movie elements in most of Cain's novels.

WILSON, EDMUND. "The Boys in the Back Room: James M. Cain and John O'Hara," *New Republic*, CIII (November 11, 1940), 665–66. The first serious commentary on Cain's novels (though only *The Postman* and *Serenade* had appeared). Reprinted, with commentary on other writers added, in *Classics and Commercials*, New York: Vintage Books, 1962.

(For reviews of Cain's novels consult *Book Review Digest*; the excerpted comments offer a fascinating overview of critical and public response to Cain's novels, from many sources which are difficult to locate in the original.)

Index

Absurd, The, 158, 173–74
Action, 17, 21, 22, 25, 62, 69, 75, 101, 124–32 passim, 146–47, 155–156, 173
Adams, Jay, 48
Adventure, 71
Agee, James, 47–48
American character, 35, 59, 71, 92–93, 104–5, 153
American Dream, 59, 74, 92, 108–10
American land, 59, 71, 92
American male, 70, 157
American Mercury, The, 34–42 passim, 58, 100, 118, 139
American public types, 164
American scene, The, 35, 39, 53, 107, 154, 176
Animal motifs, 78, 148
Anticipation, 146
Aquinas, Thomas, 160–61
Art, 56
Atonement, 85
Audacity, 27, 76, 93–97, 158
Authenticity, 126
Autobiographical elements, 51, 70

Banality, 106–7, 128–29, 138, 140, 142, 151
Basso, Hamilton, 158
Bathos, 71
Beauty, 77, 153
Benét, William Rose, 39, 80, 137, 151, 159, 176
Ben Grace (*Love's Lovely Counterfeit*), 65–66, 103, 164

Bill "Willie" Cresap (*Mignon*), 64–65, 85, 94, 130, 135, 164
Bitches, 74–75
Black Mask magazine, 19, 168
Blizzard, William, 33
Booth, Wayne C., *Rhetoric of Fiction*, 136, 144
Burbie ("Pastorale"), 106
Burnett, W. R., *Little Caesar*, 166

Cain, Edward (brother), 26–27, 32
Cain, Genevieve (sister), 27
Cain, James M.: health of, 23, 36, 57–58; as journalist, 23, 31–33, 36–39, 41, 49, 50; and music, 23, 28–29, 101; as novelist, 23, 29–30, 49–59; residences of, 23–34 passim, 37, 39, 40, 42, 44, 49, 56; as screenwriter, 23, 42–46, 51, 179n; as teacher, 23, 30–31, 33–34; grandparents of, 24; education of, 25–26, 31, 33; childhood of, 25–27, 43, 70, 178n; early jobs of, 28–31; and World War I, 32–33; marriages of, 33, 36, 39–40, 54, 56–57; and the theater, 40–41, 46, 116; and *New Yorker*, 41–42; fiction of, as movies, 42, 47–49; and World War II, 53–54; organizes American Authors' Authority, 54–56; image of, 58–59, 62; and Catholicism, 86; literary ideals of, 112; novels of, in paperback, 121; foreign publications of, 175; recognition of, 176; fiction of, reviewed, 178n,